Mercy without End

Left to right: Lavina Fielding Anderson, Marina Capella, Christian N.K. Anderson, and Paul Lawrence Anderson

Mercy without End

TOWARD A MORE INCLUSIVE CHURCH

ESSAYS BY

LAVINA FIELDING ANDERSON

FOREWORD BY JANA RIESS

SIGNATURE BOOKS | 2020 | SALT LAKE CITY

The opinions expressed in this book are not necessarily
those of the publisher.

Cover design by Haden Hamblin.

FIRST EDITION | 2020

LIBRARY OF CONGRESS CATALOGING-IN-PUBLICATION DATA

Names:	Anderson, Lavina Fielding, 1944- author.
Title:	Mercy without end : toward a more inclusive church / essays by Lavina Fielding Anderson ; foreword by Jana Riess.
Description:	First edition. | Salt Lake City : Signature Books, 2020. | Includes index. | Summary: "These eighteen essays span more than thirty years of Lavina Fielding Anderson's concerns about and reflections on issues of inclusiveness in the Church of Jesus Christ of Latter-day Saints, including her own excommunication for "apostasy" in 1993, followed by twenty-five years of continued attendance at weekly LDS ward meetings. Written with a taste for irony and an eye for documentation, the essays are timeless snapshots of sometimes controversial issues, beginning with official resistance to professionally researched Mormon history in the 1980s. They underscore unanswered questions about gender equality and repeatedly call attention to areas in which the church does not live up to its better self. Compassionately and responsibly, it calls Anderson's beloved religion back to its holiest nature"— Provided by publisher.
Identifiers:	LCCN 2019059903 (print) | LCCN 2019059904 (ebook) | ISBN 9781560852834 (paperback) | ISBN 9781560853824 (ebook)
Subjects:	LCSH: Church of Jesus Christ of Latter-day Saints. | Christian life— Mormon authors. | Excommunication—Church of Jesus Christ of Latter-day Saints. | Mormon Church. | LCGFT: Essays.
Classification:	LCC BX8656 .A5195 2020 (print) | LCC BX8656 (ebook) | DDC 289.3/32—dc23

LC record available at https://lccn.loc.gov/2019059903
LC ebook record available at https://lccn.loc.gov/2019059904

CONTENTS

To Paul, Christian, Marina,
and the good Saints
of Whittier Ward

Foreword

JANA RIESS

I was baptized into the Church of Jesus Christ of Latter-day Saints on September 25,1993, the day after Lavina Fielding Anderson was forced out of it. Her stake disciplinary council had convened the night before to determine her fate, and she learned of the council's decision on the morning of the 24th via a letter from her stake president. "You are outside of the principles of the gospel and are leading others with you," he wrote. And then the icing on the cake: the excommunication, he insisted, "has been done out of love and concern for you."

The good Lord must have a sense of humor, or perhaps there is a subtle Principle of the Conservation of Feminists at work in the church, because the date of my own baptism is almost too bizarre for me to think of it as a mere coincidence. It had taken me more than two years of studying what Mormons call the restored gospel before I was ready to join the church. At the time I was living far from Utah in Princeton, New Jersey, but I was aware of the unsettling purge that was unfolding in the church, since it made the *New York Times*. I did not know who Lavina Fielding Anderson was, but I understood that the church I was about to join was in the process of excommunicating individuals who sounded a lot like me, and I was afraid. Which is, I think, largely the point of any excommunication: to strike fear in the heart of anyone who questions, doubts, or dares to be different.

As this beautifully written collection of essays makes clear, though, Lavina's life as a Mormon did not end on September 24, 1993. Her son, Christian, notes that her religious faith has never wavered, and her attendance at their family ward's sacrament meetings has been impeccable. More than twelve hundred times, Lavina has sat in sacrament meetings since her excommunication, and more than twelve hundred times, the now-forbidden bread and water have passed her by.

As a reader, it is impossible not to be moved by the spiritual and emotional implications of a fellow Latter-day Saint living in a state of exile within the very heart of Zion. It is remarkable to me how Lavina keeps on keeping on, despite judgment within the institutional church (though not, I was glad to learn, within her tight-knit ward community). As I read her story, I wondered whether I would respond in the same way if I were ever excommunicated. Would I continue offering myself on Sundays? Would I give of my time to an institution that had spurned me? I do not think that I would. That is part of what makes this book a wonder to me. It's a chronicle of covenant faithfulness in which the other party to the covenant has not been especially faithful in return: a gentle jeremiad.

As a work of history, Lavina's memoir chronicles a quiet revolution within the church. In literary works of tragedy, timing is always critical: Romeo, for example, doesn't get the memo in time that Juliet's seemingly fatal poison was just a sleeping draught, so he kills himself just moments before she wakes up. I think the historians of the future will see the timing of Lavina's excommunication as tragic. She was punished in 1993 for raising a flag, for blowing a whistle, for being a harbinger. Documenting events the church wanted buried was enough of a sin to be worthy of excommunication for either "apostasy" or "conduct unbecoming a member." Calling out ecclesiastical wrongdoing in a public way was simply not done in 1993.

I wonder how different Lavina's story would have looked if the conflict had occurred just ten years later, when the internet was a reality, personal blogs had begun to proliferate that sometimes criticized the church or its leaders, and it was impossible for the centralized institution to control the flow of information any longer. Lavina was excommunicated in 1993 not because what she said was factually untruthful but because she was among the first to say it publicly. And her excommunication was upheld in 2019 not because it was ever the most moral course for the church to take, but because the church still has no precedent for admitting its own errors, despite all the positive changes that have occurred in the intervening quarter century to humanize the institution.

At forty-nine, I am the same age now that Lavina was when she was excommunicated, and I'm keenly aware that I am able to persist as a progressive Mormon because she and other pioneers made it possible for me to do so. Yes, I get hate mail from total strangers, but I have never received ecclesiastical discipline for anything I have written in my Religion News Service column or said on a podcast. That's not due to any virtue on my part but simply because the times have changed, and Lavina was among those whose precedent helped to change them. The tragedy is that her church membership was needlessly, senselessly, considered collateral damage in that process. I'm grateful that here, at least, she is accorded the dignity of being able to tell her own story.

February 2020

... and mercy shall go before thy face and have no end. —Moses 7:31

Introduction

I wrote the first draft of this introduction on Friday, March 29, 2019. Five days earlier on Sunday, March 24, David J. McLean, president of Salt Lake Liberty Stake of the Church of Jesus Christ of Latter-day Saints, had reconvened the high council disciplinary council that had excommunicated me twenty-five years and six months earlier for "apostasy" on September 24, 1993. I thereby had joined Avraham Gileadi, Lynne Kanavel Whitesides, D. Michael Quinn, Paul J. Toscano, and Maxine Hanks. We collectively became the September Six, a house-cleaning initiated by Apostle Boyd K. Packer in the leadership vacuum left by President Ezra Taft Benson's dementia. Later Janice Allred, David Wright, Margaret Toscano, and others were added to the body count. Gileadi's controversial interpretations of Isaiah had made him a target, but the rest of us were "liberals"—with interest in a wider inclusiveness for LGBTIs, feminists, and the new Mormon historians (see "Intersections on Life's Journey," chap. 1 herein).

TWENTY-FIVE YEARS AGO

In the spring of 1993, Marlin S. Miller, president of Wells Stake, called me in over an article I had published in *Dialogue: A Journal of Mormon Thought* documenting impact points between the institutional church and its scholars. I concluded that article by urging more collaborative and mutually respectful interactions. When it became apparent that he and I were on a collision course, I thought through very carefully what some of the consequences could be, including excommunication. I was forty-nine years old, and that's old enough not to become a martyr on a whim or to step heedlessly into the paths of large trucks, but I felt that an issue of conscience and integrity was involved. I felt that I had behaved responsibly and compassionately in calling for another, and hopefully wiser, look at the distressing pattern that had developed between the church and its intellectuals, primarily its historians. As long as I was not breaking any rules of the church—and I was not—I felt that President Miller did not have the right to ask me to violate my conscience. He disagreed, and he had the power to see that his view prevailed. He announced my excommunication on September 24, 1993.

I appealed the excommunication in October 1993. Church presidents Gordon B. Hinckley and Thomas S. Monson upheld President Miller's decision in December. President Miller informed me of that fact in January 1994. After receiving this judgement, I wrote to President Miller reminding him that I had never received any instructions about what might be necessary for rebaptism, even though the *General Handbook of Instructions* specifies twice that such information must be provided. I asked if he had any counsel for me. He did not answer this letter. I wrote again three months later, in April 1994, repeating my request for information.

This time he responded: " I sincerely wish to see you return to membership and full fellowship in the church. In order to do so, you must put away any items or conduct that makes [sic] you feel that the 'Lord's anointed' are wrong or unrighteous. They are and will be personally accountable to the Lord, and it is His place, not ours to pass judgment."

Well, this response was something of a red herring. He had never suggested that he had any grounds for ecclesiastical action against me except for the *Dialogue* article. I had been charged with conduct unbecoming a member in the letter summoning me to trial. I was excommunicated for apostasy. I might mention that President Miller did not specify the grounds in the letter informing me that I was excommunicated but said, when I telephoned him to find out the reason, that it was apostasy. When I noted that I had actually been charged with a different offense (conduct unbecoming a member), he paused, then explained, "Apostasy *is* conduct unbecoming a member," suggesting that he saw the two categories as equivalents. In either case, what I had apparently done wrong was refuse to repudiate (his word) the article and agree not to publish other information about ecclesiastical abuse.

Now the grounds had apparently shifted to the presumption—never discussed and certainly never proved—that I judged all of the church's general authorities as wrong and unrighteous. I wrote back on April 14, 1994:

> President Miller, I have never felt nor said that General Authorities are unrighteous. I have never questioned their motivations, their intentions, their authority, or their goodwill. On every issue I have been more than willing to give them the benefit of the doubt.
>
> But it sounds almost as if you expect me to believe that they are never wrong or are incapable of being wrong or that they are always right or that whatever they do is right. Is this what you mean? If it is, I think you are asking me to do something that the Church does not require of its members. If it is not what you mean, then I need you to explain what you do mean.

President Miller never responded. Although his five successors as stake president visited my husband, Paul, and me once apiece and had a cordial conversation, they never asked to meet with me a second time. I did not hide or disappear. I lived in the same house, attended the same ward meetings, and even sat on the same bench that we had occupied ever since we moved into the Whittier Ward in 1977. I have the same testimony of the Savior, of Joseph Smith, of the Book of Mormon, of the church, and of the current prophet that I always have. I keep the same rules of the church.

The leaders of the church, beginning with my stake leaders and extending to the First Presidency, have the authority to say that I can't go to the temple, can't take the sacrament, can't speak or pray in church, and can't be a member of the church. I acknowledge their authority. I agree that they can make those decisions.

But my relationship with my Heavenly Father and the Savior lies within my power. Naturally, I think often about being excommunicated, but I have always felt a great sense of peace that I made a moral decision, an ethical decision, a decision of integrity and conscience. There might have been a different decision that would have yielded a third alternative to silence or excommunication. But I didn't know what it was then, and I still don't. I did the very best I knew how to do, the thing that I felt was the right thing to do. I regret being excommunicated, but I don't regret standing up for what I felt was right. It's a great blessing that, in the intervening twenty-five years, I have not wasted any energy thinking, "If only I'd done such-and-such."

An unexpected benefit of excommunication is that Paul would almost certainly have spent most of the intervening twenty-five years in a bishopric or on a high council. He had already been a counselor in our bishopric and served on the high council. He would have been a compassionate and insightful bishop, but he wasn't a born administrator; and both of us were uncomfortable with some of the negative marital consequences of "confidentiality." Instead, Paul was able to volunteer for his favorite callings: as ward choir director and as Gospel Doctrine teacher for most of that quarter century.

And our son, Christian, has had two full-time parents. I had spent eleven years in the Primary teaching Sunbeams; and Christian, when boredom became too acute in his own class, could always slip into our room to feed snacks to the three-year-olds, help act out Bible stories, and comfort a distressed child. He and Paul were home teaching companions until Christian left for Stanford. Paul was assistant scoutmaster while Christian was getting his Eagle. Christian and I both sang in the ward choir that Paul led. In other words, Paul had no callings since 1993 that Christian could not be included in.

After Paul's death in 2018, I found a letter he wrote to President Miller, a tender love letter to me, a respectful call to President Miller to think about his behavior. I cherish Paul's sense of justice, his clarity, and his balanced view. It is dated September 22, 1993, the day before the disciplinary council:

Dear President Miller:

I have been thinking that you and I have at least one thing in common—we are both caught somewhere in the middle of a situation that we wish had never happened.

Happily, all my life I have tried to be a good Latter-day Saint. I have loved the Church, enjoyed its programs, sustained its leaders, and have tried to make its ideals the center of my life. Sadly, now I find that I am the husband of the wonderful, affectionate, sincere, and brilliant woman whom you are threatening with the harshest penalties that are in your power to give. I realize that you are doing this under the direction of your priesthood leaders, using the one-sided documentation supplied to you by them, as they have supplied similar materials to so many other stake and ward leaders in recent months. I am sorry for the painful position that you must be in.

I realize that under the circumstances there is probably nothing I can say to you that will make much difference in the outcome of this sad situation, but as a man who loves both his wife and his Church, perhaps I ought to say something anyway.

In all the years I have known her, Lavina has been a person of deep spirituality and genuine goodness. She loves the Church and its teachings and exemplifies its ideals in her life to a remarkable degree. She has faithfully and diligently fulfilled many callings in our ward. In recent months, she has attended Church to provide music for three consecutive meetings when she should have been home in bed because of sickness and pain. She does her visiting teaching on the first Sunday of each month and gives much love and service to those whom she visits. In our home, she has insisted that we pray together, read the scriptures, and sing hymns regularly. She has been widely recognized in the Mormon scholarly community as a voice of moderation amid sometimes strident expressions, as a voice of faith in gospel ideals amid negativeness and anger, and as an example of faithful activity while many others have become inactive and bitter.

I believe Lavina's only crime has been to speak some unpleasant truths more loudly and clearly than Church leaders like to hear them. She has tried to give a voice to the quiet pain of friends and acquaintances who have been hurt. She has done this believing that Church leaders, if only they realized the unnecessary damage the Church has done to some members, would wish to do something positive about it. Unfortunately, they have decided to punish the messenger instead of receiving the message.

Last Wednesday, the First Presidency released a statement about Arab–Israeli peace that had particular poignancy for me. It said, "We are always grateful when opposing sides can reason together in good faith and come to an agreement intended to resolve their difficulties. We are confident that when there is enough of a desire for peace and a will to bring it about, it is not beyond the possibility of attainment." In our case, and in the cases of many of our friends, they were never willing to do this.

I cannot help wondering what might have happened if the first time Lavina and I met with you, you had said, "I disagree with parts of your article, but I respect your motives and am moved by the pain you describe. Would you stop publishing such things if you had another way of communicating your concerns to Church leaders? What if I arranged a meeting with the area president and attended it with you, not to agree with your position, but to help you find an acceptable way to share your concerns." Instead, you advised her to be silent and threatened her with sanctions. It seems to me that the gospel of Jesus might have provided some better alternatives.[1]

At the leadership meeting of our stake conference you made a memorable statement: "Men should be careful how they treat women, because God counts their tears." I have seen Lavina's tears in recent days, and I believe that God may be counting them, just as you said.

Over the years we have been acquainted, I have valued your friendship and respected your sincerity. As an active member of the Church I sustain you as my stake president. I believe that you wish that this situation had never landed in your lap. Lavina, Christian, and I have prayed for you daily in our family prayers in recent months, that you will be guided to lead our stake in wisdom and in love, and we will continue to do so. We will also continue to pray that the spirit of understanding and forgiveness will fill our hearts.

God bless you to do the best you can.

Sincerely,

Paul L. Anderson

DEVELOPMENTS IN 2018–19

Over the summer and fall of 2018, I had had a number of cordial and candid conversations with Bishop Mahonri Madrigal and Stake President David J. McLean.[2] I had described to them the distinct inspiration received in the summer of 1993 that I would be

---

1. An earlier draft included this paragraph: "Bishop Burgon told me that you said to him what I have heard you say before, that you strive to fear God more than man. I hope that some of the men you will try not to fear are the ones in white shirts and ties who have supplied you with a very one-sided set of accusations against my wife. They have accused her in secret, leaving you to perform the dirty work while Lavina will never have an opportunity to know the identity or motives of her accusers or to confront them directly as Church guidelines direct. I also hope that you will remember that the God you fear is my wife's loving Father."

2. Paul and I have lived in the same house since we married in 1977, but reorganization of stake boundaries in 2017 meant that we were living in Liberty Stake, not Wells Stake.

excommunicated, that I should not attend the court, and that it would take "a long time" before I was reinstated. I accepted this message as revelation to me and, for my part, privately pledged to stay worthy of membership. Both men extended themselves in courteous, helpful ways. Bishop Madrigal met with Christian and me on September 24, 2019, and confirmed plans to move forward with reinstatement with President McLean. Bishop Madrigal did not know, but it was exactly twenty-five years to the day after my excommunication.

Paul had died on March 23, 2018.[3] I spent the summer overseeing the remodeling of our home to allow Christian and his wife, Marina Capella, to merge households with me in October 2019. President McLean invited me to write him a letter to serve as the basis for "conversations" with his counselors and the stake high council. As a result, he reconvened the high council court on March 24, 2019, another resonant anniversary date, twenty-five years and six months exactly after the excommunication.

Disciplinary Council, March 24, 2019

This statement is, in essence, the letter that I wrote in December 2019 to President McLean at his invitation. I modified it slightly for presentation to the high council by adding a tribute to my ward:

> The members of Whittier Ward have continued to accept me as a sister in the household of faith. I have not heard one accusatory

---

3. Paul was born and grew up Pasadena, California, graduated as an architect from Stanford and Princeton, served his mission in Japan, worked with Florence S. Jacobsen, the first LDS Church Curator, on designing the Museum of Church History and Art (now the Church History Museum) adjacent to Temple Square and its exhibits in downtown Salt Lake City. Then he worked with James Mason designing the Museum of Art on the campus of Brigham Young University in Provo, Utah, where he ended his career as chief of exhibit design in 2016. Although he had done frequent residential remodelings and from-the-ground-up plans, he then plunged into a long-deferred desire to explore landscape paintings. He had produced about a hundred when he died very unexpectedly; we were able to share many of these paintings with friends and family who came to his memorial service.

or negative syllable from any of them. They have made it easy for me to keep the promise I made twenty-five years ago to keep my covenants and remain close to the Church. Christian and Marina have lived in many wards, and it has brought me happiness to hope that Whittier Ward will become their "home ward" as well.

I then continued with my affirmation of faith:

> I very much appreciate your [President McLean's] invitation to share some aspects of my testimony with you. Its foundation is my knowledge that God lives, that he cherishes each one of us, and that the mortal experience is designed to teach us his own two great characteristics of love and respect for agency.
>
> Key in that experience is the mission of our Savior, who came into mortality to teach us the gospel and to offer himself to atone for our sins and also to set an example that we can follow as we strive to become like him. I have been blessed with sacred revelatory experiences that have taught me more about these members of the Godhead and helped instruct me in how the Holy Spirit operates. My gratitude for these blessings fills my heart.
>
> Words fail to express that gratitude and also falter as I try to comprehend the great blessing of the restoration of the gospel to Joseph Smith, his bringing forth the Book of Mormon, and the establishment of the Church. You specifically wanted to know if I sustained the leaders of the Church—which I do, not only since the days of Joseph Smith but also of each man who has been called and ordained as Church president since that period.
>
> I do not need or expect perfection from these Church leaders. I'm grateful that the Lord works with us in our imperfection and extends his mercy as long as we strive to repent, exercise our faith, love each other, and provide service where we can.

I then spelled out my reservations:

> Three current Church policies are troubling to me for their exclusionary aspects. One is the exclusion of some worthy couples who are legally and lawfully married from full Church participation.

Their children are also excluded from those blessings.[4] Another is the exclusion of worthy and righteous women from full priesthood service. The third is the exclusion of Mother in Heaven from her place in our understanding of family life, both in the preexistence, family life in mortality, and in the eternities.

I have faith that these policies are among the "great and important things pertaining to the Kingdom of God" that are yet to be revealed, and I anticipate those eventual developments with joy.

As a matter of personal integrity, I had shared my concerns about these three issues with every ecclesiastical leader with whom I had had a conversation about reinstatement. I did not want, by silence, to leave a false impression that I accepted the church's policy on these issues.

The disciplinary council continued with a supportive statement by my son, Christian, who was thirteen when I was excommunicated.

Christian's Statement

It is my understanding that church discipline is to be administered in such a way that it will ultimately work for the good of the person being disciplined. The person must show a willingness to live a Christ-like life and "demonstrate ... reliably by righteous actions over a period of time" that they remain dedicated to the Church of Jesus Christ of Latter-day Saints; the only recommended length of excommunication is one year.

Lavina was excommunicated in 1993, over 25 years ago now. Two weeks ago a deacon insisted on trying to pass her the sacrament over me after I'd handed him back the bread tray. Lavina's excommunication was older the day that deacon was born than

---

4. In a leadership meeting on April 5, 2019, preceding the church's semi-annual general conference, Second Counselor in the First Presidency Dallin H. Oaks announced that the restriction on ordinances for children had been rescinded, also that LGBTI couples would no longer be assumed to be apostates, even though their unions constituted a "grave transgression." I felt it was also significant that these exclusions, previously considered doctrines, then policies, had retreated to "adjustments." I anticipate continued "adjustments" in these exclusionary areas.

that deacon is now. In that long quarter-century, Lavina has never stopped attending her meetings and contributing to her ward in any way she was permitted to. This means she has had to watch the symbols of Christ's universal love and acceptance go past her over 1,200 times—incidentally an attendance record better than that collected by the seven bishops who have served in Whittier Ward in that time period. Clearly, the period of probation has long since elapsed.

Whatever good might come from the rededication a disciplinary action causes has long since passed. Prolonging Lavina's exile from the ward family she loves and who love her cannot possibly be prompted by a spirit of love and concern for her well-being. Her sincere belief in Jesus and determination to follow him no matter the adversity faced within or without the Church should be commended, and this good and faithful servant should be rewarded. She embodies, more than anyone else I know, the ideal of a "broken heart and contrite spirit" which has influenced me so strongly that I, the last time I checked, was one of only two of the twenty-one children of the September 6 who is still an active member.

This court happens a year and a day after the death of my father. Almost the last thing he did in life was drive with Lavina and me to BYU, to attend a lecture honoring her work, then to a formal banquet in the top floor of the Student Union where she was given a lifetime achievement award in the heart of an institution where two senior apostles, who will probably be our next two prophets, were presidents. We all know that would not have happened in 1993. But we also all know the church is a different, bigger place than it was then. I pray that you agree it is big enough for my entire family.

As you consider her rebaptism, remember Nephi's list of the things Christ invites all of us to do, and the things Christ will never say to us (2 Ne. 26:23–26):

"For behold, my beloved brethren, I say unto you that the Lord God worketh not in darkness.

"He doeth not anything save it be for the benefit of the world; for he loveth the world, even that he layeth down his own life that he may draw all men unto him. Wherefore, he commandeth none that they shall not partake of his salvation.

"Behold, hath he commanded any that they should depart out of the synagogues, or out of the houses of worship? Behold, I say unto you, Nay.

"Behold, doth he cry unto any, saying: Depart from me? Behold, I say unto you, Nay; but he saith: Come unto me all ye ends of the earth, buy milk and honey, without money and without price."

Bishop Madrigal had, in his comments at Paul's memorial service, read Paul's testimony that was part of a ward millennial project in 2000. Now, with emotion, he read the testimony I had written for the same collection and affirmed that it was "the testimony of a believer."

At my invitation, the service missionaries who had been assigned to minister to me, also made brief statements. Both had been warmly supportive and proactive since the fall of 2018. When we entered the high council room, for instance, Sister Melanie Hepworth Neville promptly rearranged the chairs, repositioning mine—originally isolated—so that Christian's flanked mine, with Melanie's and her husband's clustered close around. In Melanie's statement, she said that she had been aware of my writing "for many years," due to a shared interest in Mormon history, and that when I told her it was "the desire of my heart to be baptized," she literally "clapped her hands for joy." Her husband, Roark B. Neville, added his report: "I've been in Sister Anderson's home, I have taught her, I have prayed with her, and we discussed the gospel. I see no reason that Lavina should not be welcomed back." Two high councilors, who were members of our ward, gave specific and supportive testimony of my sincerity. Only two or three high councilors asked questions.

After consultation, the disciplinary council's decision was to forward to the First Presidency a recommendation for reinstatement.

President McLean stressed that only the First Presidency would decide when to act and that their decision could be positive, negative, or something unpredictable.

Post-Disciplinary Council Events

In early April 2019, my bishop passed on a form labeled "Applicant Instructions," which asked for information on such reasonable topics as "The reasons you desire to be readmitted" but also such committee-generated topics as "Whether you are current in all financial obligations related to divorce." I returned my answers to my bishop in early May. The "reviewer" of this document expressed concern that my statement did not show sufficient "remorse." To his credit, President McLean responded that it might be because I didn't feel I had done anything wrong. He, Christian, Marina, and I consulted over a clarifying addendum to the draft in which I expressed "deep regret whenever anyone leaves the Church for whatever reason." I hoped that the last phrase would suggest, without spelling it out, that those reasons could (and often did) originate in the abusive actions of individual leaders or official church policy. I said:

> Discussing difficult issues is precarious, but not discussing them leaves many feeling alienated, unheard, and in pain. I sincerely respect the decisions of those who feel that the Church is not a safe or nourishing place for them or their children, but I have never intentionally tried to influence anyone to leave the Church.
>
> I've been greatly blessed to be able to remain attached to our ward family over the past twenty-five years, and my hope has always been that others will experience and contribute to their own loving community. … I have waited with patience and hope to once again partake of the sacrament, worship in the temple, and participate more fully in my ward.

The remainder of this addendum spelled out points I thought I had already made in earlier statements and letters. This version went off to the reviewer on June 9, 2019. The next development was that, on July 21, a beaming Bishop Madrigal said I should expect "very soon" to get a telephone call scheduling an interview with a general authority, whom he named. No call came. Instead, President McLean asked us to meet with him on August 27.

At that meeting, he read a short letter dated August 7 and signed by all three members of the First Presidency. In it they stated they had evaluated the information and were not accepting his recommendation for reinstatement "at this time." He read it twice, at my request, and said he was "perplexed" by the decision since the current openness to "diversity" had led him conclude that this was a good time to request reinstatement. He said he had no information about the decision beyond the letter itself but cheerfully engaged in "speculation" with us. I speculated with him that the unnamed church employee who had found my statement lacking in "remorse" may have submitted a negative recommendation. The conversation triggered a couple of charming stories about President McLean's father when he disagreed with a church action. President McLean tried to find a reason for optimism in the phrase "at this time" and invited me to meet with him again if I wished to approach the First Presidency at some point in the future. I thanked him and extended the same invitation to him to continue the conversation if he felt inclined to do so.[5]

I spelled out my three conclusions as our meeting ended: "First, I'm not angry, and I'm not disappointed. Second, I feel that my efforts to live my covenants have been accepted, and this matter is

---

5. Perhaps another explanation is that President Russell M. Nelson, "Closing Remarks," *Ensign*, November 2019, 121, announced revisions to the temple recommend questions. Interview question 7 asks, "Do you support or promote any teachings, practices, or doctrine contrary to those of The Church..." Given my own clarity in resisting the exclusion of LGBTI members, Mother in Heaven, and priesthood ordination for women, it seems likely that the First Presidency disqualified me for reinstatement. President Nelson's public explanation occurred in October, two months after President McLean received the letter refusing reinstatement.

unfinished business for the First Presidency, not for me. Third, my relationship with the Savior is in my control, where it's always been, and this action by the First Presidency doesn't change that." I realized that I had hoped for a positive outcome but I had expected a negative one. As with my excommunication and the rejection of my appeal to that First Presidency, I plan to let it affect my life as little as possible. Sundays will still find me in the Whittier Ward chapel, third bench from the front on the north side.

THE ESSAYS

The essays published here were almost all written by invitation and presented at conferences sponsored by the Mormon Women's Forum, Pilgrimage (an annual women's retreat that began in a single national event in 1981 in Nauvoo, Illinois, at the same time as the LDS temple dedication and in subsequent years met mostly but not always in Salt Lake City), and the Sunstone Foundation. They span thirty-three years—from 1985 to 2018—and fifteen of the eighteen are published here for the first time.

I sent the proposed essays to both my bishop and stake president, explaining that I was not asking for their permission but that I did not want them to be surprised. Both accepted this gesture as one of courtesy, and President McLean not only surprised me by reading them but also warmly discussed two of them with me. I found this attentiveness remarkable, given the time demands on a stake president.

It is possible to argue that these essays are interesting but quaint historical artifacts of what Mormonism was like in the late twentieth century because the landscape is very different now. The ongoing publication of the Joseph Smith Papers has made historical topics treated repressively twenty-five years earlier widely available and has created a vigorous cadre of well-educated younger scholars who publish widely with a variety of professional tools. Although there are still troublesome questions, the knee-jerk suspicion of the academic treatment of Mormon history has, for most practical purposes, dissolved.

Mormon women have been included more fully in decision-making and in public roles, and troubling topics like racism are receiving careful scholarly attention as well as energetic public debate. Twenty-five years ago (and still at the present) I saw myself as a progressive. Elder Boyd K. Packer designated feminists, homosexuals, and "so-called intellectuals"[6] as the most troublesome members of the church. As an ardent enthusiast for the New Mormon History nurtured by Church Historian Leonard J. Arrington, one of the finest human beings I know, I considered myself an unqualified supporter of intellectuals. The gays and lesbians (also transsexual and intersexuals) I knew were outstanding human beings, living their lives with integrity.[7] As for feminism, I considered myself a proponent of women's equality and an expanded, public recognition of Heavenly Mother even before I knew about feminism. The unanswered questions about the ordination of Mormon women and Heavenly Mother's role include perhaps the largest number of unanswered issues.

But there is much, much more to be done before the church can be said to have achieved full racial equality and especially full gender inclusiveness. I would therefore argue that these essays, in looking back a quarter century, highlight still-shadowy areas in our institutional life. (Church President Russell M. Nelson issued

6. Boyd K. Packer, "All-Church Coordinating Council Meeting," May 18, 1992, photocopy of typescript in my possession.

7. The last formal project of the Mormon Alliance before it transferred to inactive status was the publication of the most detailed history of the LDS Church and LGBTI members, which also includes a careful and thoughtful scriptural analysis that opens the door to their theological acceptance of full membership. See Duane E. Jennings, *Stumbling Blocks and Stepping-Stones: Including Lesbian, Gay, Bisexual, Transgender, and Intersex Children of God in the LDS Plan of Salvation*, ed. Lavina Fielding Anderson, 2 vols. (Salt Lake City: Mormon Alliance, 2016).

instructions to use only the full name of the church in the fall of 2018, but nearly all of these essays were written before that fiat, and I have my own reason for using the term, namely, that the LDS Church, of which I have not been a member, is narrower than "Mormonism," in which I claim a place. I have not attempted to replace "Mormon" where it originally appeared.)[8]

In preparing this collection, I found it significant that I still subscribed to the same views. I did not find my positions or insights outmoded. In 2019 I still embraced the sense of God the Father, God the Mother, and Jesus Christ that I had cherished as a younger woman. It might be possible for someone to argue that I was merely grappling with the same issues and refusing to develop a broader range of insights. Instead, to me it feels as if my life experience had deepened these aspects of my faith. I felt no impulse to discard them.

I begin this compilation with my most recent essay. In 2018 I had agreed to present an overview of my life in a popular session at Pilgrimage called "Life Journeys"; but between accepting the invitation and delivering it, my husband of forty years died. That event gave me the focus of "Intersections on Life's Journey" and let me explore the ways in which I negotiate my Mormon identity. It also serves the purpose of providing an autobiographical orientation and background for the essays that follow.

I felt that one of the powerful tools the church used to induce conformity was the shaming and presumed-guilty labeling of those excommunicated. In contrast, I took the position with others of the September Six that the church should be accountable for its decisions and that transparency should replace secrecy. I was then

8. "Roundtable Responses," *Dialogue: A Journal of Mormon Thought*, 52, no. 3 (Fall 2019): 19–55, consists of thoughtful and insightful reflections on the attempted retirement of "Mormon" by Michael Austin, Rebbie Brassfield, Loyd Isao Ericson, Peggy Fletcher Stack, Mette Ivie Harrison, Clifton H. Jolley, Kalani Tonga, and Ronald Wilcox.

editor of the *Journal of Mormon History*, where I served for a total of nineteen years and was somewhat startled when a handful of leaders in the intellectual Mormon community encouraged me *not* to resign. Since I had not contemplated resignation, I was somewhat bemused, though appreciative, of this support. I received numerous invitations to speak on the topic of my excommunication and accepted all of the invitations that were practical. Both *Dialogue* and the Sunstone symposiums continued to offer invitations to discuss my situation. This was enormously important, since both organizations had struggled with how to balance orthodoxy and faith explorations in authors, participants, and presenters. At stake for these struggling organizations was whether they could avoid censure by both general authorities and orthodox supporters.

The next five essays deal specifically with aspects of how I processed that event: "Mercy without End," "Sacrament Meeting, Whittier Ward," "A Testimony of Presence," "Excommunicant," and "Eternal Perdition? Bureaucratic Limbo? The Theological Ramifications of Excommunication." I chose to remain active in my ward,[9] and I credit the members of Whittier Ward with, in essence, ignoring the social strictures of excommunication. I was greatly aided in

---

9. Avraham Gileadi, as noted, was not identified with the liberal causes that made it possible to group the rest of us. Michael Quinn and Maxine Hanks had already chosen low profiles where their wards were concerned. Janice Merrill Allred's bishop held a grueling series of interviews in which he declined to discuss the issues he chastised her for. He disfellowshipped her in October 1994 for her theological investigations and excommunicated her in May 1995. She has continued to attend her Provo ward with her husband, but except for her oldest daughter, who was married and out of the home at the time of these events, her children have all disengaged from the church. Janice has continued to attend Sunday school. Margaret Toscano, her sister and Paul Toscano's wife, was excommunicated in 2000 for her feminist writings. Paul and Margaret's four daughters, who rejected the stake president's action against Paul, had refused to attend church after Paul's excommunication. Margaret attended their ward for a few months to demonstrate a willingness to discuss the issues, but their daughters resisted her continued presence at church as "disloyal." In the interests of family unity, she stopped attending church meetings.

this decision by Christian's youth leaders and teachers, and Paul's unwavering support. No one in the ward felt called upon to lecture me for my presumed failings, a result, I believe, of the sixteen years we had already spent as active members of the ward. The media coverage, especially religion reporter Peggy Fletcher Stack's articles in the *Salt Lake Tribune*, had been both fair and detailed. I suspect that most people who were interested probably felt they had a reliable picture of my views.

Others, both those who had been excommunicated in September and those who followed, had less ward support. Their children, in particular, were the subject of sneers from age-mates that may have begun with the parents. I took it as a particular blessing that my disciplinary council was first scheduled as a high council court, then reassigned to my bishop who accepted the assignment but willingly gave me a blessing and was relieved when the stake president took the responsibility back. This step is a departure from the official church procedure specifying that women are to be disciplined in bishops' courts. As a result, ward members did not need to take sides, either with me or with the bishop. In essence, what happened at the stake stayed with the stake. Typically, those with questions would ask, "How's Lavina doing?" Paul had a friendly but firm way of saying, "*We're* fine" that did not invite further comment.

The excommunications highlighted ongoing and intensifying tensions between individual faith and conformity to institutional mores that we now tend to term a "faith crisis." The easy accessibility of the Internet has provided innumerable forums in which members can share their experiences, offer lessons of their own experience that may be helpful, and find like-minded individuals and groups. This forum, indeed, the topic itself, was less readily available during the 1980s and 1990s. The next seven essays span the period both before and after my excommunication: "Dealing with Our Divine and Human Church," "Many Mansions—But

No Doghouses: Toward a More Inclusive Community," "Modes of Revelation: A Personal Approach," "Covenants and Contracts: Re-negotiating Membership in the Church," "The Spiritual Power of Gratitude," "Loving the Questions," and "In the Garden God Has Planted: Explorations toward a Maturing Faith."

The next four essays may be most valuable historically because they identify what I saw as key issues in Mormon feminism. Some of them have become obsolete as Mormon women have become more visible and empowered. Genuinely encouraging are developments such as revisions to the LDS temple endowment, a women's session of general conference that trades off annually with the priesthood session, more encouragement to serve missions, and harsh media attention for illegal actions at BYU against rape and abuse victims that has generated corrected policies. "The Grammar of Inequity," "Fear Training," "'The Only Life You Save': The Seduction of Sacrifice," and "Women in the *General Handbook of Instructions*" suggest a baseline from which these more contemporary developments can be measured.

I conclude with "Circles," a meditation on temple worship, an experience that has been barred to me for twenty-five years. Fortunately, I had been a weekly temple-goer as a single woman, and Paul and I went as frequently as we could manage around our schedule and Christian's needs, so I had memorized the endowment ceremony, which has since been revised and is readily though unofficially available on the Internet. It was a genuine consolation to me to consider that having the temple in my heart and mind manifested my willingness to God that I would be ready when my body could follow my heart through those doors.

Finally, at the suggestion of my publisher, I have sometimes made minor word and other changes to the original versions of the essays to facilitate the reader's understanding of people, places, events, etc.

ACKNOWLEDGMENTS

I acknowledge the enormous debt I owe to roommates, women's and other conferences, scripture study groups, and individual friendships. Although individual friendships have remained staunch and nourishing across this span of years, I choose not to name these individuals lest the public acknowledgment redound negatively among their families and other friends. I cherish these relationships. It is both sad to me and ironic that so many friends have distanced themselves from the church and that the friends who have found ways to remain attached to church are possibly at most risk if I were to publicly acknowledge their support.

I express my appreciation to the organizers of Sunstone and past publisher of its magazine, especially Elbert Peck, who provided calm and sympathetic leadership during the most turbulent days. The source notes for the essays acknowledge those that were originally addresses or panel presentations for Sunstone. The editors of *Dialogue: A Journal of Mormon Thought* also provided thoughtful guidance. Again, the source notes trace the publishing history.

This compilation had its origin in the invitation of Gary James Bergera, managing director of the Smith–Pettit Foundation and company director of Signature Books Publishing LLC. The nearly four decades during which I have served on Signature Books's editorial advisory committee have provided less advice, on my part, than free-flowing arguments, a lively awareness of trends in Mormon scholarship, and delightful friendships with Gary, Ron Priddis, George D. Smith, Richard S. Van Wagoner (now deceased), Martha Bradley-Evans, Lisa Orme Bickmore, John Sillito, and Kenneth L. Cannon.

My son, Christian, helped with compiling the essays, refining the original candidates, and providing updated notes that left the original essays substantially intact. He was supportive in a dozen technical ways and, with his wife, Marina Capella, provided a nurturing emotional climate. We all appreciate the irony that the bureaucratic processes for reinstatement were moving forward at the same time as the preparation of this anthology.

I acknowledge with the tenderest of feelings and the deepest gratitude the humor, wisdom, and steadiness of my husband, Paul, whom I miss in scores of ways, not least in recognizing how he quietly and consistently kept the foundation of our family intact. It is a task I believe he is still fulfilling.

Salt Lake City
2020

1

Intersections on Life's Journey

I presented these remarks at Pilgrimage in Salt Lake City on June 2, 2018. My husband of forty years, Paul Lawrence Anderson, had passed away unexpectedly less than three months earlier on March 23.

I was asked to speak about my life journey—a powerful metaphor since it implies a departure point and an arrival and that we are somewhere between the two of them.

My life has been shaped by my effort to approach and understand Jesus, by my desire to know him and to be known by him, to speak the language of prayer and worship, to dwell in hope and faith. The initial impetus comes from my parents. My mother's mother, for whom I am named, clung to her faith while my grandfather traded horses, never held a steady job, and drank what little money he did make instead of parenting their seven children. My father was an orphan by the time he was twelve, but his six surviving older siblings cherished their mother's faith and their father's sense of honor and wove them into a strong commitment to the church. My five siblings and I grew up with that commitment. They taught us clearly that life was a journey and gave us the most reliable map we could have to achieve it.

Several decision points reinforced the shape of that journey. For instance, BYU was the only university I considered attending.

When I was mission age, I accepted that calling and went to France. France was a great place to test my commitment since there were certainly no distractions from French people clamoring to hear the missionary discussions or join the church. In graduate school at the University of Washington, I included Institute classes and ward activity with my scholarly endeavors. I was still in graduate school when I was hired by the *Ensign* as its women's editor. That position gave me entry into the world of Mormon women's history, which had become a litany of losses and the terror of the institutional church over the rising feminist movement in the United States.

So: education, a mission, and employment only reinforced my commitment to the church and the gospel. The relationship between the two was, up to that point, almost synonymous. After Christian's birth in 1980, I established my editing company, having already seen enough bureaucratic shenanigans that I perceived a serious separation between the church and the gospel in several ways. By then Paul and I had married and were deeply involved in what LDS Church Historian Leonard Arrington called the "unsponsored sector" of Mormon culture. Unquestionably, the decision to marry Paul was the most important of my life.

Paul was an architect from Pasadena who had first come to Salt Lake City on a fellowship with Leonard Arrington's office to do some research on Mormon architecture. We have not been able to reconstruct how we met, but I do remember that, at the time, he was fetchingly bearded. He had to shave off his facial hair when Florence Smith Jacobsen[1] hired him as a manager of historic sites for the church's Arts and Sites Division. When I met Paul, I was thoroughly and happily single. Paul became a delightful addition

---

1. Florence was a granddaughter of LDS Church presidents Joseph F. Smith and Heber J. Grant, former general president of the church's Young Women's Mutual Improvement Association, restorer of the Lion House, and, as Paul admiringly noted, "the smartest person in the room—any room."

to the social life that swirled through the home I shared with my roommates, and I was genuinely surprised—and even a little angry—when he proposed. He later told me he was more than a little angry himself to show up for a date and discover that I'd invited two or three other people to join us. Since I was asking him to events about as often as he asked me, I wasn't defining what we were doing as dating, let alone courting. Deciding to marry was difficult; it took me about six weeks.

Those six weeks were a very significant spiritual education in learning how to pray. I discovered that Heavenly Father's respect for free agency is so profound that there are many times the Holy Ghost cannot give us an answer because we have not yet asked the correct question. I have a mental picture from that time of the Holy Ghost (you'll have to pardon the irreverence) hopping frantically around on one foot while I blundered through bursts of static into a clear signal of what the right question was. Interestingly enough, it was not "Should I marry Paul?" A series of right questions followed, and they included: What would marriage be like? What would be the hard places? What would be the easy places? What will the changes be? What strengths and what inadequacies would I take to marriage? I don't particularly want to be married; do I need to be married?

I received extremely clear information about all of those topics. I received insight into my attitudes about privacy, money, work and children, priesthood, professionalism, and ability to communicate that was somewhat shocking though not, I have to admit, very surprising. But possibly the most important question that I asked was, "What kind of person is Paul?" In answer to that question, I had the closest thing to a vision I have ever experienced. I saw a personage with a definite personality, occupying a definite space, who told me, almost in so many words, "Let me show you how I feel about Paul," and I then experienced that person's feelings for Paul: the deepest, most profound sensations of love and a respectful savoring of personality. There was no question in my mind that I was in the presence of someone who knew Paul differently and better than I did or possibly could know him, someone who loved him totally. I acquired an awesome amount of respect for Paul quite suddenly.

There were other issues to be worked through, but one sunny day, as I knelt again in prayer, I asked again, "Should I marry Paul?" expecting to learn of a new question I should ask. Instead, I was distinctly told, "You have enough information to make that decision now." I double-checked. *I* was supposed to make the decision? Yes. There was a long internal pause, a kind of mental breath-holding, then I said, still on my knees, "Yes, I will marry Paul." The reaction could not have been more vivid, an explosion of pleasure and excitement like being in the center of a fireworks display. It surprised me, pleased me, gratified me, and humbled me simultaneously. I knew that not all of those emotions were my own, and the delight shared with other presences who cared about the decision was reassuring in ways I don't even know how to begin to describe. One of the consequences has been that I have never had to question the initial rightness of the decision nor had to wonder if I made a mistake.

Our first pregnancy resulted in the baby's prenatal death, but the second brought us Christian, who has been an utter delight from the moment of his birth. I don't know what we would have done with an ordinary, normal child. Christian liked classical music AND the music we had liked as teenagers. He and Paul worked out complicated rebuses for the closing song in sacrament meeting. Christian amused himself by constructing a formula for pitting the recommended speed of the hymns against the organist's actual performance. He liked piano lessons, poetry, and messing around with computers.

In 1993, President Ezra Taft Benson's lengthy decline toward death became Elder Boyd K. Packer's moment to enforce more orthodoxy, and I was one of the six who were disciplined in September with others, like Janice Allred and Margaret Toscano following later. Interestingly, Paul also used the metaphor of a journey, an interrupted one, in describing his feelings about my excommunication. Speaking at a prayer service in the White Memorial Chapel on the eve of my excommunication, he said:

I feel as though I have been in an accident, a collision on the highway. A large and heavily loaded truck, an 18 wheeler with tremendous power and momentum, has collided with several small cars filled with passengers. The cars are smashed and run off the road. Windshields are broken. Some people are bleeding and crying. Everyone is in shock. The press has arrived, taking photographs and describing the scene. It is a little hard to tell just how it happened. Those of us in the cars say we were travelling along, heading in the same direction as the truck, in an adjacent parallel lane. There were a few honks on the horn, some screeching of tires, followed by a collision. The truck driver isn't telling how he sees it. There were many witnesses, but they don't agree on what happened or whose fault it was.

We wander through the scene, talking with the injured, feeling our own sore places, comforting the frightened, assessing the damage. We are bleary with shock and sick with fear. Then slowly it dawns on us. There are many cuts and bruises, a few broken bones, but we have all survived. There are no life-threatening injuries. Healing may take a good long time, feelings of fear and insecurity may persist for a while, especially in the presence of big trucks, there may be a danger of infection for some wounds if they are not properly tended, but we have all survived substantially intact. All of us can hope to heal completely. We are going to be all right. We are suddenly filled with a sense of relief and gratitude, and we put our arms around our family and friends with increased feelings of appreciation and love.

This could have been another point of dramatically intersecting roads in my journey, but Paul and I were committed to seeing that thirteen-year-old Christian have as normal a Mormon experience as possible. Paul had been on the stake high council two years earlier but had resigned to teach Christian's Primary class after a series of unprepared and unimaginative teachers. My excommunication meant that Paul was not called for the second time into the bishopric. He would almost certainly have been called as bishop, but my excommunication gave him immunity and meant, ironically, that Christian had two full-time parents as a teenager. That was good for all three of us.

There were other points of intersection: Christian's decision to serve a mission, his meeting Marina Capella,[2] and their participation as full partners that has filled Paul and me with pride and joy as we have watched their lives unfold.

And now Paul's death. I have tried to explain my feelings that, after the numbness and shock have worn off—and I'm still not there yet—I will know that the very decisiveness of Paul's death is a blessing. We have not had to deal with the agony of a prolonged dying, in which Paul's personality was stripped away before his body gave out, or with the anguish of asking ourselves, "What if we'd done this or that differently?" Or "If only we had known or done something else or been somewhere else." It was about fifty minutes—not even

---

2. I certainly won the daughter-in-law sweepstakes when Christian married Marina. I can think of no greater compliment from a daughter-in-law than that Marina, not Christian, originated and lobbied for their move to Salt Lake City in the aftermath of Paul's death. In return here's my own compliment to Marina. Christian was in Salt Lake City for an event on Friday, March 23, 2018. We had just walked into the house, and I proposed hot chocolate before we went to bed. Paul said, sounding rather puzzled, "I think I might be going to faint." He sat down at the kitchen table and slumped forward. It was obvious that he was in distress, and I said urgently to Christian, "Call Marina!" Fortunately, he called 911 instead and immediately began CPR. We did not know that Paul was already dead—that he would never take another breath; but I pay this tribute to my wonderful daughter-in-law: At this moment of crisis when a catastrophe was upon us, I wanted Marina to be with us.

a full hour—from the time we entered our home until the paramedics packed up, told us to call the mortician, and left. I thanked the ward officers and members who had showed up simultaneously with the paramedics and begged them to go home, since it was already midnight; they did so, except for Pam and Lynn Carson who said, quietly but firmly, that they would stay until the mortician arrived. They told us family death stories, some of them comical, discussed the mixture of church doctrine and folklore that sudden death brings out, brought us to laughter, and shared our tears.

And now two insights that I've learned from Paul's death. The first is what I call proxy housekeeping. Those of you who have visited our home in the past eight or ten years have noticed the accumulation in corners and under desks of many boxes of miscellaneous items and papers. Paul had boxes going back to his days at Pasadena High School, Stanford, Princeton, the Church Museum of Art, his work at the Brigham Young Museum of Art, and his father's papers. I was always so happy whenever we had visitors for dinner or overnight because Paul had to clean his snowdrifts of papers off the guestroom beds or the kitchen table. His method was to put everything in a box and then pile the box on top of other boxes. As I tackled the job of sorting those papers, I wondered if I would feel angry at Paul for not doing it himself or feel pain because I was disposing of things he had accumulated and kept, whether for good reasons or not. I think Paul may have been a bit of a hoarder; and so, in sorting his papers, I'm doing for him something that he could not do for himself. I have felt increased affection and appreciation, not anger or pain—hence, proxy housekeeping.

And the second is that we really can call down the blessings of heaven for each other. I have always prayed for those who were suffering or put their names on the temple prayer roll because I so desperately want to do something and usually there's so little that lies within my power. But now Christian, Marina, and I have been the recipients of many prayers, and I can literally feel them, like a touch on my shoulder or a kiss on my cheek.

I'll close with a prayer by a nineteenth-century clergyman, Henry Twells (1823–1900), that Paul's best friend in the ward, Lynn Carson, has set to music:

> At even ere the sun had set,
> The sick, O Lord, around thee lay
> O, with how many pains they met!
> O, with what joy they went away.
> Once more 'tis eventide, and we
> Oppress'd with various ills, draw near.
> What if Thyself we cannot see?
> We know that Thou art ever near.
> O Savior Christ, our woes dispel,
> For some are sick, and some are sad,
> And some have never lov'd Thee well,
> And some have lost the love they had.
> And some are press'd with worldly care,
> And some are tried with sinful doubt
> And some such grievous passions tear
> That only Thou can cast them out.
> And some have found the world is vain,
> Yet from the world they break not free;
> And some have friends who give them pain,
> And have not sought a friend in Thee.
> And none, O Lord, have perfect rest,
> For none are wholly free from sin—
> And they who fain would love Thee best,
> Are conscious most of wrong within.
> O Savior Christ, Thou too art man;
> Thou hast been troubled, tempted, tried,
> Thy kind but searching glance can scan
> The very wounds that shame would hide.
> Thy touch has still its ancient pow'r,

No word from Thee can fruitless fall;
Hear, in this solemn evening hour,
And in Thy mercy heal us all.

2

Mercy without End

When my disciplinary council was scheduled for September 23, 1993, I told Paul I wished there was a way to let people come together in a community expression of support and affirmation of the liberal aspects of the gospel that we both felt were among the finest expressions of Mormonism. It beggared belief that six ecclesiastical officers in almost as many LDS wards/stakes had spontaneously decided to clean house that fall, and evidence emerged later than the church's area presidents, primarily Elder Loren C. Dunn, acting on Apostle Boyd K. Packer's instructions, had been told to discourage intellectual and feminist activity. The "September Six" coalesced in two weeks into a small group who were, for the most part, not unwilling to explain issues to the media that their ecclesiastical officers refused to hear. They were Lynne Kanavel Whitesides (disfellowshipped September 14), Avraham Gileadi and D. Michael Quinn (excommunicated September 15), Paul J. Toscano and Maxine Hanks (excommunicated September 18), and I (excommunicated September 23). By my count, an additional twenty people had formally resigned from membership in the church between September and November. My husband, Paul, promptly arranged to rent the White Memorial Chapel on Capitol Hill (downtown Salt Lake City), a recreation of the Eighteenth Ward Chapel (built after Brigham Young's Death. It was jammed to the walls when the meeting convened on the evening of September 22. I had asked the incomparable Ardean Watts, past associate conductor of the Utah Symphony, to accompany our hymn singing, which he did with the verve of a full-scale orchestra. I had selected as a theme Enoch's description of God from LDS canon: "And naught but peace, justice, and truth is the habitation of thy throne; and mercy shall go before thy face and have no end" (Moses 7:31). At my invitation, Maxine Hanks addressed the topic of peace, Lynne Whitesides spoke on justice, Mary Ann Morgan shared insights about truth, and Martha Sonntag-Bradley spoke passionately about the brutality women experience from childhood of being vulnerable to punishment for asking questions. I felt particularly drawn to the last phrase: "Mercy shall go before thy face and have no end." These remarks were integrated into a larger article, "Freedom of Conscience: A Personal Statement," and published in Dialogue: A Journal of Mormon Thought *26 (Winter 1993): 196–202.*

My dear brothers, sisters, and friends, I don't know how to express my gratitude for your presence tonight. I woke up very early this morning with a feeling of happy anticipation thinking about tonight. Even though this evening is not primarily for me, I feel it as part of an extraordinary support and love that have surrounded me for the last week and a half. One friend appeared on my doorstep yesterday with hugs and apricot jam. Another nourished us with lasagna and her love simultaneously. A third stopped by and said, "I thought maybe you could use a roll of stamps." Friends from the Reorganized Church of Jesus Christ of Latter Day Saints sent devotional thoughts and five boxes of chocolates. Flowers have sprouted all over the kitchen. A pot of chili appeared on the stove. There have been literally scores of phone calls, letters, notes, and cards. People have asked to be witnesses for me at the disciplinary council and have been disappointed when I've explained that I won't be attending. Paul, Christian, and I will never forget this kindness and generosity.

I also want to thank those who disagree with me and discuss it with me. I'm committed to the process of communicating in respect and love about our differences. I don't think any of these people have changed my mind, and I don't think I've changed theirs, but the process of talking through those differences has affirmed our relationship. I honor these people as an important part of the process of dialogue in our community.

So thank you for being at this meeting, bringing your diversity of approaches, motivations, and concerns with you. This meeting isn't even on behalf of the September Six. It's for all of us, here and elsewhere, who feel a need for healing, reconciliation, and new peace in the church.

I've been thinking lately about metaphors for the church. I'm becoming increasingly uncomfortable with military metaphors that compare the church to an army, with corporate views, or with the mechanical model that treats a member like a defective toaster that can be unplugged and thrown away while a new one is plugged in. I've heard the church called a family, though a dysfunctional one.

I find myself returning with new appreciation to the Apostle Paul's metaphor of the church as a body (1 Cor. 12:27–31). I've always thought of this metaphor in the simple, straightforward, seminary way where the body is diversity, not only diversity in the callings we have in the church but also diversity in our personalities and gifts. I've been thinking lately of what the body does for a member in pain. A couple of weeks ago, when I started to pick a dead hornet off the window sill only to learn that it was quite alive, my brain didn't say, "Boy, what a stupid finger. Chop it off! We'll have to get a new one." No, my body gave that finger top priority and immediate attention. The feet carried that finger to the sink and the other hand poured ammonia over the sting. The eyes were stinging in sympathy. I'd been on my way to the refrigerator to make lunch, but my stomach suspended all distress calls for the next few minutes to give full attention to the finger. And then, a few minutes later when the crisis was over, both hands, even the still-shocked finger, helped make the sandwich that the stomach wanted. For the rest of the day, there was a tender place on the finger, and the other fingers returned to it frequently during the day to rub it and make it feel better.

I like the way the metaphor of the body feels. Even if amputation has to occur and the body compensates, it goes throughout the rest of its life acknowledging its crippledness, mourning its incompleteness.

My message tonight is simple: This month we stand revealed as a crippled and a crippling body of Christ, not functioning very well some of the time and apparently headed in an insane way toward functioning worse. I call on us to reject this metaphor and instead think of the healthy body, in touch with all its parts and members, tending and nurturing all of its parts with the whole in turn being nurtured by those parts. I say that there is a place in the church for all of us because there is room in the grace of Christ for every human being in the world. Mother Teresa says that Christ would have died for you if you were the only person in the world who needed his redemption. I want us to feel that grace, that redemption.

The Apostle Paul makes another important point: "Those parts of the body that seem to be weaker are indispensable, and the parts that we think are less honorable we treat with special honor. And the parts that are unpresentable are treated with special modesty, while our presentable parts need no special treatment" (1 Cor. 12:27, NIV). Being placed on probation, disfellowshipped, or excommunicated have always represented shame, separation from the body of the church, dishonor, and diminishment. But that does not necessarily represent people's experience. For some, the severing of ties with the church represents freedom and exhilarating spiritual growth. Among such are one of my dearest friends from college and another is a former missionary companion. For both of them, I'm convinced that their choices were right. For a second group, such judgment represents a humble choice, part of a necessary repentance, like surgery to correct an infected fingernail. And in a third group of cases, it's brutal amputation, without anesthetic, producing wounds that remain unhealed.

As one of those under ecclesiastical sanction, even though the court will not meet until tomorrow, I stand before you. Whether the discipline is something that you sought and welcomed as part of your repentance or accepted as marking a new stage in your spiritual journey that took you in another direction, I feel a kinship with you. Could I ask those of you who have also felt the sting of being told you are an unworthy member, for whatever reason, to join me in standing up? [We applauded for them—about half the audience.]

Thank you. I'm through drawing lines between sheep and goats. That's not my job. I'm a feminist and an intellectual, and I'm *not* a danger to the Church of Jesus Christ. Homosexuals have long been the most stigmatized group of Mormons. I'm through believing that they also are dangerous. I say that there's room for all of us.

This is a night for miracles. It's time to seek a different paradigm, time to create other metaphors, to see with new eyes, hear with new ears. That's why this is a prayer service, rather than a protest rally. We are met here tonight in power—the power of faith, of praise, and of worship. We are calling down miracles.

As Paul has explained, each speaker will address one aspect of Enoch's description of God in Moses 7:31: "And naught but peace, justice, and truth is the habitation of thy throne; and mercy shall go before thy face and have no end." I've taken the last phrase for my text: "Mercy shall go before thy face and have no end." John Donne's sermon, given at St. Paul's Church in London, on Christmas day 1624, illuminates the concept of mercy:

God made sun and moon to distinguish seasons, and day, and night, and we cannot have the fruits of the earth but in their seasons. But God hath made no decree to distinguish the seasons of his mercies. In paradise, the fruits were ripe the first minute; and in heaven it is always autumn: his mercies are ever in their maturity. We ask [for] ... our daily bread, and God never says "You should have come yesterday." He never says "You must [come] again tomorrow"; but today if you will hear his voice, today he will hear you.

If some king of the earth have so large an extent of dominion, in north and south, as that he hath winter and summer together in his dominions; so large an extent east and west, as that he hath day and night together in his dominions; much more hath God mercy and judgment together.

He brought light out of darkness, not out of a lesser light; he can bring thy summer out of winter, though thou have no spring. Though in the ways of fortune, or understanding, or conscience, thou have been benighted till now, wintered and frozen, clouded and eclipsed, damped and benumbed, smothered and stupefied till now, now God comes to thee, not as in the dawning of the day, not as in the bud of the spring, but as the sun at noon to illustrate all shadows, as the sheaves in harvest to fill all penuries. All occasions invite his mercies, and all times are his seasons.[1]

This is the God we worship, the God whose mercy has no end.

---

1. John Donne, "St Paul's. Christmas Day in the Evening, 1624," in *Renaissance England: Poetry and Prose from the Reformation to the Restoration,* Roy Lamson and Hallett Smith, eds. (New York: W. W. Norton, 1956), 834.

3

Sacrament Meeting,
Whittier Ward, Salt Lake City, 1993

I prepared this talk as an evening fireside address for a study group in Salt Lake City, February 18, 1995. This is its first publication.

December 12, 1993. Sacrament meeting in Whittier Ward. Paul and I are sitting on the north side of our two-aisled chapel, the third row back, a row that has become our family territory since we moved into the ward three months after marrying in June 1977. Christian is passing the sacrament to our section, his face set in deacon deadpan but his eyes flickering quickly to my face. I wink at him. He holds the tray for Paul, who has been staring at his scrawled notes about next week's Christmas program. Absently, Paul lifts a piece of bread to his mouth, then takes the handle to pass the tray to me. Christian's eyes widen. He grips the tray harder, not relinquishing it. Paul looks up in surprise, then remembers. His hand drops. We all smother grins. Christian goes to the next row.

Then I feel the pain somewhere under my ribs. Not really pain. A pang. These are my husband and my son, the two men I love most, the two men who love me most dearly. My husband began a gesture of inclusion because he forgot. My son completed the gesture of exclusion because he remembered.

I have been excommunicated for eighty days.

✦

I was reared by parents for whom the church was family and more than family. Both of them had ancestors who crossed the plains before the railroad, but Daddy was orphaned by the age of twelve and Mama's father was never active. She tells of her mother, for whom I am named, contriving to shield her and her sister as they sneaked out the back door to Primary. Both parents served missions in the South at immense sacrifice. One of the forces bringing them together was their mutual commitment to the church, their testimonies of its truthfulness. Daddy was twice a ward bishop, both times building a chapel when that job meant coordinating the volunteer labor of the members and raising most of the money. Mama worked in and/or presided over every women's auxiliary on both the stake and ward levels, but Primary was her special love.

There was never any question in my mind when I was growing up of what the church meant. All six of us children went to all of our meetings, read scriptures, married in the temple. I earned every individual award available except for Golden Gleaner, then the height of a ladder of achievement awards for girls. Both brothers and I served missions. My sisters served stake missions and, with their husbands, have since served at least two full-time missions apiece. Our son, Christian, like most of his cousins and in-laws, served a mission and married in the temple.

I thought my excommunication would devastate my parents, who had spent their honeymoon doing endowments at the Logan temple (Utah). They served as ordinance workers in the Seattle temple from 1980 to 2001, crossing the Cascade Mountains for the four-hour drive from their home in Othello, Washington, twice a month, no matter how bad the winter weather was. When the Columbia River temple opened in 2001, they became ordinance workers there until my mother's health became too fragile. After her death in 2007, my father continued his service at that temple every day until he was in his nineties.

Their loyalty to the church has been so passionate, so deep, that we grew up without a vocabulary for discussing it with them. It was simply part of the family weather. When I wrote to them, during the summer of 1993, sketching the "disagreement" with my stake president over my *Dialogue* article on the institutional church's discomfort with its intellectual community,[1] I did it because the Spirit that had been whispering to me all summer told me I must. Time was running out.

I imagined every kind of accusation and recrimination; but my parents, siblings, and in-laws did not play from that script. "We love you," they say, even when they don't fully understand what I did or don't share my feelings. Paul's family has been the same. My father recruited my brother Lynn to help him write a long letter to my stake president for the disciplinary council. I liked the whole letter, but especially two paragraphs:

> We have had a family member hung by a mob in Nauvoo for the Church, and we have had a family member jailed for six years without trial, (also Nauvoo) but we have never had one disfellowshipped and certainly not for accurately telling some uncomfortable truths. ...
>
> I am 78 and just an old potato farmer but even I find it difficult to believe that the trial/hearing of six scholars and writers in the same week in Utah is the result of local action.

The stories we never heard around the dinner table growing up are being told now. Lynn told me that Daddy spent eight months trying to extract payment from the Church Building Department for the contractor who installed Warden Ward's furnace, then walking in just before October conference and announcing to the scowling official, "The church pays its bills. I left seventy acres of

---

1. "The LDS Intellectual Community and Church Leadership: A Contemporary Chronology," *Dialogue: A Journal of Mormon Thought* 26, no. 1 (Spring 1993): 7–64. Winner of the Lowell L. Bennion Prize for Essays in Gospel Living.

beans in the field to come to conference, and I'm telling you that I'm not leaving Salt Lake City until I have a check for that contractor." He left town with the check the Monday after general conference.

Daddy also told me a story I'd never heard before. When he was a new bishop, the stake president instructed him to hold a court on a man who had been inactive for years. Daddy reluctantly did and excommunicated the man in absentia. The man died a few weeks later and Daddy, who had not talked to him before or after the court, looked back on that fifty-year-old event with unslaked remorse. "I know I'm going to have to answer for that," he told me. "I shouldn't a done it, and I knew I shouldn't a done it."

✛

My entire family is active in the church. Even me. Even now. In the weeks since my excommunication, I have been out of town on Sunday once and had the flu once. On the other Sundays, even when Paul is gone, I sit on the third row back, north side. When the deacons come by, I shake my head at the tray and look away from their puzzled glance.

I sing the hymns. Some of them now have meanings that I had never imagined. I say "amen" to the prayers. I follow along during the lessons, only occasionally raising my hand when the teacher asks a question, taking notes. "I'm an archivist," I tell people, "not an activist." They always laugh.

For the first time since age eighteen, I am not a visiting teacher. People with flu are happy for the soup anyway. As a family, Paul, Christian, and I continue our custom of family prayer, of reading the scriptures and singing hymns every night after supper.

✛

This path probably started at the *Ensign*, where I was hired as the women's editor in 1973. I met Leonard Arrington, who had become Church Historian two years before. I instantly loved Leonard—his sunny cheerfulness, his astonishing erudition, his serene faith that testimony and scholarship could function hand in glove, or perhaps hand *and* glove, his contagious joy in his work. Thanks to Leonard, the same mood prevailed with his staff of people, mostly around my age, who were rediscovering the documents, reinterpreting and rewriting Mormon history. It was a zestful, heady time.

I frequently joined the historians at their big round table for lunch in the church cafeteria, where the gossip and politics about the dead circulated with as much relish as about the living. I had dutifully filled out my four-generation sheets, but I'd always recoiled from genealogy itself, associating it with one family of obsessive compulsives in Warden, Washington, who, in an annual sacrament meeting mandated by the stake, saturated us with guilt. Around that lunch table, I began to realize that the dead were also the living. That was the beginning of loving them.

It felt right to bring their lives, their hopes, their demolished dreams, and their triumphs out of obscurity and out of darkness. It was a work of love. Many people, mostly of my generation, felt this same desire to love the Lord with all their minds as well as all their hearts. *Dialogue, Sunstone*, and *Exponent II*, were all born, as I saw it, out of an urgent love that demanded reconnections with the past. Something sang in me at the power of that past and the joy it brought to the present.

The rediscovery and recovery of the Mormon past were interwoven with two other values: my growing awareness of and dislike for church bureaucracy with its emphasis on loyalty, management, and control, and my loathing for the Nixon cover-ups of Watergate and the many paths leading to other pockets of corruption.

I would rather trust the truth, I thought. Yes, truth is not simple, it's not just one thing, it's not always expedient, and maybe it can shake faith. But the antidote isn't less truth, more management, more silence. It's to keep talking, keep asking the questions, keep looking. How else can we know the truth? What else is worthy of the Church of Jesus Christ?

The institutional backlash began almost immediately during the late 1970s and early '80s. When the voices of fear began, when rifts developed between the institutional church and the historians, when LDS feminist Sonia Johnson's excommunication set the boundary beyond which Mormon feminism should not pass, when Elder Packer threatened church employees who did not "keep confidentiality," when Linda Newell and Val Avery were forbidden to speak in sacrament meeting because of their biography of Emma Smith,[2] I insisted that these were aberrations, that the real model to follow was the smiling serenity of Leonard Arrington, who saw truth—the whole truth—as the friend of faith, not its foe.

I think I made my choice then. Against silence, against fear, against an anxious tending of other people's testimonies lest they be "shaken." I made a choice for love, for responsible truth-telling, for trusting that with truth and love come understanding and forgiveness, for believing that the most important kind of obedience is obedience to conscience, that the most important loyalty is to Jesus Christ and the principles of his gospel. I bitterly regret that I never wrote to historian Juanita Brooks in the early 1970s before Alzheimer's claimed her, stammering my gratitude that she had told the truth about the Mountain Meadows massacre. I would have told her, "I would rather know the truth, even a hard truth, than a pretty lie or a soft half-truth."

As the betrayals and blood of Mark Hofmann's forgeries came into focus through the dust and smoke of his bombs and the violation of trust became clearer, so did my conviction. *Tell the truth, more truth, more sides of the truth, deeper levels of the truth.* I watched

---

2. Linda King Newell and Valeen Tippets Avery, *Mormon Enigma: Emma Hale Smith, Prophet's Wife, "Elect Lady," Polygamy's Foe* (Garden City, New York: Doubleday, 1984).

the church employ new and more sophisticated management techniques to control its history, trying to flash-freeze one version of an organic, healthy, growing process into awkward permanence. I saluted Linda Sillitoe and Allen Roberts for writing *Salamander: The Story of the Mormon Forgery Murders*, for dealing immediately with the violence, with the collusion and betrayal of a community. I thank them for saving us from the century of festering silence and lies that Juanita Brooks ended for the whole church by her truth-telling. I sorrow over the price they paid for theirs.

During these *Ensign* years (1973–81) of questions and exploration, I never missed church, even when it was boring and unfulfilling. I never stopped going to the temple, even when my awakening feminism asked increasingly painful questions. I never refused a calling. I never stopped believing that the church was true, no matter how some of its leaders and members behaved. I never stopped loving it. I never thought of leaving it.

But I also never tried to persuade myself that everything that came across the pulpit was true. I never believed it was right to punish historians (or sociologists or artists or writers or feminists or journalists or economists) for telling the truth. I never believed it was right for someone to win an argument just because he had the heavier title.

In August 1991 when the joint council of the First Presidency and the Quorum of the Twelve issued a solemn warning against unauthorized "symposia," a nightmare feeling came over me. I saw the church taking a step into a dark age of its own creation. I had watched Maureen Ursenbach Beecher, Jill Mulvay Derr, Carol Cornwall Madsen, and others around that historians' lunch table reconstruct the Nauvoo vision of women from their documents because no one alive knew the stories of our great-grandmothers. A whole generation of Mormon women's history had been erased by the women themselves in silence and self-censorship, eradicating the living memory of women's spiritual gifts that came into being with the Nauvoo generation. That's when I thought of becoming an archivist—to create a record of my own ward, my friends' experience, my own thoughts. If the church can stop the explorations of the Mormon intellectual community, I thought, it will only last for two generations at most. Is there some way to be sure we won't have to start completely over? To understand the time of silence so we can guard against it?

I took minutes in every church meeting I attended, talked to friends about their experiences, and started sorting the shambling heap of newspaper clippings and manuscripts that had been accumulating in my filing cabinets.

All through the winter, spring, and summer of 1992, as I researched and wrote, I prayed, as I had for years, over similar issues: "Am I just being proud? Am I just being stubborn? What's the right thing to do?" The answers were simple Sunday School phrases: *Tell the truth. Love unconditionally. Cherish freedom.* As autumn became winter, as I proofread the editing on my *Dialogue* article, I kept praying. I read the Book of Mormon once, then again. I underlined the warnings against rebellion, against contention, against pride. I knew I had stepped over a line marking the limits of orthodoxy, like the yellow tape the police string around a crime scene. Surely I should feel darkness, a stupor of thought. Surely I was walking on quicksand. But the next step was always clear, the ground was always firm, the sense of peace was always strong.

The darkness had come earlier, when I was trying to find a way to stay inside the yellow tape. During the winter of 1991–92, I had a cold that developed into laryngitis. During its hardest clamp on my vocal cords, I dreamed of being a stick figure that was being erased from a chalkboard. I knew that keeping the records wasn't enough. I felt the prompting to speak out, to go on the record, to stand up and say, "Look at this pattern. It's hurting people. It's hurting the church. It's not necessary." I prayed. I hoped that general authorities would read my article and, if not immediately, still feel that there was a healthier direction in which to steer the church. But I also knew what happens to messengers who deliver bad news.

I prayed, "Is speaking out the right thing to do?" The answer was an instantaneous, "Yes." Simultaneously I heard a click, the creation of a solid core of resolve in myself I had never felt before that turned and locked into place. I did not ask, "Will I be punished?" I think, on some level, that I didn't want to know. I've never been a candidate for Martyr of the Month. I knew that my hope was deep and suspected that my courage was shallow. I wanted to act out of hope.

✢

I reported my research on the troubled relationship between the institutional church and its members at the Washington, DC, Sunstone symposium in the spring of 1992. I continued to pray. The core of steadfastness in myself was still there, stronger than my spine, my skull. In August, I delivered a fuller version at the Salt Lake City symposium. *Dialogue* asked to publish it in the spring 1993 issue. I continued praying. "Is this right?" "Yes," the answer came. "For the captives shall go free."

An RLDS friend wrote in June 1993:

I'm most of the way through your "contemporary chronology" in *Dialogue*. I find it both fascinating and disturbing. One of the really vast differences between our churches is in our attitudes toward and tolerance of authority. Some of our dissidents have complained about our First Presidency's supposed arbitrary use of their authority in the recent disputes. ... Compared to what you have described, they have nothing to gripe about. ... At their most authoritarian moments, our general authorities have never exercised the kind of control you describe as commonplace in the LDS church. I skipped ahead and read your proposals. They are excellent, rational, and reasonable. I can't imagine that anyone would have problems with any of them. But of course, someone will. I vigorously applaud your courage for writing the article, and may God be with you!

✦

I've always been suspicious of people with causes. The John Birch zealots at BYU gave me a slithery feeling. I turn off the television when I see pickets and yelling mouths. I don't like seeing my face on the evening news or reading my name in the newspaper. But now I have a cause. It probably could have been civil rights in the sixties or Vietnam in the seventies or neighborhood beautification, or the PTA, or the poetry of W. B. Yeates, or, if I'd married in college like my three sisters, a family of six or seven children. Maybe. I don't know. Maybe other people can choose their causes. Mine choose me.

Mormonism chose me. I grew up in the smallest of small towns, first, Moore, Idaho, with one paved street, until the fifth grade when we moved to Warden, Washington, which could boast paving on two streets. Moore was very Mormon. I knew only one child in my elementary school who wasn't Mormon. In Warden, thanks to the Grand Coulee Dam, Mormon farmers from Idaho were moving onto land that could be newly irrigated, displacing a previous generation of comfortable German dry farmers. Everyone in town got along in a respectable Community Church that worked out acceptable inter-denominationalism—except for the Catholics, who were nearly all Hispanics, and the Mormons. We were different and mildly ostracized for it. The teasing set my identity the way hot water sets dye.

Maybe if I hadn't hated farm labor so much, maybe if we'd had a television instead of books, maybe if I hadn't loved reading so much, maybe if my parents hadn't sacrificed their present and their future to see that we all got to BYU, maybe if I hadn't loved learning so much, maybe if I hadn't taken those scriptures so seriously about knowing the truth and becoming free, about light and truth being the glory of God ...

Somehow, perhaps because I was at BYU and then on a mission, I missed the 1960s. Maybe if I'd rebelled then—marched and chanted and called policemen pigs—I would have got it out of my system.

But it doesn't feel like rebellion, like defiance. It feels right, organic, like a plant lifting its leaves toward the light. I am what I am because of who I am. I'm a Mormon.

A friend wrote: "I saw you on the television news last night and thought what a peculiar religion we belong to, [where a true believer like you is excommunicated but] where a disbeliever but ostensible member like myself will be hounded until I die to participate—and after I'm dead mystic rituals in holy places will be performed to make up my lack of belief. ... Perhaps the only thing more disconcerting than unbelief is real belief."

✦

In June 1992 when Paul Toscano asked me to become a trustee of the Mormon Alliance, I refused. I wished them well, but I was just too busy. But people who had heard versions of my paper in Washington or Salt Lake City were calling me, telling me about a friend, an uncle, themselves. I had just read *The Subtle Power of Spiritual Abuse* by David Johnson and Jeff Van Vonderen (Minneapolis: Bethany House Publishers, 1991).

I listened, I took notes, I asked questions as people told me their stories. Often, when I used the term "spiritual or ecclesiastical abuse," they would stop me. "Spiritual abuse!" they would say, their voices lifting with discovery. "I didn't know what to call it but that's what happened to me. That's what it was."

I listened to their stories. I heard their pain. Many of the stories were terrible. Sometimes I felt anger and horror crawl over my skin as I listened. Sometimes I cried. Sometimes I was so exhausted after listening that I had to go to bed for an hour. Sometimes the spiritual strength of the person on the other end of the phone reached through to my spirit, and our conversation was a kind of prayer, glowing and affirming.

"I'm so sorry that happened," I would say. "That's a terrible, terrible thing. It's not the gospel. It's not what God intended to happen in his church. You know that God loves you, don't you? I'm here to tell you that he does." Those conversations felt like a calling. Not in the church but in the kingdom. I realized that I had accepted that calling just by saying, "Yes, I'll listen."

"I don't know how to do this," I prayed. "What if I hurt someone instead of helping them?"

"Mourn with those who mourn, and comfort those who stand in need of comfort," came the answer. I felt my heart turn toward those who felt they no longer had a place in the church. It felt right to say, "That shouldn't have happened. I'm so sorry."

"Nobody's ever listened before," said the voices on the other end of the line. "They've always said it's my fault. They've always said I must have misunderstood. They've always told me how to fix it."

When Paul Toscano asked me again to become a trustee, I said yes. Janice Merrill Allred and I jointly chaired the case reports committee and began meeting in the fall of 1992. The phone rang steadily. Strangers. Ordinary members of the church. Not the friends and acquaintances, the academics, historians, feminists, and intellectuals whom I had written about in *Dialogue*. Believing people like my family. Faithful women like my mother.

They told me about years of service, about their testimonies, about their sacrifices. They thought they belonged, thought they'd proved their loyalty, thought they were valuable members. They told me how none of it mattered when a leader turned on them. The details changed from story to story—the shape of the coercion, the outline of the punishment, the silhouette of dismissal—but the story was always the same: a leader who used his office to compel, to intimidate, to silence.

"He wouldn't listen."

"Everything I'd done—it counted for nothing."

"I was so angry. I'm still so angry. I can't force myself to walk into the chapel."

"I felt wadded up and thrown away."

"I wanted to die."

✛

Elder Loren C. Dunn, the area president, gave my stake president a photocopy of the *Dialogue* article and the invitation, printed in the letters section of the same issue, to contact the Mormon Alliance. President Marlin S. Miller called my husband and me into a meeting with him and his two counselors the first week in May 1993. They asked questions and listened courteously for an hour. When we left, Paul said, "Well, nothing we said made any difference."

President Miller had made two conditions: I needed to repudiate the *Dialogue* article—apologize for it; and I needed to stop talking to people about their negative experiences with their leaders. Otherwise, he didn't feel I was worthy of a temple recommend.

When I prayed that night, I was surprised to find gratitude springing up inside me. Then I recognized the blessing. President Miller had made it so easy. What if he'd said, "There are times when we have to sacrifice one thing we love for another thing we love"? I could have been on the rack for weeks over that question. "He's asked you to apologize for telling the truth." The voice that usually answered my prayers sounded as if it were smiling. "He's asked you to turn away from people in pain, to say 'It's not important. You don't matter.' Is this a hard choice?" It wasn't.

President Miller and I spent the sweltering summer of 1993 in a stately exchange of correspondence, I from the cool clarity of our mountain cabin east of Salt Lake City, he from his office in the stake center behind the Arctic Circle on Seventeenth South. I tried repeatedly to reframe the question of responsibility for spiritual and ecclesiastical abuse in a way that he could see it. I failed. He kept explaining that the issue was one of not embarrassing the church.

He insisted that I return my temple recommend. I refused because I did not feel unworthy but promised not to use it "until this matter is resolved." He called the temples and told them not to honor my recommend. In my whole life, I had never been treated like a liar before. It hurt.

I asked again and again for President Miller to arrange an appointment for me with Elder Dunn. He refused. When I wrote directly to Elder Dunn, it was President Miller who answered. He said Elder Dunn agreed with him that this was a local matter. It hurt again, to realize that I was not worth even the twenty-nine-cent stamp it would have taken for Elder Dunn to tell me "no" himself.

That was when I knew, when the voice became distinct: *There will be a disciplinary council. You are not to attend. You will be excommunicated. You will not be reinstated for a long time.*

I didn't think it would come so fast. I thought that, once we moved back from the cabin at the end of August, President Miller and I would meet again, that I'd try again and probably fail again to meet with Elder John E. Fowler, Elder Dunn's replacement, that President Miller would read other things I'd written (he probably wouldn't like them either), and that the show-down would probably come in the spring of 1994 when the first volume of case reports appeared.

I woke up the Sunday morning of stake conference, September 12, with the words of a letter running through my mind—the explanation to President Miller about why I would not attend the disciplinary council. "I don't need to worry about this now," I thought.

Paul, Christian, and I sang in the family choir at stake conference. The letter summoning me to a disciplinary council for "conduct unbecoming a member" was delivered an hour after we got home. I wrote my letter explaining that I would not attend.

People were astounded. "But why won't you go?" they asked. One reporter, an inactive Mormon, turned off the camera and said, "I'm disappointed in you. You should fight for your membership."

I explained dozens of times that I accepted President Miller's jurisdiction over me but not over the problem of ecclesiastical abuse. Not going was a way of keeping the two issues separate. It sounded plausible, reasonable. But it was not the real reason. The real reason was that constraining spirit, whispering cool and clear in the canyon: *You will be excommunicated. You are not to attend.* I had been saving up arguments all my adult life for this court. I had long lists of things to say. But I felt utterly at peace.

The high council of Wells Stake met on the night of September 23. Three friends made statements and came away feeling downcast and depressed. By then Lynne Whitesides had been disfellowshipped. Avraham Gileadi, Paul Toscano, and Maxine Hanks had been excommunicated. Michael Quinn's court was scheduled for the next Sunday. To no one's surprise, he was also excommunicated.

I had made a statement at Lynne's disciplinary council and another at Paul's. Virgil Merrill, Lynne's bishop, and Kerry Heinz, Paul's stake president, had looked straight at me as I read my statement. There were no interruptions. The few questions afterward were courteous. Their eyes were expressionless. It was very clear that nothing I said would make a difference. I said it anyway—for the record, on the record, to make a record.

✦

The letter, delivered the morning of September 24, said "excommunicated." I looked for the reason. "You are outside of the principles of the gospel and are leading others with you. ... This has been done out of love and concern for you." I still wasn't sure why I'd been excommunicated. I telephoned President Miller. "Apostasy," he said. "I'd be happy to revise the letter."

I realized that it didn't matter very much, but I wondered when the charges had been changed, what would have happened if I'd gone to the disciplinary council, prepared with a defense against conduct unbecoming a member.

My brother Lynn, my husband, Paul, and I were up most of the night of October 22–23 working on the appeal to the First Presidency. It was thirty-seven pages long with nineteen attached documents, neatly organized in two sections—procedural problems and the substantive issue of ecclesiastical abuse, each with orderly, numbered lists. We got punchy in the middle of the night, giggling like undergraduates slugging through a research paper. After I turned in the appeal, I noticed, to my professional embarrassment, that it was misdated October 13. There was also a typo in the third paragraph.

When Paul and I drove away after delivering it, I felt an enormous burden lift, one I didn't even know I was bearing. *It's out of your hands now,* the voice whispered. *Your part is over. You don't need to be anxious about what happens from here on.*

My stake president sent me a note a couple of weeks later saying he had sent it on to the First Presidency. He explained that the charge was initially "conduct unbecoming a member" instead of "apostasy" so it would be "less embarrassing" for my family. Paul and I looked at each other. Had we heard right? Less embarrassing to have people think I was excommunicated for adultery, for being convicted of a felony? The stake president added that, furthermore, apostasy *is* conduct unbecoming a member.

What does apostasy mean? All summer, all fall, the definitions have swirled confusingly. How can people who love the church, believe it's true, believe that the general authorities are prophets, seers and revelators, have testimonies of the Savior—how can they be apostates? At October's general conference, Elder James E. Faust read the triple definition of apostasy from the church's handbook:

opposing the church, teaching false doctrine, sympathizing with a cult. The real definition was in his long quotation from George Q. Cannon who squelched the Godbeites in the 1860s: disagreeing in public with the general authorities.

It was inevitable, this slide toward simplicity. The need for something as behaviorally clear-cut as adultery was desperate. But now President Miller and those he reported to could be determined by a simple catechism:

Was it in public? Of course it was. We have the published article. We have the Sunstone tape.

Was it disagreement with the general authorities? Of course it was. Otherwise Elder Dunn wouldn't have sent it to us.

But was it true? True? What does that have to do with it?

I worried about two things. First, I did not want to feel bitter toward President Miller, the high councilors, or the general authorities involved in the excommunications. I knew President Miller was a good soldier, a decent man, doing what he thought was right. Would I still feel the same way after he'd excommunicated me?

Second, I had already made a commitment to keep attending church. If Juanita Brooks, never formally disciplined but almost totally ostracized, could do it, so could I. But how hard would it be? Would I have enough strength? And what if people were mean to Christian or made nasty remarks to Paul?

On Wednesday, September 22, the night before the disciplinary council, about 150 friends filled the White Memorial Chapel on Capitol Hill.[3] We prayed, sang, and bore testimony. It was an affirmation of love. As Ardean Watts led us in the spine-tingling "Lord's Prayer," Larry Toscano jumped to his feet on the front row, his face radiant with exultation. Then the rest of us were on our feet, singing

---

3. See Chapter 2, "Mercy without End."

the power, the glory. That feeling tingled about us as Jack Newell pronounced the benediction.

The first problem—my feeling for those involved in the excommunication—was taken care of. *Fear not, I am with thee, O be not dismayed ...* Wednesday night and the White Chapel is me, I thought ungrammatically. Whatever happens Thursday night is them. I started to understand one reason why I was not to go. It freed me to love and forgive them. I hope it did the same for them.

The second problem was easy, too. Kevin Jones called up. "I want to go to church with you," he said abruptly. "If you think you're going to have a hard time or if nobody else is going to sit on your row, I want to be there." Kevin, a fast-talking attorney with a quirky sense of humor, had had a long stretch of inactivity during his early twenties when he was struggling with a serious illness and botched surgery. It was while he was on *Dialogue's* executive committee that he had come back to church, gone to the temple, and become elders' quorum president in his ward.

"I think it'll be all right," I said. "I promise I'll call you if it's not."

The first Sunday after my excommunication, I sat on the second row from the back in Relief Society, listening to someone else play the piano. When the lesson was over, a half-dozen older women crowded around me to hug me. "We love you," one of them murmured. "Keep coming," said another. "Did you see how many were in opening exercises at Sunday school?" asked a third. "I think it's because of you. You're making people search their souls. I know I'm searching mine."

The bishop was standing at the door to the chapel. He took my hand and pulled me into a hug, smiling warmly. Paul was on the stand that day, leading the choir. Christian was sitting with the deacons until after the sacrament was passed. I would have to walk alone to the third row from the front, north side, and sit there alone, at least until after the sacrament was over and the choir had sung. It was a very long walk, but it wasn't a hard one. People kept stopping me, hugging me. When I sat down, it took me a minute to realize what I was feeling. Pride. I was so proud of my ward. They were behaving exactly as you'd hope a Christian community would behave.

"We can do it," I thought. "How long was it for you, Juanita? Thirty years? We can do it."

✢

People ask Paul how we're doing. "Fine," he says. "We're fine. Lavina's doing what she thinks is right. There should be room in the church for her." He sounds calm, but every now and then his own anger surprises him.[4]

People ask Christian how he feels about what's going on. "I'd probably be upset if Paul and Lavina were upset," he says matter-of-factly. Is anyone giving him grief at school? No, in fact, the kids come up and say, "I saw your mom on television." They're not sure what excommunication is, but they think that knowing anyone on TV is neat.

Blithely, he carols Paul Toscano's parody around the house to the tune of "Count Your Blessings" : "Excommunicate them one by one / Excommunicate them, it's such fun …" I can't help laughing.

"Isn't this hard on Christian?" people ask. I call Linda Newell and ask what happened to her children during the ban. She thinks

---

4. Speaking at Paul's memorial service on March 29, 2018, Paul Larsen, our next-door neighbor for twenty years who had volunteered to be a witness at my disciplinary council, found an occasion to sit in a hot tub with my husband a couple of years after the excommunication and ask directly, "How do you feel about it?" Paul Larsen continued: "I saw something I'd never seen before in Paul. I saw anger. This look came over him; he was furious, and the anger was coming through the water. … I climbed out of the hot tub, that's how intense it was." Feeling this way was deeply troubling to Paul, and he asked a close friend for spiritual advice. This friend quoted the commandment to "pray for them who despitefully use you and persecute you" (3 Ne. 12:44). With considerable misgivings about the sincerity of such a prayer, Paul did so and, in a surprisingly short time, discovered that the sincerity came. His anger dissolved, replaced by peace and genuine forgiveness.

being thirteen may be an advantage. Eric, their son who returned just before Christmas from his mission, was about thirteen then. I look for subtle signs of depression, uncertainty, regression. Christian is not subtle. "Are you on the phone *again*?" he demands.

I switch on the answering machine. We play Clue after supper and make a jigsaw puzzle, listening to the old comic records Paul and I accumulated during college: PDQ Bach, Tom Lehrer, the Smothers Brothers. From this island of serenity, the sea doesn't look so rough.

✦

Riddle: What are the two kinds of sheep Utah raises?
Answer: Blind and black.

✦

The phone never stopped ringing in those mostly pre-internet days. Twenty, thirty, even forty calls a day. Cards and letters stuffed the mailbox. I don't know how many. They bulged out of folders I labeled "Letters, excommunication, September." I made another for October. When we wrote my appeal to the First Presidency, due on October 23, Paul counted them. There were more than 200. I made another folder for November. Almost every Christmas card and letter came with a note, a letter. I haven't even started filing those yet. People wrote letters to my stake president, to the First Presidency, to us. Marti Esplin apologized for her angry missive to the First Presidency. "I just couldn't write one more sweet letter," she said.

Paul and I were stunned by the outpouring of love, of encouragement, of generosity. I had been braced for hostility, threats. There were many letters and calls from strangers but no anonymous ones. Not everyone approved, of course. Some told me I was wrong, raised questions, even chastised—but the tone was never harsh. When Steve Benson, Pulitzer Prize-winning cartoonist for the *Arizona Republic* and Ezra Taft Benson's grandson, told me in November that the response to his and wife Mary

Ann's withdrawal from the church was running about 60 percent for, 40 percent against, I blinked. At that point, I'd received a total of *seven* letters expressing disapproval. The count is still fewer than two dozen.

Pat Scott, the stalwart correspondence manager for the *Journal of Mormon History* and later co-executive secretary of the Mormon History Association, brought a bouquet of white roses the day after I received my letter about the disciplinary council and another on December 11, almost the three-month anniversary of the first letter. Leonard Arrington and his wife, Harriet, sent a note, called, brought flowers, took us out to dinner. At one point, we had eleven flower arrangements filling the house with exotic shapes and scents. They came from Los Angeles, Boston, Washington, DC, and Ann Arbor, as well as Utah. Ron Priddis and Gary Bergera brought five loaves of bread, one of each kind Great Harvest had made that day. Marti Bradley arrived with a pot of chili, Shauna Cook Clinger with lasagna, Perry Porter with homemade spaghetti sauce and French bread. I'd never even met Perry; he'd been following the situation on Mormon-L (an early Mormon-themed Internet forum). The son of a Chicago friend left four quarts of just-bottled peaches on our front porch. Two friends gave me tapes of music that had brought them solace. Another gave me scented soap, a third bubble bath. A grandmother in her eighties drove to my house to bring me a roll of stamps. Barbara Howard, leading the devotional at the John Whitmer Historical Association annual meeting, spoke of reconciliation and sent a package of sweet basil seeds to me, delivered by Richard Jensen. Every night in family prayer, we thanked God for the kindness being shown us.

A friend, observing the welter of cards, the counters loaded with flowers, commented, "It's like a funeral."

Paul smiled, "But everybody's still alive." We are. Alive and well!

+

I spent the autumn writing letters and talking on the phone. *We're fine. We're really doing okay. No, Paul isn't in any jeopardy [at work] that we know of. Christian's fine. Our ward's been great. I'm fine, too. I thought I'd cry a lot, be paralyzed with depression. I thought I'd be angry. But none of that has happened. Of course it's horrible. It can't be anything but horrible. Still, I feel … peaceful, at peace, at ease. Thank you so much for calling, for writing. Thank you for caring. Thank you …*

+

There are always reasons for not speaking the truth. It is not always expedient. It does not always edify. It always conflicts with someone else's view of the truth. It can be economically dangerous. It will upset your family. Someone with more authority or power can always tell you why your version is not the best version. The church owns the truth—not the members. Don't counsel the Brethren. Don't steady the ark. Don't get out of line. Don't wash dirty linen in public. The church's enemies will use it against us. Have a little more patience. Trust us.

There are dozens of reasons—good reasons—for remaining silent. How many reasons does it take to speak out? At what point does silence become a lie? I do not regret my decision to speak out. I feel honored that I could testify to the truth.

+

It also seems as if I spent the fall bearing my testimony—to reporters, to lapsed Mormons, to non-Mormons, to strangers, to friends struggling with their own pain, explaining over and over again the plan of salvation, the nature of agency, the eternal identity of the individual, the unfailing love represented by Christ's atonement, the goals of religious community. Three weeks before my excommunication, I bore my testimony in Relief Society. I could not guess how many years would pass before I would be allowed to bear that same witness to my ward members.

A man who had been my home teacher more than twenty years earlier wrote, asking me a long list of questions, demanding if I had lost my testimony. I wrote back:

> Thank you for asking me about my testimony. The answer to all of the questions you asked in your letter is yes. I do have a testimony of all those things. Every Sunday in church I make the covenants of the sacrament in my mind and in my heart, just as I have always done. It is a great sorrow to me that I cannot manifest my acceptance of those covenants by physically partaking of the emblems of the Savior's atoning sacrifice, but I feel that my covenants are accepted of him. As I review the temple ceremony in my mind and as I think of the questions of the temple recommend interview, I can honestly answer [yes] to all of those questions—that I am keeping my temple covenants, including sustaining the leaders of the church.
>
> I love the church and believe its teachings. Speaking the truth in love is an act of supportiveness, trust, and confidence.

I meant the thanks. Opportunities to bear testimony are precious to me. I know that God lives and that he loves us and answers prayers. I know the Savior's love for us. I know that he died for us. I know the power of the atonement in my life. I know the power and beauty of the Book of Mormon. I started rereading it in January, as I have started every new year since President Ezra Taft Benson challenged the members of the church to make it more central to our lives, and I am struck anew by its intensity and energy. I know Joseph Smith was a prophet and that the truth which he shaped and cut loose from the mountain is rolling forth. I know these things by the witness and power of the Spirit. I say with Nephi, the Book of Mormon prophet, "I do not know the meaning of all things. ... nevertheless, ... I know that he loveth his children" (1 Ne. 11:17).

+

A bouquet of a thousand white roses, Sunday Gathering, the Olive Branch, postcards of peace and love to the general authorities throughout December, study groups, discussion groups, worship groups coming together, the Circle of Love in April ... Energy is running through the network.

Christian had a great time at the vigils but didn't want to go to the Olive Branch service in December. "More church," he said.

"Well," I tempted, "Ardean Watts is doing the music."

Christian's face lit up. "All *right*!" he exclaimed.

✦

"Was it worth doing?" a friend asks, apologizing if the question is too personal. "I mean, you can't change the church."

I didn't do it to change the church. I hope for change in the church, but changing the church isn't my job. I did it to change myself, to affirm myself, to confirm myself. I did it to be free. Each time someone tells the truth, the amount of truth in the world increases. When there is enough, then we will be free indeed.

I hold the personal belief that Mormon theology is an immensely enriching, empowering, and powerful intellectual system and that its reduction to the boring and predictable level of most Sunday school classes is one of the criminal acts we have all endured within the last quarter century. (I make an exception for Paul's Gospel Doctrine class, which has been known to draw such accolades from the often elderly, ill-educated, and faithful Saints of Whittier Ward as, "That lesson was better than TV!")

✦

January 6, 1994

A letter arrives from President Miller. It was absolutely what I expected, down to the last syllable, but I still feel heavy-hearted. I tell Paul, "I guess this proves that hope can exist in the face of certain knowledge." President Miller writes:

I have recently received a letter from the First Presidency. ... They ... deliberated and pondered [your appeal] carefully and concluded that there was no reason to alter the decision reached by the stake disciplinary council.

... These special servants of the Lord have asked that I convey their love and deep concern. ...

I add my love and concern for you as well.

I read the words. I believe they were written sincerely. But it didn't feel like love. "Rebuking betimes with sharpness," the scripture reads, "when moved upon by the Holy Ghost; and then showing forth afterwards an increase of love ... lest he esteem thee to be his enemy" (D&C 121:43). After our initial conversation in May, President Miller and I have spoken only three times, each time at my instigation. At our stake conference in early September, I went to him in the foyer. He smiled pleasantly and shook hands warmly. On Friday he had written the letter summoning me to be tried for my membership. At that very moment, it was in his pocket, or in the pocket of the counselor who delivered it. On the morning of September 24, I telephoned him, holding the letter that told me I was excommunicated, to ask him why. He was pleasant as he told me it was for apostasy. At ward conference in November, I went to him and his counselors, standing in a sort of reception line inside the chapel, and shook hands with all three of them before Sunday school began. President Miller was pleasant. They were all pleasant.

I wonder if the scripture should read, "Then showing forth afterwards an increase of love ... lest *ye* become the enemy of the one whom thou hast reproved." We are only now starting to understand how, throughout our history, we have demonized the gentiles who opposed Mormons in their communities. We have far to go before we understand how quickly and how easily we demonize and dehumanize those within our own community with labels of liberal, conservative, feminist, gay, intellectual, John Bircher, zealot. It seems we can do almost anything to the label, never seeing the hurt person behind the label.

My parents were shocked. They had been hoping, too. My father wrote to President Gordon B. Hinckley, reminding him of several shared experiences, asking if he'd read the appeal. A letter from the secretary to the First Presidency assured my father that he had. Daddy asks me, "What are you supposed to do to be rebaptized?" I answer, "I don't know." I wrote back to President Miller asking that very question. He didn't respond.

✝

January 16, 1994.

President Miller attends a missionary homecoming in our ward. Christian is assigned to pass the sacrament on the stand. I watch as my son, the child of an excommunicated apostate, reverently serves the symbols of Christ's body and blood to the man who ruled that I was no longer worthy of them.

For a moment, we are all suspended in holy timelessness. President Miller, Paul, Christian, the emblems of the sacrament, and I. We are all together within dedicated walls, all beloved children of God, all mortal human beings, imperfect and broken. For all of us, Christ suffered and died to bring healing and wholeness. Something hallows this moment. I feel at peace.

4

A Testimony of Presence

I made this presentation to Pilgrimage, a retreat held near Salt Lake City on May 13, 1994, seven months after being excommunicated.

I came to Pilgrimage last year with an unanswered invitation from my stake president for Paul and me to come see him. We were pretty sure it was about the article that had just come out in early April in *Dialogue: A Journal of Mormon Thought* about the impact points in the church's increasingly tense and hostile relations with LDS scholars and intellectuals.[1] We were right, but it was also about my work on the Case Reports Committee of the Mormon Alliance, since that same issue invited people who felt that they wanted to talk to someone about cases of ecclesiastical abuse to contact me or Janice Allred, my co-editor.

My stake president made his position very clear. Such things embarrassed the church; therefore I could not remain a member in good standing unless I apologized for the article and promised not to talk to people about their negative experiences. I spent the summer unsuccessfully trying to find some way to engage him

---

1. Lavina Fielding Anderson, "The LDS Intellectual Community and Church Leadership: A Contemporary Chronology," *Dialogue: A Journal of Mormon Thought* 26, 1 (Spring 1993): 7–64. This essay subsequently won *Dialogue*'s Lowell L. Bennion Prize for "Essays in Gospel Living."

in a discussion of spiritual and ecclesiastical abuse or to help me meet with the area president. In September, I was excommunicated with five other high-profile scholars and feminists. One was Avraham Gileadi, a conservative scholar whose views on the prophecies of Isaiah and the apocalypse gave active members more substance than the bland but virtually sacrosanct Sunday school manuals. The other five, all from Salt Lake City, were part of the small but active Mormon liberal community. Lynne Kanavel Whitesides, president of the Mormon Women's Forum, a feminist organization, was disfellowshipped—still a member but barred from the sacrament, public participation, and the temple. She had joined the church as a teenager, as had Paul J. Toscano, an attorney, who had appealed to the general authorities to "choose love, not power." Feminist Maxine Hanks, editor of a compilation of essays called *Women and Authority: Re-emerging Mormon Feminism,* followed. D. Michael Quinn, a former professor of history at Brigham Young University and a former member of a stake high council, has held the cutting edge in Mormon history since the 1980s with his intensive research and brilliant analyses of the succession crisis after Joseph Smith's death in 1844, Joseph Smith's participation in folk magic, Joseph Smith's establishment of temple rites that included women as priests, and the continued private authorization of polygamy after the church had officially abandoned the practice in 1890.

Each person who was disciplined and those close to him or her have stories of their own. I want to thank each one of you who called, who wrote, who gave me a hug, or who prayed on behalf of any of us and our families. In our home, we could feel the prayers and support as warm and nourishing as chicken soup. They made it possible for us to stay strong and calm during this hideous tempest.

People usually ask me if I'm still going to church. Yes, I am. I haven't heard one negative syllable from one person in my ward. They've made it very easy for all of us.[2]

People say, "Even so, it must be hard." Well, yes and no. Paul's comparison is that we've been in a terrible multi-car pileup on the freeway. We've been banged around. Our ears have been filled with the terrifying shriek of brakes, the crash of cars hurtling into each other, and the wail of sirens. The ground crunches underfoot with broken glass. But we're not bleeding. We don't have any broken bones.[3] My best explanation is that the excommunication simply did not recognize who I am, so it did not speak to who I am and it cannot change who I am. The term "apostate" means nothing as it applies to me. It's nonsense syllables.

But it's not easy in another way. One of the hard things is simply facing the fact that I gave—and still give—my allegiance to a church that does not value me and other people I respect and love. I've been dealing with that recognition a lot lately. During our ward's Easter service, the choir sang "The King of Love My Shepherd Is." I suddenly found myself in tears at the line: "and on his shoulder gently laid and home rejoicing brought me." It's just so clear to me that the church right now has no under-shepherd who cares whether the sheep are home. In fact, as one friend pointed out, the shepherds are busy drop-kicking the sheep off the cliff. Michael Barrett's disciplinary action on April 24, 1994, brought to eighteen the number of excommunications over related issues since January 1993, and, as I recall, an unspecified number, perhaps

---

2. As of this writing, that is still true. No one in my ward has ever expressed negativity or disapproval of me, either directly or to Paul. Christian's youth leaders were particularly sensitive in making sure he felt welcome. When he and Marina merged households with mine on Roberta Street after Paul's death in March 2018, ward members went out of their way to express happiness with Christian's "return" and to make Marina welcome despite her complicated shift schedule as an Insta-Care pediatrician.

3. For Paul's written comparison, see Chapter 1, "Intersections on Life's Journey."

as high as forty or fifty more excommunications in central Utah over conservative theological interpretations. This number does not include those for whom courts have been scheduled but not held, those where the court resulted in probation or disfellowshipping, the lengthy list of those who have withdrawn from membership in the church in the last few months, and the longest list of all, which is of people who have been interviewed, scolded, and threatened, and who have lost recommends and callings, though no formal action has been taken.[4]

French professor Karl Sandberg's powerfully written and persuasive analysis of the trial of the Puritan poet and theologian Anne Hutchinson contains the poignant sentence: "The hungry sheep look up and are not fed."[5]

These are two sheep quotations, and I don't consider myself or any other member of the church to be a sheep. But I think my emotion responds to those images of confusion, bewilderment, betrayal of trust, and the rebuffed longing for love and acceptance. I think this is a rocky time for the church. None of us is without sin, but stones are flying through the air. The leaders are casting stones at the members, the members are casting stones at each other and at the leaders; and when people aren't throwing stones, they're trying to feed them to others who are starving for the bread of life. Tory Anderson writes about his mission as an experience of "feeling extreme pressure from leaders who always told me they love me but who were often less than mere acquaintances."[6] This situation is confusing at best, and it can be crazy-making.

---

4. These figures are small compared to the hundreds of mass resignations, following the gay-exclusion policy in 2015.

5. As quoted in Karl C. Sandberg, "Mormonism and the Puritan Connection: The Trials of Mrs. Anne Hutchinson and Several Persistent Questions Bearing on Church Governance," *Sunstone*, Feb. 1994, 28.

6. Tory C. Anderson, "Where Have All the Questions Gone?" *Wasatch Review International* 2, 2 (1993): 6.

I come in contact every day with people who are exhausted, angry, ashamed, afraid—and by and large, they are this way because of mixed messages from the church or local leaders. They wonder whether they can say or write something, go to a certain meeting, participate in a certain way, speak from their hearts. They silence themselves and bind themselves, and hope that the bindings and gags and bandages will somehow shield them and keep them safe. They're trying to preserve their faith, but it won't work because they're simply denying their fear.

Thomas Moore, a contemporary psychologist, writes about the importance of acknowledging doubt as the shadow side of faith:

> If we don't allow some uncertainty into our faith as we practice it, we fall victim to neurotic excesses: we may feel superior, or entitled to berate those who have betrayed us, or we may become cynical about the possibility of trust. Not owning unfaithfulness, we find it split off from ourselves and embodied in others. "These other people cannot be trusted." "This person I put my faith in is despicable, completely untrustworthy." [I think we have all seen the process of demonization at its unchecked ugliest in recent months.] Living only the positive side of faith, the other side creates a nagging paranoid suspicion of others and of the changes life brings.

> Also, if we don't acknowledge the shadow side of faith, we tend to romanticize our belief and keep it in fantasy, apart from life.[7]

I've made two discoveries about myself since I've been of but not in the church (so to speak). One is that I've stopped being afraid; and only now did I realize how deeply afraid I have been for most of my life—even though I've never thought of myself as particularly fearful. The worst has happened and I'm still myself. That's a marvelous, freeing feeling.

---

7. Thomas Moore, *Care of the Soul* (New York: Harper Perennial, 1994), 254. My thanks to Sally Emery and Irene Bates for sharing this insight with me.

The second discovery is that I've stopped being judgmental. It was wonderful to participate in a downtown demonstration called Circle of Love that circled Temple Square in April and truly felt in myself the willingness to take the hand of any other person who wanted to be there for whatever reason—liberal, conservative, gay, lesbian, believer, nonbeliever, excommunicant, orthodox. It didn't matter. For an hour we could come together in a transcendent desire for peace and inclusiveness.

I think every good Mormon internalizes all kinds of secret codes. "I'm okay, but you're even more okay because you're a man, and the bishop is more okay than both of us because he's a man with a higher position," etc. I think we learn subconsciously to use any difference as a marker of value. Married women are more valuable than single women. Mothers are more valuable than the childless. The active are more valuable than the inactive. The orthodox are more valuable than the unorthodox. Boys who don't go on their missions aren't valuable at all until they've repaired this terrible flaw. Girls who do go on missions are slightly more valuable but also slightly more dangerous.

The list goes on and on, unendingly. I'm ashamed to realize how carefully and meticulously I maintained such lists, without even realizing it. I'm grateful to feel that burden slip away. We all memorize, "Judge not, that ye be not judged." In my case, I had to learn it backwards: "You've been judged. Have you learned to judge not?" I hope I'm learning.

I realize that the stand I have taken and my excommunication may have made it more difficult for some of you to feel the same about the church. I hope you'll forgive me. I know that some feel I am in great need of forgiveness. If you feel that way, I hope you will offer me your forgiveness. I also know that some of you feel that the church has much to be forgiven of. I hope you can extend that forgiveness as well. Let me share with you a hymn text that appears in the RLDS hymnal created especially for worship in their temple, a beautiful building that was dedicated as a place of "reconciliation and peace." It reads:

> Gentle God, when we are driven
> Past the limits of our love,
> When our hurt would have a weapon
> And the hawk destroy the dove,
> At the cost of seeming weak,
> Help us turn the other cheek.
>
> Gentle Spirit, when our reason
> Clouds in anger, twists in fear,
> When we strike instead of stroking,
> When we bruise and sting and smear,
> Cool our burning, take our pain.
> Bring us to ourselves again.
>
> In the mirror of earth's madness
> Let us see our ravaged face,
> In the turmoil of all people
> Let compassion find a place.
> Touch our hearts to make amends,
> See our enemies as friends.
>
> Let our strength be in forgiving
> As forgiven we must be,
> One to one in costly loving,
> Finding trust and growing free.
> Gentle God, be our release.
> Gentle Spirit, teach us peace.[8]

---

8. Shirley Erena Murray, "Gentle God, When We Are Driven," #16 in *Sing for Peace: A Collection of Hymns and Songs for Congregational Worship* (Independence, Missouri: Herald House for Temple Worship Center/Reorganized Church of Jesus Christ of Latter Day Saints, 1994). Tune by Jillian Bray. Text and tune copyright 1992 by Hope Publishing Company.

May 23 will be the eight-month anniversary of being excommunicated. I do not think there is any way I can be rebaptized for years—ten, fifteen, even twenty years. During those years, what I want to do in my ward is to offer the testimony of presence.[9] I want to be there—not allowed to speak from the pulpit, forbidden to teach or pray aloud, but still testifying by my presence. Let me tell you two stories to illustrate what I mean by the testimony of presence.

The first is about Elder Helvécio Martins of Brazil, the first black man to be called as an LDS church general authority in April 1990. He and his wife "gained a testimony" the first night they met the missionaries in 1972 and, even though he was barred from holding the priesthood, were baptized. "When the Spirit tells you the gospel is true," he told an *Ensign* reporter, "how can you deny it?" He also told the reporter of working "for the construction of the temple just like other members," even though they "didn't expect to enter it." Then he tells this story: At the cornerstone-laying ceremony in March 1977, President Spencer W. Kimball "took hold of my arm and privately told me, 'Brother, what is necessary for you is faithfulness.'"[10]

I think of President Kimball, eighty-two years old, short, wearing those glasses with the special microphone attached to spare his ravaged voice, surrounded by caucasian apostles and mission presidents, looking into that crowd and seeing the black face of Elder Martins. In his autobiography, Elder Martins continues: He was helping "reporters from various newspapers, magazines, and television-radio stations" before the meeting began when he glanced at the speakers' platform and saw President Kimball beckon to him. "I turned away, not believing his gesture could be meant for me," said Elder Martins. "Still, I couldn't help looking at him again. Smiling, the prophet

---

9. I am indebted for this concept to Sharon Conrey Turnbull, who addressed the Circle of Love service on the "ministry of presence" on April 2, 1994, in Salt Lake City.

10. "Elder Helvécio Martins of the Seventy," *Ensign*, May 1990, 106.

repeated the signal," then, when Elder Martins still could not believe it, sent Elder James E. Faust for him. Elder Martins went to the stand where President Kimball embraced him, introduced him to President Marion G. Romney, then "put his arm around me, looked me straight in the eye, and said, 'Brother Martins, what is necessary for you is fidelity. Remain faithful and you will enjoy all the blessings of the gospel.'" At the end of the ceremony, when President Kimball was leaving, he stopped in front of Elder Martins, gripped his hand strongly, held his arm with the other hand, and said, "'Don't forget, Brother Martins, don't forget.'"[11] Something about the presence of a black man, standing in the presence of a prophet with other members of the church—come to celebrate the cornerstone laying of an edifice he and his family had sacrificed to construct but which he could not enter, where he and his wife, who had sold her jewelry for the temple fund, could not be sealed, where no ordinance to unite them to their children could be performed, where their two sons and two daughters could not enter as missionaries, brides, or grooms—I say, something in the presence of Helvécio Martins called to President Kimball as a Christian and as a prophet. That was in March 1977. In June 1978, the revelation extending priesthood to all worthy black men was announced.

What if Helvécio Martins had stayed away from that cornerstone laying? What if he had said, "We just can't take it any more"? That would have been a valid decision. I honor and respect the decisions of those who feel they can't take it any more or take it right now.[12] But I think that by being there, he bore a testimony of

---

11. Helvecio Martins with Mark Grover, *The Autobiography of Elder Helvecio Martins* (Salt Lake City: Aspen Books, 1994), 66.

12. Martin E. Marty, a historian of religions, has observed, "It is always easier to invent a new religion and give it a new past, than it is to deal with real-world religions with real pasts, with all their terrible flaws and exciting ambiguities." As quoted in "Spiritual Amnesia," *Signs of the Times*, May 1994, 7. I agree with Joanna Brooks who, during a Sunstone Symposium West panel presentation (Burbank,

presence that made his continued exclusion intolerable to President Kimball. I thank the Lord for the strength of Helvécio Màrtins.

The second story again involves the issue of race, this time a woman in the RLDS tradition,[13] Amy Elizabeth Thomas Burke Robbins, the granddaughter of slaves who escaped to Canada from the American South. She joined the Reorganized Church of Jesus Christ of Latter Day Saints in Detroit as a widow with one child. When she remarried, she moved to Battle Creek, Michigan, where a congregation was later organized. She brought up her children, eight by the second marriage, in the Reorganized faith. She did this even though the pastor explained to the other members that her skin was the visible sign of God's curse; the white members at summer reunions (somewhat comparable to Education Week at BYU) refused to let her and her children use the same beach as they; the president of the RLDS church, whom she revered as a prophet, opened a local conference with a racist joke; and her children, gifted with wonderful voices, had to stand behind a curtain as they sang with the choir. Then some members told the pastor they were ashamed to bring friends to church because blacks attended. In her autobiography, Amy wrote:

> Only the Master could know the humiliation I underwent, ... for spiritual food for which I was starving. ... There was a motion made ... that I stay away from Church, for a while at least, that they have a chance to bring their friends; there was much discussion and finally the motion was lost, however, I offered to remain away

California, March 12, 1994) sponsored by the Southern California chapter of the Mormon Women's Forum, said that she would not leave the church: "These are my people. This is my language. And this is what I know how to do." She made this comment during the question-and-answer session (audiotape in my possession); for the prepared portion of her remarks, see Joanna Brooks, "Gender and Spirituality, or Why the Guerrilla Is the Most Feminine Creature in the Spiritual Jungle," *Mormon Women's Forum: An LDS Feminist Quarterly* 5, 1 (Mar. 1994): 6–7.

13. Effective April 6, 2001, the Reorganized Church of Jesus Christ of Latter Day Saints changed its name to "Community of Christ."

from the Church for a period of six months or longer and though some were much opposed to it, I did stay away ... which was about the hardest thing I have ever done. What they did not know was that I did, as it were, "lick up the crumbs that fell from the Master's table," when I would stand under the window and get what instruction might sift through, and, in my heart sing the songs of Zion with them.[14]

Helvécio Martins and Amy Robbins bore testimony with their unflinching presence of how their church should behave. They are my models for the next twenty years. Without anger, without accusation, and without apology, I want to bear the testimony of presence in Whittier Ward. I want that testimony to say, "I'm here. I've been excluded from fellowship for speaking the truth and following my conscience, but I'm still here. Don't be afraid. We don't have to hide our history, silence our scholars, abuse our members, exclude our gay and lesbian members, and marginalize our women. We can understand the gospel better and we can live it better. The Savior who died for each one of us calls each one of us to come to him. And if we're good enough for him, we can be good enough for each other."

---

14. Roger D. Launius, "White Woman in a Black Man's Church: Amy E. Robbins," *Journal of Mormon History* 19 (Fall 1993): 75–78.

5

Excommunicant

This is the draft of an article I prepared in July 1995 at the invitation of Sojourner, a feminist journal published in Boston, Massachusetts. The following September 1995 was the second anniversary of my excommunication. I have updated the text and notes with more contemporary material.

I have come to believe over and over again that what is most important to me must be spoken, made verbal and shared, even at the risk of having it bruised or misunderstood.

—Audre Lorde[1]

Excommunication is a complicated issue. It's a feminist issue because, in the Church of Jesus Christ of Latter-day Saints, women are barred from the all-male priesthood, priesthood otherwise available universally to boys beginning at age twelve.[2] Of course, men are excommunicated too; but in a disciplinary council, women appear only as the accused or as witnesses, never as the judges.

Excommunication is a social issue. It divides families, stigmatizes excommunicants, and is viewed very differently by excommunicators and excommunicants. A quasi-legal procedure, it does not follow legal rules.

---

1. Audre Lorde, *Sister Outsider* (Freedom, California: CrossingPress, 1984), 40.
2. Or at age eleven if they would turn twelve within the calendar year, according to a policy change effective January 2019.

It's a spiritual issue because it casts people out of their spiritual homes. It bars them from partaking of the bread and water that represent Christ's flesh and blood, broken and shed to redeem humankind. It excludes them from the temples where Mormonism's holiest rites are performed. It cancels the baptism that made them a member of a religious community. It suspends the temple sealings that make marriage a union that transcends death and that links parents and children eternally.

Above all, it's a personal issue. I was excommunicated for "apostasy," a term that makes little sense to me. Apostates are people who hate the church, don't believe or follow its teachings, and who try to destroy it. I'm fifty-one years old, a sixth-generation Mormon. I served a two-year proselytizing mission in France in my early twenties. I graduated (twice) from the church-owned Brigham Young University in Provo, Utah. I was married in the temple. My father was a bishop twice of our local congregation (ward) and, both times, oversaw the construction of a chapel—the first meetinghouse also served as the Lost River Stake (Idaho) meetinghouse. Members were expected to bear most of the costs of these buildings and to contribute their labor. As an elementary school child, I carried bricks to the walls being mortared into place. As a teenager, I swung a hammer to help construct the ward meetinghouse in Warden, Washington. As a missionary, I spent our once-a-week "preparation day" shoveling and screening sand for the concrete that went into the walls of Marseille Branch's beautiful chapel, the first to be constructed in my mission.

Mormonism differentiates between "active" and "inactive" (also "less active") members. "Active" means that you go to church at least once a month and preferably every week, contribute at least 10 percent of your income to the church, and accept callings, or assignment by your local ward bishop, to carry out one of the teaching or leadership callings required to staff a ward of about 200 people. I did all of that and more. When I was forty-five, I calculated that I had contributed about seventy years worth of service to the church through overlapping assignments, beginning as a teacher of a Primary class when I was fourteen. At the time I was excommunicated I had three such assignments.

So what happened? Maybe I believed too much, hoped too much. In the spring of 1993 I published an article documenting about 130 impact points between the institutional church and its scholars—primarily its historians—in a dialogue that has been going on, with increasing tension, since the 1960s.[3] I wrote with love for the church and its history. I expressed concern about the ways in which their dialogue seemed to be breaking down. I pointed out the behavior we might expect from a church that prized the truth, believed in on-going revelation, and had canonized the statement: "The glory of God is intelligence, or, in other words, light and truth" (D&C 93:36). What could it fear from its past? I hoped for mutual forgiveness and better communication.

As a continuation of that article, I also began to document the ways in which ordinary members—not academics or intellectuals—sometimes found themselves grappling with injustice inflicted by an ecclesiastical leader who held all the cards. They were bewildered, their trust betrayed. In a church of untrained lay leaders, you expect imperfection, ignorance, insensitivity. But not brutality, coercion, threats, and intimidation.

My stake president said I had to repudiate the article and stop collecting these accounts. I thought about it for a long time—about three months. I couldn't accept his conditions. He excommunicated me. I have nothing against him. He's a decent, hard-working man. He makes his living as a medium-level government employee,

---

3. See Lavina Fielding Anderson, "The LDS Intellectual Community and Church Leadership: A Contemporary Chronology," *Dialogue: A Journal of Mormon Thought* 26, 1 (Spring 1993): 7–64. Awarded *Dialogue*'s Lowell L. Bennion Prize for Essays in Gospel Living.

but he contributes probably another forty-hour week in managing a stake in downtown Salt Lake City that covers aging neighborhoods with a rising number of widows, welfare recipients, and single-parent families. The disciplinary council he convened consisted of him, his two counselors, and the twelve men who constitute the stake high council. My husband had served on that high council, after a three-year stint in our ward bishopric, for almost five years until he resigned to become our son's Primary teacher. We've lived in this stake for seventeen years. These fifteen men were neighbors. They all wore white shirts and ties. Nobody raised their voice. The stake president kept assuring me that he loved me. They made me not-a-member. It didn't feel like love to me. The clear spiritual instructions I received prepared me for excommunication and, very clearly indeed, told me I should not attend the disciplinary council. I was puzzled but obeyed. Only later I realized that this spiritual guidance meant that I could meet these fifteen men without hostility or resentment for their role in canceling my membership.

How do things like this happen? The Mormon church is a young church, organized in 1830 as a restoration of Christ's New Testament church. That's the Mormon story. I believe it. My ancestors lived through that founding and its fiery early history when it was expelled from three states and its founding prophet, Joseph Smith, was assassinated in 1844 by some of Illinois's solid but outraged citizenry, with the help of former Mormons disturbed by the secret practice of polygamy. I love its history, its heritage of faith, sacrifice, human stupidity, and human transcendence.

The Mormon church is authoritarian and relentlessly patriarchal. Apostleship is for life. Men call women to preside over the Relief Society, the Young Women, and the Primary. Women have a place—an auxiliary, ancillary, unquestionably secondary place. I don't like this arrangement, but I accept it even while I hope it will change. I respect and sustain these men even when I disagree with them.

The Mormon church is an American church, even though more than half of its 16 million members (2019) live outside the United States. Managing this growth, as President Gordon B. Hinckley repeated endlessly in interviews in national media, is the church's greatest challenge. I rejoice in this growth. I believe that the international church will help the core church by stripping away some of its hampering American baggage.

Was I somehow standing in the way of its hierarchy, its internationalism? It's hard to see how. People get excommunicated all the time in the Mormon church. But usually it's for adultery or being convicted of a crime. They repent, say they're sorry, say they won't do it again. A year later, they're rebaptized. A year after that, their temple and priesthood blessings are restored. Sonia Johnson was excommunicated in 1979 for her pro-ERA stance. She didn't say she was sorry. Kate Kelly, the most public face of the Ordain Women movement, was excommunicated in June 2014. She wept as her stake president communicated the decision of his court, but she didn't say she was sorry either.

But why now? Why this? Why this wave of ecclesiastical terrorism? It wasn't a purge, insisted church public relations spokespersons. This was purely a local matter, taken up by individual bishops and stake presidents. The passive voice is comfortingly vague. "She was disfellowshipped," we say. "He was excommunicated." That's correct, but it's not complete. Someone *did* this. Marlin S. Miller excommunicated me. And it was not his own idea. Loren C. Dunn was the area president—the general authority to whom all of these stake presidents reported with the exception of Avraham Gileadi. Dunn sent my stake president a copy of my article. He talked with Lynne Whitesides's stake president, with Michael Quinn's, with Maxine Hanks's. Ironically, Michael and Maxine lived in the same stake. Even more ironically, that stake president was Maxine's distant cousin. Since the 1960s, Dunn has been a protégé of a powerful conservative apostle, Boyd K. Packer, who in May 1993 announced in a meeting of department heads and mid-level managers that the three greatest dangers facing the church were feminists, homosexuals, and "so-called intellectuals." Packer met personally with Paul Toscano's stake president, who admitted to Toscano that the "fair implication" of that meeting was that Packer wanted Toscano out. Packer personally replaced Gileadi's stake president with a BYU religion professor only weeks before Gileadi found himself facing the disciplinary council who excommunicated him.

These disciplinary actions have not stopped. David P. Wright, a biblical scholar at Brandeis, was excommunicated in April 1994 for applying some of the tools of critical scholarship to the Book of Mormon. That same month, Michael Barrett, an attorney with the CIA in Maryland, was also excommunicated. His "sin" was writing letters to editors filling in historical background on statements, particularly about the exclusion of worthy black men from the priesthood, from 1847 to 1978—statements that church public relations people had left misleadingly vague. His stake president, who was the church's lobbyist and full-time PR employee in Washington, DC, admitted that Barrett's letters had always been factually accurate. In December 1994, Brent Metcalfe, editor of the book on the Book of Mormon, was excommunicated. Janice Merrill Allred, Provo (Utah) homemaker, mother of nine, and theologian, was disfellowshipped in October 1994 for her theological investigations and excommunicated in May 1995. Margaret Toscano, her sister and Paul's wife, was excommunicated in 2000 for her feminist writings. Less publicized were a series of excommunications over doctrinally based disagreements from people in central Utah who have since formed another church.

Does any of this make sense? Perhaps in some world I don't understand of expedience, of power alliances, of control. But not in my world. Not in the freedom and grace of Mormon theology. Not in the context of Jesus Christ's redeeming love.

I sit in church every Sunday. I cannot speak or pray publicly, but I sing the hymns I love and join in the communal "amens" that echo after the closing words of a sermon or prayer. For my husband and our teenage son, Christian, the damage has been minimal. Our active, orthodox parents, brothers, sisters, and in-laws have been unanimously supportive. Our ward still welcomes us. For most of the others, attending church has been too painful for them and their children. Of the twenty-one children involved, only two are still affiliated. The Sunday after her excommunication, Janice Allred had to sit through a Sunday school lesson about how the Pharisees were unrighteously eager to cast people out of the synagogue but how excommunications in the Lord's church are inspired.

I understand why such punished people have to stop going to church. I think of my weekly walking into my ward chapel as proxy attendance for those whose suffering precludes their own attendance. I think it does me good to be there—to be surrounded by ordinary people who are trying to do their best and to become better. I think it does them good to have me there, cast out but not departed, and therefore someone who cannot be forgotten.

When I was praying about my decision to publish the article (I knew some people wouldn't like it) and later when I was praying about whether I could accept my stake president's silencing of me, I didn't ask if it would be prudent or safe or expedient. I asked if it was right. The answer was always the same. It is right to tell the truth. It is right to speak up for those who have been silenced. "Right" does not mean easy or uncomplicated, but it is not as hard as turning away from the truth, turning away from those who have been hurt.

I'm still a Mormon. I'll always be a Mormon. The church leaders have control over my membership, but I have control over an even more important relationship—the heart, mind, might, and strength that I offer to Jesus Christ as I pray for strength to endure and to thrive. I have faith that someday I'll be a member of the Mormon church again.[4] But in 1993, I think the church took a turn toward rigidity and narrowness that it will take a generation to discard. That generation has passed and there are signs that Mormonism is rediscovering its more essential self: its belief in the sanctity and eternality of the individual, its cautious recognition of the silent and exiled Mother in Heaven, its historic recognition of women's spiritual gifts, its affirmation of the individual's potential for godhood, its fundamental faith that human beings are children of God and essentially good, its faith that God is eager to speak to individuals, not only to the hierarchy.

Only four months after Marlin Miller excommunicated me, he was attending our ward. I watched as Christian, with the other teenage deacons, took the tray of broken bread to his assigned position—the stand where the priesthood leaders were sitting. I watched as the child of an excommunicated "apostate" reverently served the symbols of Christ's body and blood to the man who cut his mother off from the Church of Jesus Christ. For a moment, I felt as if hands—hands pierced with the nails of crucifixion—were lovingly encircling the entire chapel. There was room for Marlin Miller. There was room for thirteen-year-old Christian. And there was room for me.

---

4. At this writing, my current stake president, David McLean, has reconvened the high council court, heard my statement (see the Introduction) and statements of support from my son, the "visiting ministers" assigned to me by the intervention of my bishop with the stake president (ordinarily excommunicants may not have visiting or home teachers, callings replaced as of January 2019 by a "ministering" program), my bishop, and two members of the high council who are also members of my ward. See the introduction for developments since that reconvened disciplinary council.

6

Eternal Perdition?
Bureaucratic Limbo?

THE THEOLOGICAL RAMIFICATIONS OF EXCOMMUNICATION

I made the following remarks at the Salt Lake Sunstone Symposium on August 5, 2010. I and other panelists were responding to four questions posed by the moderator. At this point, I had been excommunicated for one month short of seventeen years.

The first question asks: Why does excommunication not require a ritual? I think, in fact, that it does—or, at least, is—a ritual, but that like most Mormon rituals, it looks and sounds an awfully lot like a meeting. I remember being very impressed when I read some piece of claptrap fiction as a teenager about a Catholic excommunication—or maybe it was an exorcism. A visible and quite impressive ritual was involved. The bell was silenced. The book was closed. And the candle was quenched. All of these symbols had metaphoric meanings, obvious even to me, of termination. If you were on the receiving end of the bell, book, and candle, you'd know it was not just another Sunday school class.

But a Mormon excommunication begins when two priesthood holders deliver a letter and a "Hope you have a nice day." The excommunication itself begins and closes with prayer. The participants shake hands. In my stake, it's not inconceivable that afterward everybody could just go next door to the Arctic Circle for a milkshake. In other words, it seems terribly anticlimactic if what's really at stake is eternal salvation and/or damnation and if you're being delivered over to the "buffetings of Satan."[1]

Excommunication functions as a ritual in terms of communal life with a certain sequence of interviews, the predictable meeting time and place, the procedures outlined for the course of the meeting, the adjustment of the individual's status in the community, and especially the creation of a record.

I uphold the church's right to maintain standards that define some offenses as worthy of excommunication, but I assert that, like most rituals, excommunication functions best in a non-contested environment when all of the parties participate voluntarily. I think it's very important for some individuals to recognize that they have engaged in activities that damage their souls and that damage their relationships with those around them. It can be very important for such individuals not only to confess and forsake their sins but to undergo rituals that represent repentance, both to their community but especially to themselves. (I don't think excommunication is the only way that message can be communicated, but that's another topic.)

Every so often the *Ensign* will publish an article by that prolific author "Name Withheld" that deals with a voluntary confession and submission to excommunication. A couple of years ago, I remember one by a man who had engaged in either pornography or adultery. The article, written in first person, described his anguish, his mortification and suffering as he sat in sacrament meeting without partaking of the sacrament or participating in ordinances for his children, the suffering but steadfastness of his equally mortified wife, his regular meetings with a stern but encouraging bishop, his determined study of the scriptures, and finally his dawning appreciation of the power of Christ's atonement in his life. Name Withheld's article ended with his joyous rebaptism and his fervent

---

1. This phrase was common in nineteenth-century excommunications but seems no longer to be employed much.

testimony of the value that excommunication had in getting his attention and saving his soul.

But what about the involuntary excommunicant? What about the careless sinner who doesn't value his or her membership and isn't going to let a little thing like fear of excommunication make him stop beating his wife, incesting his child, embezzling church funds, or spraying his neighborhood with an AK-47? I still think the church has a right to say, "You can't do those things as a member of the church." The ritual has no meaning to the excommunicant, but it has some value to the community.

And then there's my category. I'm not quite sure what to call it, since, from my perspective, the actions that the church found so offensive were some of my most sincere attempts to live the gospel, to mourn with those who mourn, to comfort those in need of comfort, and to testify of the Savior. I was not a voluntary participant in being excommunicated. On the contrary, I found the church's actions wrong-headed, politically motivated, and morally offensive. Rather than being motivated to repent, I felt more strongly committed to continuing the actions for which I was being punished. I can see that, from the institutional perspective, such an attitude was even more shocking evidence of my rebelliousness; but no one has proposed this perspective to me face to face. I trust that, were such a thing to occur, I would seize it as an opportunity to exercise the Christian virtue of forgiveness, which would probably be considered even more insufferable than my original attitude.

So, the bottom line of this discursive answer is that I think excommunication is a ritual—a Mormon-style ritual—and that like most Mormon meetings, some are more successful than others.

The second question is: If blessings are "restored" to an excommunicated person who returns to the church, what became of those blessings in the interim? Well, institutionally speaking, those blessings existed only on paper in the first place. And if there should,

God forbid, be a discrepancy between your claim that you were baptized and a record that fails to substantiate it, you have to be rebaptized. Nobody is going to accept mere Christian behavior as evidence of being a Christian unless the piece of paper also exists. How do you know you've been ordained to the priesthood? You have a piece of paper that says so and there's a notation on your permanent church record giving the date, place, and officiator. But here's the point. The Holy Spirit of Promise seals those blessings—it grants the real remission of your sins, it confirms the eternal love and mutual service that are the heart of a marriage and the parent-child bond, and it links an individual's faith in Christ with the power of the atonement; but those are activities that the church can't promise, can't control, and can't regulate. So the church does what the church *can* do; it promises, controls, and regulates the pieces of paper.

The follow-up question was: Is it reasonable that God would give fallible human leaders the power to separate people from him or their families in eternity? This question leads to the deeper question of whether God exists (and yes, in my world, he does), whether he cares about such things (and yes, in my world, he does), whether we'll have families in eternity (and yes, in my world, we will), and whether he's willing to acknowledge the binding and loosening authority of fallible human leaders (and, in this world or the next, if you've got human beings, what other kind of leaders are you going to have?).

Think of all of the sincere, self-sacrificing souls who diligently go to the temple every Thursday at 5:30 a.m. and perform proxy ordinances, investing two hours and forty-five minutes of their day in the belief that the accident of having your name recorded in a sixteenth-century parish register has just made the remission of your sins possible. Obviously, if God is really serious about remitting the sins of the millions of people who lived and died without making it as far as the parish register, he has more efficient means at his disposal. But maybe he doesn't have any better way to make materialistic, stressed-out Americans develop self-sacrifice, love, and service than tell them to get to that 5:30 a.m. session on Thursday mornings. And maybe calling a fallible plumber to be a bishop and a fallible interior decorator to be a Relief Society president is the best way God can get them to be more compassionate, more loving, and a little less fallible. I don't have a problem with that, nor do I have a problem with God saying, at whatever form the judgment takes, "You know, you really did okay about 65 percent of the time, and you've already beat yourself up enough over the other 35 percent now that you see the consequences."

Let me invite your reflection on two historic accounts of excommunication. The first is John D. Lee who received the blame as the architect and perpetrator of the Mountain Meadows Massacre in 1857. He was not innocent. Juanita Brooks, in her still-unsurpassed biography of him, saw him as a scapegoat; and it is true that he bore the punishment alone when others, including Brigham Young, in my opinion, should have shared that responsibility. Instead he was exiled, expelled, and excoriated. David O. McKay, to his everlasting credit, was church president in 1961 when the First Presidency and Quorum of the Twelve authorized John D. Lee's reinstatement and restoration of blessings, a moment of institutional forgiveness and shared responsibility that survived the spiteful threat to Juanita Brooks of rescinding Lee's restoration.[2]

---

2. Levi S. Peterson's magisterial biography, *Juanita Brooks: Mormon Woman Historian* (Salt Lake City: University of Utah Press, 1988), recounts Brooks's courage and continued commitment both to the church (she and her husband were both denied significant callings) and to truth-telling. See Harvard S. Heath, ed., *Confidence amid Change: The Presidential Diaries of David O. McKay, 1951–1970* (Salt Lake City: Signature Books, 2018), 424–25, for McKay's dismay that Brooks announced Lee's reinstatement in her biography of him but his more mature reaction not to allow rescinding the reinstatement.

Amasa Lyman's experience may be less known. Amasa was ordained an apostle during Joseph Smith's lifetime and was even called to be a counselor to the First Presidency. He served diligently and faithfully in many mission fields in colonizing San Bernardino and Utah. But according to Leo Lyman's splendid biography, Amasa developed some doubts about whether the literal blood of Jesus was required for the atonement. (I think it may be significant that he developed these doubts after the Mountain Meadows Massacre, when there had been altogether too much attention to bloodshed.) He recanted his views, recanted his recantation, and became a Godbeite and a spiritualist, though arguably without the same fervor he had applied to being a Mormon. He was excommunicated in 1870 and died at age sixty-three in 1877.

Three years later, his son, Francis Marion Lyman, was ordained an apostle. Ten years later in an 1890 quorum meeting, Marion claimed that he had succeeded in "winning" nearly all of his family, alienated by Amasa's excommunication, back to the church and confessed in tears that he was "very anxious to do something for his father," which obviously hinted at Marion's hopes for reinstatement. Lorenzo Snow, who was then president of the Twelve, comfortingly stated that Amasa "would be required to pay the penalty for his sins, but … he would certainly also be rewarded for his good deeds." Five years passed. Wilford Woodruff and George Q. Cannon died. Lorenzo Snow became church president, then he died. Marion, who was close to the next president, Joseph F. Smith (who, in fact, had been called as an apostle to fill the vacancy left by Amasa's ouster), made several overtures, asking to be baptized and ordained by proxy for his father. Nothing happened. More time passed. Marion became senior apostle and president of the Quorum of the Twelve.

What seemed to tip the balance was a dream by Marion's sister, Martha Lyman Roper. She dreamed of seeing Amasa and running to embrace him, only to be warned back from a "great chasm" that separated them. Amasa told her he was "weary and tired of his black clothes," in which he had insisted on being buried, although it seems unlikely that he could have been buried in temple white unless the family had held a secret funeral. He confessed that he "did so want to be with his family, his wives and his children whom he loved and longed for." One of those wives, Caroline, died in 1908 at Oak City where she had been Relief Society president for thirty-two years. President Joseph F. Smith and Marion both spoke at the funeral, then ate dinner with the family where Martha, at Marion's request, told Joseph F. her dream. "President Smith listened, then remarked, 'Well, Marion, it looks like your father has suffered long enough. We will see what can be done for him.'"

Eight months later, Apostle John Henry Smith, a cousin of Lyman's, baptized Marion in the Salt Lake temple for his father, and Joseph F. Smith confirmed Marion as proxy for his father, "restoring his former priesthood ordinations and temple sealings in the same ordinance." Leo with both compassion and judiciousness notes, "Lyman's status in the hereafter must (with ours) be left to the supreme judge of all humankind."[3]

Both of these examples raise the question of the role suffering plays in repentance. A considerable body of Mormon theology, including Spencer W. Kimball's influential works, gives suffering an even more important place than behavioral change. Who decides whether that suffering is sufficient? Now, the decision seems to be left to the same bishop (or his successor) or the same high council (or their successors) who determined guilt in the first place. Living individuals are still rebaptized—that well-known ritual of entrance into the church—but less well-known is the fact that the

---

3. Edward Leo Lyman, *Amasa Mason Lyman: Mormon Apostle and Apostate—A Study in Dedication* (Salt Lake City: University of Utah Press, 2009), 492–94. See also Scott H. Partridge, ed., *Thirteenth Apostle: The Diaries of Amasa M. Lyman, 1832–1877* (Salt Lake City: Signature Books, 2016).

membership record is "updated" with the date of the original baptism but not as a new baptism. I assume the same procedure is followed for confirmation, priesthood ordinations, and sealings.

I want to answer a final question. Do I want to be rebaptized? Do I see value in becoming again a member of the church? Yes and yes. I recognize and applaud other religious communities, but Mormonism is mine. I think that God loves, honors, and validates the sincere efforts for good of all his children, but it was as a Mormon that I made my initial covenants and it is as a Mormon that I strive to keep them. I consider that my task in living the gospel is to not create or widen the breach that the church has put between us so that, when it is time for our paths to flow together again, they will do so easily and joyously.

7

Dealing with Our
Divine and Human Church

This essay was first delivered in 1985 at Pilgrimage at a time when LDS-related historical issues, including plural marriage and early folk beliefs regarding magic, were especially hot-button topics. It is one of my early explorations of how to address potential faith crises and preceded my excommunication by eight years.

I've sensed, in the past few years, a deepening concern among people like me about historical issues in the church. I think during the previous ten years, the issues were somehow farther away. When Elder Boyd K. Packer was upset because Dean Jessee's book[1] documented that Brigham Young counseled a son to stop using tobacco on his mission, it was fairly easy to say, "That's funny, but it's also really silly to make an issue out of it. The Word of Wisdom barely existed beyond a good idea in the nineteenth century." Similarly, when Dean May documented the high rate of experimentation and failure among cooperative movements in Utah[2] and this upset Elder

---

1. Dean C. Jessee, ed., *Letters of Brigham Young to His Sons* (Salt Lake City: Deseret Book and the Historical Department, Church of Jesus Christ of Latter-day Saints, 1974). For Packer's reaction to this and other publications, see Gary J. Bergera, ed., *Confessions of a Mormon Historian: The Diaries of Leonard J. Arrington, 1971–1997* (Salt Lake City: Smith–Pettit Foundation, 2018).

2. Leonard J. Arrington, Feramorz Y. Fox, and Dean L. May, *Building the City of God: Community and Cooperation among the Mormons* (Salt Lake City: Deseret Book, 1976).

Ezra Taft Benson because the Lord doesn't "experiment" and besides "communitarianism" sounds so much like "communism," it was also easy to say, "But who expects a prophet never to make mistakes? Do current prophets think they never make mistakes?"

Within the last three years, though, much of the most interesting research has focused on the very beginnings of Mormonism—not just *a* prophet but *the* prophet: Joseph Smith. Linda King Newell and Valeen Tippetts Avery's biography of Emma Hale Smith has been deeply disturbing to some for the documentation it provides about Joseph Smith and the origins of polygamy in Nauvoo.[3] Michael Quinn's examination of the termination of polygamy raises some of the same questions about intention and deception on the part of Joseph's successors.[4] Richard Bushman and Jan Shipps and others have examined the strains of folk religion in the first decade of Mormonism.[5] What do we do with this information? How do we integrate it into our faith? What difference does it make to how we live our lives, treat other people, do our work, approach God?

When Jill Mulvay Derr and I were roommates and both working in the Church Office Building in the 1970s, she on the second floor in the History Division and I on the twenty-third floor in the *Ensign* office, we would drive home to our drafty house on 1300 South in the Princeton Ward and speak with real appreciation of how the waves of rumor, policy changes, and power shifts that rocked the Church Office Building flattened to a ripple as soon as you set foot on the sidewalk and were nonexistent by the time you

3. Linda King Newell and Valeen Tippets Avery, *Mormon Enigma: Emma Hale Smith: Prophet's Wife, "Elect Lady," Polygamy's Foe* (Garden City, New York: Doubleday & Co., 1984).

4. D. Michael Quinn, "LDS Church Authority and New Plural Marriages: 1890–1904," *Dialogue: A Journal of Mormon Thought* 18, 1 (Spring 1985): 1–105.

5. See, for example, Richard Lyman Bushman, *Joseph Smith: Rough Stone Rolling* (New York: Alfred A. Knopf, 2005); Jan Shipps, *Mormonism: The Story of a New Religious Tradition* (Urbana: University of Illinois Press, 1987).

got to 1300 South. Events of major theoretical importance simply had no practical impact in the Princeton Ward where the problem was still caring for each other's spiritual and physical needs.

At the same time, this approach, a healthy celebration of the church as a Christian community, does not discuss the legitimate question raised by historical sensations and contemporary ecclesiastical politics. This question could be phrased: "It *does* make a difference to how I live my life. I'm living it now in accordance with teachings of the church. Sometimes these teachings are very rewarding and sometimes they're inconvenient and sometimes they're downright painful. Why should I do painful and inconvenient things for the church if the church is somehow flawed from its very foundation, if Joseph Smith made it up, if it's not 'the true church'?"

The first position begins with the notion that truth is what you make it; you existentially validate your reality by living it out. The second approach sees truth as something discrete and external to ourselves that we must approach and grope toward an understanding of before we can possess.

For me, both approaches must work together. Let me tell you how it works for me.

I love the church—although it sometimes makes me mad, bores me, or disgusts me.(By that I mean that the organizational operation strikes me as oppressive and bullying at least some of the time.)

I love the Book of Mormon. I love its sense of peace and purpose, despite its absence of women and the amount of space devoted to slaughter. It is scripture to me in every sense of that ambiguous word.

And I love Joseph Smith. This is a recent love—only within the last ten years. My first feeling about the Doctrine and Covenants when I read it in my early teens was that it was supremely weird. Joseph Smith was weird. The church was weird. I liked my comfortable 1950s and 1960s church. I didn't want it to be weird. I feel differently now. I know that I also am weird. Weird is part of the game. I came to this quite delightful conclusion, not by avoiding the Doctrine and Covenants so as not to be exposed to Joseph Smith's weirdness, but rather by reading everything I could get my hands on: the Doctrine and Covenants, *The History of the Church*, B. H. Roberts, lives of the presidents, Fawn Brodie, Donna Hill, *Dialogue: A Journal of Mormon Thought*, Sunday school manuals … the works. As Irene Bates has been known to say, "I have an immense trust in truth if you follow it to the end. It's when you stop asking questions and stop wrestling for the answers that you are left with limited truth, and, because it's limited, it's nearly always false."[6]

I do not feel betrayed and angry if Joseph was wrong or mistaken or misled—and I think that sometimes he certainly was. Those times were direct results of his free agency. Certainly, God spoke to him. God speaks to everyone. But Joseph listened better than a lot of us and actually entered into a dialogue that lasted for the rest of his life. It is the listening and the dialogue that are the models for us, I believe, not whatever notes he jotted down in the course of that ongoing conversation.

I was shocked and disgusted to discover that Joseph Smith married a fourteen-year-old girl, probably consummated that marriage, and concealed it from Emma.[7] My image of "prophet" did not accommodate this kind of behavior. I could not begin to find holy motives for such behavior. I also felt deeply guilty, naturally, to feel this way about a prophet—not just *a* prophet, either, but *the* Prophet. I took my indignation and guilt to the Lord in prayer over a period of time. I don't recall being particularly sophisticated or eloquent in my petition. It was more along the lines of, "If Joseph Smith did this—and it looks as if he did—then he was a real jerk. What do *You* have to say about it?" On some level, I wasn't even expecting an answer. But I got one. From that attentive, loving

---

6. Personal conversations.
7. Newell and Avery, *Mormon Enigma*, 46–47.

Presence—gently, tenderly, and with finality—came the words, "Joseph is mine. He is in my hands." God did not agree with me that Joseph was a jerk. He did not even agree that Joseph had made a mistake. He acknowledged my grief and upheld me in those same hands that were holding Joseph and that upheld Helen Mar Kimball Whitney, not only at age fourteen, but for the rest of her long life.

I have the feeling, though, that if I hadn't acknowledged my outrage and hadn't protested it to the Lord, that I probably wouldn't have got that answer. As a result, my affection for Joseph Smith is, if anything, increased by this new information about him, and I want to know more. I want to know everything I can *because* I love him—not because I'm trying to decide whether he is worthy of my love. Freedom and diversity intersect—not in rules, not in regulations—but in relationships.

The ultimate value of that experience for me was not what I learned about prayer or even about Joseph Smith, but what I experienced in that loving relationship. So far so good. But in some ways, the church we have today is much different from Joseph's church. The important question to me is: Does God speaks to me now through this church? And the answer is yes. He doesn't speak to me only through the church and he doesn't speak to me in everything the church does. But he does speak to me through the church. I therefore accept the legitimacy and the authority of the church. It is "true" to me.

Orson Scott Card in *Saintspeak* gives a wonderful definition of the phrase "only true." He says: "A synonym for *my*. For example: The only true church = my church. The only true ward = my ward. The only true way of picking cherries on the welfare farm = my way."[8]

But wait! Am I saying that the church is the "only true" church because, and only because, it is "my" church? But what happens

---

8. Orson Scott Crard, *Saintspeak* (Salt Lake City: Orion Books, 1981), n.p.

if our expectations are disappointed? If we buy a package that we think contains "the church" and take it home and open it up and then discover that it is somehow different from the package we think we bought (contains secretive polygamy, for instance, or outright bribery of major newspapers to assure statehood for Utah)? Then is it no longer either "my" church or "the only true church"? No. The church is still mine and still true, despite inevitable changes in my relationship with it.

It's no secret that our images and expectations of others, even beloved others, must undergo a great deal of alteration if we live past the age of six. We have to alter expectations of our parents that they know everything or at least always know best. And we have to forgive them for that. We have to alter expectations that if we always pay our tithing, we will always have enough money and we have to forgive our employers for that. We have to give up the expectation that if we go to BYU we will be married by the time we're seniors. And we have to forgive BYU for that. We have to give up the expectation that if we always do every church job we're asked none of our children will ever be hit by a car. And we have to forgive God for that.

Hanging onto those expectations is a sign either of childlike faith—and I firmly believe that no person should ever tamper with the childlike faith of another—or childishness, which will strangle faith more surely and more swiftly than any disappointed expectation. The church, I'm sorry to say, often contributes to childishness by making impossible promises. It promises perfect happiness, perfect safety, and perfect comfort in exchange for perfect obedience. Since perfect obedience is impossible, then it can always blame you for falling down on your bargain when you are not perfectly happy.

I like to hear children sing "I Am a Child of God." I don't like to hear adults sing it. Everybody's a child of God. This state requires only being born. The hard part is to become an adult of God.[9] Most of us plateau at being an adolescent of God, unable to stop blaming and bribing God, whining and whimpering because the magic formula didn't work, locked into a cycle of "I'll show you" types of rebellion ("I'll skip the Mother's Day program. I'll drink Coke, etc.") followed by a cycle of dependency where we try frantically somehow to make it all up—another kind of "I'll show you" ("I'll go to the temple every week. I'll do genealogy, make bread, *and* clean the closets," etc.) It seems to me that many issue-centered people get stuck here when something happens that doesn't fit into

---

9. Zina Petersen picked up this concept and launched a thought-provoking poem, creatively highlighting the genuine ambiguities and challenges of a maturing faith.

I am a child of God;
It's not an end result.
I think my Parents would prefer
That I became adult.
Leave me, hide me,
Let me find Thee,
Let me fear the night.
Let me know the mercy in not knowing I am right.

I am a child of God:
Enough, yet not to save.
Were my faith but a mustard seed
I'd walk across the waves.
Help me find me, walk behind me,
Guide my sinking hand.
Though not walking,
Yet I'll swim through doubt unto dry land.

I am a wo/man of God,
Yet always God's own child.
But innocence is ignorance, if grace has known no trials.
Try me, test me,
Defeat and best me:
Love me while I fall.
Others, fallen, will I love,
And thus will all raise all.

She did not remember the date of composition beyond "several years ago," although Facebook exchanges suggest a date of about or before 2008. Reprinted with permission.

the formula: Why did the church misrepresent its history? Why did the church kill the Equal Rights Amendment? Why did it take so long for black men to get priesthood? Why is the church so terrified of including its LGBTI members? Why did the Church Building Department destroy the Coleville (Utah) Tabernacle and gut the Logan (Utah) temple? etc.[10]

Now these are all good questions, but I hope you realize that there's only one answer: Because the church is made up of human beings, and human beings, by and large, can be jerks. That includes us. We usually are not very kind, thrifty, brave, clean, reverent, or even very smart. We're supposed to be, God wants us to be, and is, I believe, anxious to help us. But first we have to move. He accepts our disappointment when an expectation proves flawed. He accepts our anger at injustice in the church and elsewhere. Being angry and disappointed are okay. Making a career out of them is not.

Now what does all this have to do with the issues that trouble us? Those issues themselves don't matter. What we do with them does. I can accept—and even enjoy—elements of folk religion in the early church. I wonder what things we say and do now that, in 150 years, people are going to shake their heads over gravely.

I think maturity means acquiring different models and ways of looking at things. I grew up with the red telephone model of revelation: The red phone rings. The prophet, who has been just sitting there watching the phone, picks it up. It's God on the other end. God barks a crisp sentence into the phone, the prophet scribbles it down, says, "Right, Chief," and comes out into the room where we're all waiting with our notepads and pencils to say, "Now hear this. The gymnasiums will get red indoor-outdoor carpeting

---

10. The announcement by President Russell M. Nelson at April 2019 conference of plans to restore the four historic Utah temples, beginning with the Salt Lake temple, was genuine cause for rejoicing among those who had mourned the slaughter of Mormon historic architecture for half a century.

marked with basketball courts." (I did not make up this hideous, though fortunately brief, example of interior decorating.)

I'd like to propose a different model for relating to the concept of revelation, of scripture, of prophets. For who I am right now, this model fits reality better. It seems to me that nobody is really waiting in tidy rows for the door into the prophet's office to open. We're all working in a madhouse, a zoo. There are lots of phones and they're all ringing. People are talking into them as well as listening. They're also talking to each other. We say, "Just a sec, Joan. I've got a call coming in" or "Let me put you on hold, God. Somebody is waving a memo at me." Sometimes the message on the telephone is, "Joan's got the memo you need." Sometimes the messages contradict each other. There are also non-messages going on. There's background music. There are word processors clicking, printers clacking, videos flashing. You can hear birds, cars, and helicopters from outside. Some people are slamming file drawers open and shut looking for last week's messages.

And these messages are all very important. They're about lunch. Lunch is free but the schedule is uncertain: who gets to go when, what the menu is, who you get to sit by, how long you get. Depending on how hungry you are, the more numbers you punch, files you search, people you ask. And quite frequently lunch appears on your desk while you're looking because somebody ordered pizza on one of those phone calls. And even when you go to the skyroom where it's served on a lovely linen tablecloth, there are still phones, people at the same table talking, people at adjoining tables whose conversations you overhear, background music, birds, and an occasional colossal crash from the kitchen where somebody tried to enter through the exit.

I accept that revelation comes in many ways. To us. To prophets. From God. From each other. We have to grow up. We have to stop expecting each other to be perfect. We have to stop expecting the church to be perfect. We have to stop expecting Joseph Smith to be perfect. We have to stop expecting ourselves to be perfect. We have to stop expecting that a perfect God will cramp himself into our imperfect ideas about his perfection.

I wish there were more stories about women in the scriptures, but I'm glad for the ones that are there. I think we frequently see Mary as the model and try to put ourselves in her position of perfect submission when she said, "Behold the handmaid of the Lord. Be it unto me according to thy word" (Luke 1:38). We have to remember that she was talking to an angel. There are some statements you can make to an angel in safety that you really can't make to anyone else. Angels are not, as far as we know, jerks.

I'd like to suggest that perhaps we give more attention to one of those women, Hannah. Hannah was praying in the temple for a child when Eli, the high priest, saw her lips moving and thought she was mumbling drunkenly. He rebuked her. Now what if she, as a mere woman, had said to herself, "Well, he's the high priest. He must be speaking for God even though it sounds wrong to me. I must accept this rebuke and be it unto me according to thy word, Eli." Or, contrariwise, if she had said, "This jerk doesn't know what he's saying. See if I ever darken the door of *his* temple again. And you, God, how can you have a jerk for a high priest?"

Instead, she said, "No my lord, I am a woman of sorrowful spirit: I have drunk neither wine nor strong drink, but have poured out my soul before the Lord. Count not thine handmaid for a daughter of Belial: for out of the abundance of my complaint and grief have I spoken hitherto." And Eli responded, "Go in peace: and the God of Israel grant thee thy petition that thou hast asked of him" (1 Sam. 1:9–17). You'll notice that she didn't blame; he didn't apologize. She didn't demand and he didn't promise. Instead, both of them understood each other and joined in their hope and faith.

I think that's a good model for dealing with the all-too-human elements of our sometimes obscurely divine church, but it only works if there's love. Love for the church. Love for God. An awareness of his love for us. I get concerned when people pour out their souls before a conscious-raising group, in a letter to the editor, or on the bishop's desk before they've poured it out before the Lord. If that foundational relationship of loving and feeling loved is not there, it really doesn't matter very much, in my opinion, what is. Sooner or later, something will shake down the house. If we're having problems with the church, with our bishop, with racism in the church, by all means, let's keep reading, talking, puzzling, getting mad—but let's keep praying. I don't think any piece of information is very important compared to what I know and feel about my relationship with God.

C. S. Lewis puts it this way in a discussion of how prayer works:

> Religious people don't talk about the "results" of prayer; they talk of its being "answered" or "heard." Someone said, "A suitor wants his suit to be heard as well as granted." In suits to God, if they are really religious acts at all and not merely attempts at magic, this is even more so. We can bear to be refused but not to be ignored. In other words, our faith can survive many refusals if they really are refusals and not mere disregards. The apparent stone will be bread to us if we believe that a Father's hand put it into ours, in mercy or in justice or even in rebuke. It is hard and bitter, yet it can be chewed and swallowed. But if, having prayed for our heart's desire and got it, we then become convinced that this was a mere accident—that providential designs which had only some quite different end just couldn't help throwing out this satisfaction for us as a by-product—then the apparent bread would become a stone. A pretty stone, perhaps, or even a precious stone. But not edible.[11]

---

11. C. S. Lewis, *Letters to Malcolm: Chiefly on Prayer* (New York: Harcourt, Brace, Jovanovich Harvest Books, 1963), 52–53.

So what about polygamy? the Coalsville tabernacle and the Logan temple? the Building Department? the Correlation Committee? I try to remember two things. We're all jerks and God loves us anyway. Yes, it's impossible—downright unreasonable—for him to expect us to love each other. But somehow, sometimes, in some ways, he thinks we can. So do I.

8

Many Mansions—But No Doghouses

I delivered this address at a gathering of Forum for Mormon Studies in Longview, Washington, on October 4, 1992. I was excommunicated eleven months later.

Let's begin by explaining the title. At the Mormon History Association annual meeting in May this year, I responded to a session on Mormon mavericks. Sam Taylor of Redwood City, California, talked about Devere Baker who built a series of rafts that were supposed to replicate the voyage of Lehi, one of the Book of Mormon prophets. There was quite a lot of California hoopla involved, pretty spectacular failures, and a fair amount of embarrassment for the LDS Church when they failed. The second paper was about Maurine Whipple, the author of *The Giant Joshua*, by Veda Hale, a novelist and Maurine's biographer.[1] Sam is quite a colorful character in his own right, and my title comes from a note attached to the reading copy of his paper that he sent me. He called himself and

---

1. Maurine's papers, housed at Brigham Young University's Harold B. Lee Library, contained scores of short stories, regional events and historical locations, and several beginnings on her sequel to *The Giant Joshua*. Most of these works were only partly finished. Whipple's unpublished writings will be published as Andrew Hall, Lynne Larson, and Veda Hale, editors, *A Craving for Beauty: The Lost Works of Maurine Whipple* (Salt Lake City: BCC Press, 2020). Veda Tebbs Hale's biography, *Swell Suffering: A Biography of Maurine Whipple* (Salt Lake City: Greg Kofford Books, 2011), was awarded Best Biography by the Mormon History Association in 2012.

Maurine "two refugees from the Deseret dog-house." When I told him that Maurine had died in April—a month before the conference—he wrote back: "She was in the dog house for a half century because of *The Giant Joshua* and I was in the dog house for 30 years for *Heaven Knows Why*.[2] So I expect to meet her eventually in the great dog house in the sky."

I recognized the truth of what Sam said, and it made me both sorrowful and angry. As a church, we're neither very tolerant of our eccentrics nor very welcoming of our mavericks. We present our wards and our meetinghouses as safe places of warm community and sharing, of mutual belief in the Savior, and of support for each other. But the reality is that we're sometimes better at exclusion than inclusion, and we make each other pay a high price for being a member of the community. I'm not against the community. I love it. Nor am I against high prices. I'm against a system that demands a high price but doesn't deliver what it promises.

We are, in the terms of Aesop's fable, a church of diligent and industrious ants, unimaginatively and soberly trotting along our little paths, eternally preparing for an eternal winter. What do we do with gorgeous grasshoppers like Sam, Devere, and Maurine whom we don't understand and who seem to be so different from us? It strikes me as both wistful and sad that it was the strength

---

2. In this comic novel, a grandfather returns from the afterlife to get an errant grandson to shape up. It mocked many aspects of Mormon culture, such as the Word of Wisdom, and was greeted censoriously by many orthodox Mormons, including LDS general authorities. Their uneasiness with Sam's wit and especially his insistence on not whitewashing Mormon history kept Sam persona non grata for much of his life—although it did not change his fierce love for Mormonism and its people and his bone-deep skepticism that exactly paralleled the love. He was church president John Taylor's grandson and the son of apostle John W. Taylor, who was excommunicated, apparently for violating the Woodruff Manifesto with post-Manifesto plural marriages but, almost certainly, also as a scapegoat, along with his colleague in the Twelve Matthias F. Cowley, demanded by the hearings in the US Senate so Reed Smoot could keep his seat.

of Maurine's and Devere's attachments to Mormonism that made them so vulnerable to ostracism and exile. If either of them had been able to walk away, live elsewhere, take up another dream, and slip quietly into the pew of another church, they might have been much happier. And so might their friends and relations. We might have been relieved to have them at a safer distance.

This is a pretty natural human feeling. I taught Sunbeams in the church's Primary program for eight years, and I saw a lot of three-year-olds in that length of time. I'll have to admit there was an occasional Sunday when I would notice that the Holy Terror of the preschool set wasn't there and my first thought would be, "Thank God! A peaceful class."

But let me juxtapose to that feeling 2 Nephi 26:33 in which the Lord "inviteth all to come unto him and partake of his goodness; and he denieth none that come unto him, black and white, bond and free, male and female; and he remembereth the heathen; and all are alike unto God." He inviteth *all*. He denieth *none*. So I'd like to discuss two questions: What kind of dog-houses do we maintain within the church where we put members we're ostracizing? And second, how do we dismantle those dog-houses and focus on the "many mansions" instead?

First, the dog houses. Every organization has boundaries, ways for its members to tell who's in and who's out, and more subtle rules to say "how far in." The Mormon Church is an organization with very strong boundaries. You enter by baptism, but that's not all. Boundary markers are the way we dress, what we abstain from drinking, the fact that we fold our arms instead of clasping our hands to pray, our language, our sense of decorum, our sense of humor, why we sing accompanied by an organ or piano but not a guitar or a trumpet. There are many reasons why someone may not have a temple recommend; but if they do, we assume we know quite a lot about them. My father was a bishop for eleven years when I was growing up. I'm a returned missionary. My parents are temple workers now. All of my brothers went on missions. Everyone in the family who is married was married in the temple. These sentences convey an enormous amount of information to you, if you're Mormon, because you understand the culture. All of you automatically filled in a lot of blanks just with that information.

Now, one of the things you probably didn't guess is that I financed my mission by working as a go-go dancer. Do I detect some skepticism? You've got my point. Mormonism and membership are codes. We grow up learning how to read them; converts have to learn a culture, as well as learning the gospel. At least part of how successfully they convert is how quickly they adapt the markers of the culture.

These are strengths. It means there's a sense of comfort, of comfortableness when we encounter another member of the church. There's pride as well as comfort in the oft-declared observation that you know how to behave in any sacrament meeting anywhere in the world, whatever the setting or language. (The price of that predictability is, often, boredom.) Of course, we're different as individuals, but just the fact of our commonly held membership and our commonly made covenants means that we sense a kinship. We feel at home. We have a community. We belong. It belongs to us.

But the power to protect and accept has its opposite. That's the power to reject and punish. Listen to these words: diversity, difference, divergence, disagreement, dissent, disloyalty, danger. Some people go straight from "difference" to "danger." And the word that comes after danger is "dog house."

This spring, I read *The Subtle Power of Spiritual Abuse* by David Johnson and Jeff Vanvonderen.[3] They wrote this book to identify

---

3. David Johnson and Jeff Vanvonderen, *The Subtle Power of Spiritual Abuse* (Minneapolis: Bethany House, 1991). The quotations come from pp. 20–23. See also the discussion of spiritual abuse in Chapter 3 herein.

situations in their church—the Lutheran Church—where members were suffering and in despair instead of rejoicing in the love of the Savior—not because of their sins but because of their church. I felt both bewildered and amazed that so much of what they said sounded utterly familiar. Here's their definition of spiritual abuse:

> Spiritual abuse can occur when a leader uses his or her spiritual position to control or dominate another person. ... Power is used to bolster the position or needs of a leader, over and above one who comes to them in need. ...
>
> Spiritual abuse can also occur when spirituality is used to make others live up to a "spiritual standard," by making someone behave in a certain way, also without regard to an individual's actual well-being. ... In these systems, the members are there to meet the needs of the leaders: needs for power, importance, intimacy, value.

They related the example of a woman who was very depressed because she felt that she was inadequate as a Christian. Her pastor gave her a list of scriptures to memorize, which she should recite when she felt depressed. But the depression didn't go away. When she went back to her pastor, she said, "Things are worse. Our two teenage sons are misbehaving and my husband won't take any responsibility or try to help." She also reported a history of depression in her family and expressed skepticism that the scriptures would solve her problem. The pastor scolded her for arguing, and decried her unwillingness to accept his counsel. "That proved he was right. Her problem was disobedience and rebellion."[4] What had she done? She had questioned his authority. And just the fact of questioning was evidence that she was wrong.

Those of you who have taken debate in high school will recognize this tactic as ad hominem or attacking the messenger who brings the bad news instead of dealing with the bad news. Those of you who

---

4. Ibid., 17–18.

have read very much in the literature of physical or sexual abuse will also recognize it as the phenomenon called "blaming the victim."

Spiritual abuse occurs when "religious people [try] to meet their own spiritual needs through someone else's religious performance."[5] As members, we have to be righteous according to their rules. Parents pressure a son to go on an LDS mission, because otherwise someone might think they're bad parents. This is legalism, or "a form of religious perfectionism that focuses on the careful performance and avoidance of certain behaviors. It teaches people to gain a sense of spiritual acceptance based on their performance, instead of accepting it as a gift on the basis of the atonement of Christ."[6] And when we fail to do everything on the checklist, guilt just sweeps over us and washes us away. We Mormon women even have a name for it—the Patty Perfect syndrome.

Spiritual abuse is characterized by silence and secret-keeping. The abused person feels guilty and ashamed. "Admitting the abuse out loud—or even thinking that what you experienced was abuse—often feels like you are being disloyal to family, to church, even to God."[7] We deny what has happened. We conspire together, victim and victimizer, not to talk about what has happened. There are a lot of "unspoken rules. ... For instance, no one at a church gathering would ever say out loud, 'You know we must never disagree with the pastor on his sermons—and if you do you will never be trusted and never be allowed to minister in any capacity in this church.'"[8] One of the most powerful unspoken rules is "If you speak about the problem out loud, you are the problem. In some way, you must be silenced or eliminated."[9] If we excommunicate Fawn Brodie, for instance, we don't have to deal with troublesome parts of our history.

---

5. Ibid., 37.
6. Ibid.
7. Ibid., 48–56.
8. Ibid., 67.
9. Ibid., 68.

If we excommunicate Sonia Johnson, we've somehow eliminated the question of whether women are treated equally in this country and in this church.

Another characteristic of spiritual abuse is that power in relationships is lopsided. The abuser has a great deal of power, and the abused person feels absolutely powerless. Abusive "leaders spend a lot of time focused on their own authority and reminding others of it as well."[10] "The leaders require the place of honor."[11] Titles, uniforms, special places to sit, deferential treatment—all of these things are very important.

I'm sorry to say that Mormons are no more immune to spiritual abuse than Lutherans, just as Mormons are no more immune to sexual abuse than other Americans. I know people who have spent most of their lives in the doghouse, disapproved of, disdained, discarded. Such things pervert the spirit of the gospel. They blaspheme the atonement of Christ and his eternal love for each one of us. They violate our spiritual identity as children of our Heavenly Parents. Remember, "he inviteth all, denieth none." The Savior is our advocate with the Father, not our accuser (D&C 29:5).

Given that this is so, how do we go about getting out of the doghouse and dismantling it, so that we don't get back in ourselves and so that no one else can be put into it? From the bottom of my heart, I feel that the answer is the gospel. The Savior's atonement brings us freedom from the bondage of sin. He promises us rest from our weariness, living water for our thirst. One of the great burdens that he lifts from us is the burden of judgement. We are not required to judge ourselves. We are commanded not to judge others (Matt. 7:1). There is such power and such freedom in having, as the basis of our relationship with ourselves and with others, the understanding that Jesus Christ knows and loves each one of us individually.

10. Ibid., 63.
11. Ibid., 134.

When we approach someone who is different from us—whether that difference is in age, education, social class, race, culture, nationality, gender issues, politics, health, or wealth—we probably ask ourselves one of two questions that permanently shape that relationship. The first question is: Will contact with this person defile me in some way? If so, how can I set up boundaries, protect myself, avoid and limit contact? This question creates and almost certainly will perpetuate a negative relationship that will only be overcome if we are forced to spend enough time with that person to realize that we will not be contaminated by contact.

The second question is: Do I have enough love to give this person? If not, what is the lack in me? Even if the answer is "No, I don't have enough love," it still brings us into a positive relationship, for this focus leads us to perceive and grieve for our own hard-heartedness, to desire repentance, and to yearn for a fuller measure of the pure love of Christ. For me, love is the bridge that I have to walk across what sometimes seems like a chasm between my commitment to the church and my bewilderment and sorrow at the abuse sometimes inflicted on members of the church by insensitive people. It is the desire to increase the amount of love in our community that keeps me walking that bridge. It is in the spirit of that love that I am here with you now.

This spring, I was at a retreat of Mormon women where Chieko Okazaki spoke. She is the first counselor in the Relief Society general presidency, but, more importantly to our family, she is my husband's mission mother. She is one of the most generous, joyous, and loving people I have ever met. She was shatteringly honest in her address. She said she wanted to talk to those who felt hurt and marginalized by their participation in the church, and then she shared her own experience. I want to quote extensively from what she said, because I think it comes with a strong and distinctive spirit. You need to know that she was the first non-Caucasian to serve on any general board (that was the Young Women's Mutual Improvement Association general board during the 1960s), and she is the only woman of any race to serve on all three general boards—she was a member of the Primary general board when she was called to the Relief Society presidency. She said:

> With each of these callings has come an outpouring of affection, congratulations, and prayers for success from our friends, former missionaries, ward members, and family members. But at the same time, some people from whom we would expect such expressions of happiness have been silent. People who have been members of our wards, people with whom we have gone to the temple, people who have partaken of the hospitality of our home and into whose homes we have been received have been silent. Ed [her husband] and I do not know why, of course, but sometimes we have wondered if their silence stems from shock and even dismay that a Japanese American woman has been called to that position.
>
> I don't necessarily believe that it's prejudice and I have no interest in finding out. But let me put those feelings in a little more perspective for you. When I was called to Florence Jacobsen's [YW-MIA] board, no woman or man who was not Caucasian had been called previously to serve on any auxiliary board. No non-Caucasian had ever served as a mission president, a temple president, a regional representative or as a General Authority. We had lived in Salt Lake City since 1950. People stared at us when we went shopping. People stared at us in the temple. A Japanese person could not marry a Caucasian in the Salt Lake Temple at that time. Beneficial Life Insurance would not sell us insurance. All State insurance through Sears and Roebuck would not insure our cars. ... There have been many, many occasions when Ed and I could have taken offense. In fact, we have often said to each other, "If we were going to lose our testimonies, it would have been here in Zion." But we didn't lose our testimonies. We understood that we had the power to choose, and we had already chosen—we had chosen the gospel over the religion of our families, we had chosen each other over the

voices that warned about a marriage of mixed religions [Chieko was baptized when she was fifteen, Ed the year after they were married], we had chosen the mainland over the familiarity and comforts of our home island. We knew we were tougher than our problems.

And what about you? Are there some Mormon gatherings where you think, "My goodness, am I the only person who has a problem with this?" And are there some non-Mormon groups where you think, "My goodness, am I the only person here who takes religion seriously?" … I have three little mottos that I sometimes repeat to myself during interesting situations like these:

First: If both of us thought alike, one of us would not be necessary.

Second, I may be the first, but I'm going to ensure that I won't be the last.

Third—and this is really a prayer: Help, Father. I have a message they may not have heard before. How can I say it so they can hear it?

Most people will try to understand if you make these efforts; but recognize that there will be people who won't want you there, who won't hear what you say, who will misunderstand you, sometimes on purpose. Forgive them quickly so that no negative thoughts will hold you back or make it harder for them to change. If you don't forgive a person who has offended you, you create a negative relationship that becomes a second burden on top of the original problem.

Did any of you hear Dr. Olga Kolgarova, when she was here last summer? She joined the Church in Czechoslovakia nine years ago, in 1983. She was the first young person to be baptized in more than forty years in that country. Since the imposition of Communist rule after World War II, the Church had been outlawed. To be caught in a meeting, even in a private home, to be baptized, to discuss the scriptures, to perform a priesthood ordinance—any one of these offenses could bring with it a prison sentence of three to seven years. She was a professor of philosophy and ethics; but instead of teaching Marxism-Leninism, she taught a system of trust, responsibility, and love based on the Book of Mormon scripture, "Men [and women]—and yes, that's how she quoted the scripture—are that they might have joy." She taught yoga camps during the summer where she reached hundreds more of young people.

Olga lived in Bratislava, the second largest city in Czechoslovakia. Her little branch had only seven members when she first began attending meetings. By 1989, the years of Czechoslovakia's ... "velvet revolution," there were about sixty members. She talked about their meetings—of slipping into a private home after dark, having all the windows closed, the blinds pulled down, never singing a hymn. Their manuals were forty years old. There was one Book of Mormon, and it rotated to each in turn. When it was Olga's turn to have it, she stayed up all night reading it.

Olga, like all of the members, was interrogated many times by the secret police, the first time when she was twenty-two or twenty-three. She said that she went in thinking, "I could be in prison until I am thirty." And she prayed. She prayed very hard for the Lord's protection. She said, "Do you know what it is like, being called into a room where there are six people, sitting at a table, asking you questions?" This is not an experience I have had, but I know that some of you have had discussions with your ecclesiastical leaders about your beliefs. Sometimes these have been meetings of respect and love. Perhaps sometimes not. If you have felt misunderstood, I ask you to forgive them.

I ask you something else. Don't leave. Don't become inactive. You may think you are voting with your feet, that you are making a statement by leaving. You are, but your absence is welcomed and encouraged by those who don't understand or value you. They see your diversity as a problem to be fixed, as a flaw to be corrected or erased. I want you to know that your diversity is a more valuable statement. Elder [Neal A.] Maxwell talks about ... "idealists without illusions" ... I'm asking you to be idealists without illusions, to dig deep for the strength, the compassion, and the toughness you need to find your own way.

Please stay. Please be a bridge builder. We may feel marginalized, pushed to the edge, invisible, unwanted, not valuable. I tell you that we are visible, are wanted, are valuable. I love you. We need each other's support. I pray for you. Please pray for me.

Another example Olga Kolgarova used was that of the coin. We think of the coin as having only two sides—heads or tails. She pointed out that the coin has a third side—the edge. She compared one side of the coin to the view that all reality is material and physical, the other to the spiritual reality. But the edge holds both sides together. It is narrow and inconspicuous, easy to overlook, but we live our lives on the edge, drawing from both the material and the spiritual. If our place is on the edge, let us claim that place and guard it. We are making it possible for two realities to come together, not only for ourselves but for other people as well. The key to keeping these two realities together lies in Christ. We must cling to Christ with all of the energy and power of our heart, might, mind, and strength. There will always be problems in relationships until we start getting our messages from the Savior instead of people who are just as scared and limited as we. If we give power to a scared person, we've created a dangerous person. We don't have to give a peaceful person power; she has it already. There were many days in my life when I could only speak with Heavenly Father and tell him what I really felt.

When we are hurt by others in the Church who reject our gifts and diversity, I do not ask you to pretend that these wounds did not happen. I do not ask you to deny your pain. But I do ask you not to be martyrs. Don't carry the pain as a burden. Don't burden yourself with self-pity or supersensitive feelings or a willingness to take offense—even when it is intended. ... Cling to Christ.[12]

I have quoted that long passage because I think that, when our spirits have been in a safe place, when we have been loved and nourished by the good word of Christ (Moro. 6:4), when we feel his absolute advocacy for us, then it's easier to deal gently with each other, to open our hearts to others, to abandon the orthodoxy patrols along the boundaries and instead seek to serve.

12. Chieko N. Okazaki, "Cherishing Each Other," in *Pilgrimage 1992*, comp. Lavina Fielding Anderson (Salt Lake City: Pilgrimage, Sept. 1992), 58–60.

I think that there is a great deal we can do to make our wards places of cherishing and community. Sister Okazaki listed some of them. I think something else we can do is to suspend judgment, to evaluate ideas on their merits rather than on the status of the person who announced them. I am comfortable with the idea of the church as a family. I'm not very comfortable with songs about being an army. Queen Elizabeth II, in her Christmas Day address to the Dominion in 1991, said: "Democracy depends not on political structure but on the good will and good sense of the ordinary citizen. ... None of us has a monopoly of wisdom and we must always be ready to listen to and respect other points of view."[13] That feels better to me than images of hierarchy, of dominance and submission.

I long for the realization of a vision expressed by the member of another faith:

> Some Saints have chosen to leave this church and form their own because they believe it has lost some of its parts and, therefore, has fallen from God's grace. The vast majority of us, however, remain on a journey that has taken us along new paths in search of Christ's peaceable kingdom.
>
> Why do I remain? I choose to be part of a faith community that is willing to risk moments of doubt in the pursuit of truth. That kind of honesty is essential to an abundant life. How could we call ourselves the body of Christ and the people of God if we misrepresent the truth or, worse, perpetuate a lie? Here I find spiritual truth, not locked up in a preordained state or guarded by leaders who tell me what to believe but in process of revealment.[14]

And I think there are steps we can take to stop spiritual abuse. First, we must speak up. We must stop keeping "bad" secrets when

---

13. Queen Elizabeth II, "Christmas Day Message, 1991," BBC broadcast. Notes from live broadcast in my possession.

14. Richard A. Brown, "A Shoring Tower Model for Faith," *Saints Herald*, Jan. 1992, 15–17. The quotation is on p. 17.

abuse occurs. We must share our stories and our pain. When we feel isolated, judged, and rejected, it is very easy to give up, to allow ourselves to become marginalized, and to accept the devaluation as accurate. If we silence ourselves or allow others to silence us, we will deny the validity of our experience, undermine the foundations of authenticity in our personal spirituality, and impoverish our collective life as a faith community. Silence and self-censorship are terrible wrongs. Reducing the diversity of voices in a community to a single, official voice erases us. We must join in the on-going dialogue between individual and community, out of necessity and also out of love.

Second, it is not enough to protest injustice. We must uphold the beautiful ideals of justice, holiness, and goodness. When a friend of mine had his temple recommend confiscated for praising the church's actions in print, I went to my stake president and told him I was confused.[15] He was, too. We need to affirm that truth is best served by an open interchange, that disagreement can be both courteous and clarifying, and that differences are not automatically dangerous.

Third, we must defend each other. Some official actions are obviously attempts to marginalize and punish members who hold divergent views by calling them rebellious or apostate or disobedient. If we hear people being stigmatized in this way and know differently, we need to have the courage to be witnesses for them. And it goes both ways, of course. Malice and irresponsibility directed toward a leader are equally distasteful, equally deserving of setting the record straight. We need to provide honest feedback to each other. If I'm saying excessive, irresponsible things, I need to know it; and I'll hear it most clearly from my friends.

Fourth, we must directly sustain and support individuals who are experiencing ecclesiastical harassment. Such support will help

---

15. This stake president was the predecessor of the one who excommunicated me. He was later called as our stake patriarch.

prevent overreactions and speed the healing process in the survivor. Supportive observers may also help prevent some ecclesiastical abuse. I was very moved when I learned that fourteen friends, former ward members, and former ecclesiastical leaders had attended the disciplinary council of a man accused of apostasy in California. Whatever the merits of the case, there was a Christian willingness to love the sinner outside in the hall that I don't think he found inside the council chamber.

Fifth, we must be more assertive in dealing with our leaders. Our respect for our leaders, our willingness to seek and follow their counsel, and our obedience to them are all good things but only within bounds. Doctrine and Covenants 121 sets clear limits on how a person in authority may relate to a member. If those principles are being violated, then we need to say so. We need to protect ourselves from abuse, and we need to refuse to cooperate with attempts at abuse. A friend of mine pointed out that when we are baptized, our sins are washed away, not our rights.

And, finally, I think we must seek humility as a prerequisite for a more loving, less fearful, community. The apostle Paul queried, "Am I therefore become your enemy, because I tell you the truth?" (Gal. 4:16). Oliver Cromwell pleaded: "I beseech you, in the bowels of Christ, think it possible you may be mistaken."[16] These are questions we must ask ourselves, each time we pose them for someone else.

Perhaps it is necessary for someone to guard the boundaries. Perhaps it is necessary for someone to be a judge. I thank God that is not my responsibility or calling, and I pray for those who bear that burden. I listen willingly to their counsel. But I do not give my agency into their hands. If they label my behavior and evaluate my motives, I reserve the right to decide if they are truly describing me. When I have felt misjudged, stereotyped, or stigmatized, I have

---

16. As quoted by C. Robert Mesle, *Fire in My Bones: A Study in Faith and Belief* (Independence, Missouri: Herald House, 1984), 204.

sought consolation in passages like this one: "O then, my beloved ... come unto the Lord, the Holy One, ... [T]he keeper of the gate is the Holy One of Israel; and he employeth no servant there; and there is none other way save it be by the gate; for he cannot be deceived, for the Lord God is his name" (2 Ne. 9:41).

In Nauvoo, Illinois, a black convert to the LDS church, Cathy Stokes, changed my life forever by telling me, "When I went to the temple, I consecrated all of me. That included my blackness. If the Lord can use it, it's his."[17] She set me on the road to realizing that the Lord wanted all of me, even the parts that the church does not currently want and cannot use. I think for the most part that my intellectual and scholarly interests fit into that category. Maybe it's also true for some of you. I applaud you for coming. If you find fellowship and companionship here tonight, I ask you to continue to support such gatherings. And if you do not feel drawn to it, I ask that you regard without disdain or hostility those who find that it meets some of their needs,

I am a sign-seeker. I seek signs that Mormonism is becoming a more inclusive community, one that is confident in its strengths rather than apprehensive about contamination, one that separates the absolute worth of an individual from the worth or worthlessness—and there is a sliding spectrum—of that individual's works. I seek signs that Mormonism is becoming a community that listens, asks questions, and affirms rather than one which interrupts, accuses, and punishes. I want us to be a community in which we can hear the voice of the Lord saying:

---

17. Cathy has, in fact, been an influential spokesperson both for and to the church, helping to lift prohibitions against the church in Ghana, appearing on panels, and doing both formal and informal interviews to explain the church's position and to tell her own story. A medical professional, she retired as the most powerful health administrator in Illinois and had, at one point, shut down the enormous Cook County hospital for failing to meet mandated standards.

Come unto me, all ye that labour and are heavy laden, and I will give you rest.

Take my yoke upon you, and learn of me; for I am meek and lowly in heart: and ye shall find rest unto your souls.

For my yoke is easy, and my burden is light. (Matt. 11:28–30)

9

Modes of Revelation

A PERSONAL APPROACH

*I presented this essay at the 1992 Salt Lake Sunstone Symposium.
This is its first publication.*

As I have read some of the hundreds of diaries and reminiscences produced by nineteenth-century Latter-day Saints, I have been repeatedly struck by the nature of their spiritual experiences—not that they had them, nor that they had so many. Such events are not uncommon among us today. Rather I was struck by the range of types and qualities. Divine messengers appeared in night visions, people spoke in new tongues or interpreted them, broken bodies healed, departed loved ones or individuals who were far away came with messages and reassurance. In short, both the scriptures and our own history suggest that revelation can come in many ways. It is my sense, however, that modern American Mormons have a much shorter list of "respectable" or accepted ways in which revelation can come. These ways primarily seem to be answered prayers, healings, and feelings of enlightenment about the scriptures.

Matthew Rowan, who wrote a detailed reminiscence of joining the church in Scotland in 1844 when he was eighteen, recounts many spiritual experiences. He was baptized on a "cold and sleety" night in February, but his "burning desire ... kept all cold and fear from [his] heart." In bed one night, he felt a hand touch his shoulder. He turned over to see a dark-visaged man in dark clothing whose face was full of "earnestness and authority." The visitor assured Matthew that he could "speak with the tongues of angels." This description of dark apparel and features is not, I think, how most contemporary Latter-day Saints would see an angelic messenger, no doubt because of Joseph Smith's compelling description of the white-robed, light-surrounded Angel Moroni; but Matthew was probably influenced by the association of a cleric and a dark suit instead of work clothes. Trying to reclaim a friend who had drifted away from Mormonism because of ridicule, Matthew bore testimony in tongues so powerfully that it drained all the strength from his own body and left his friend quaking. The next day, this friend told him he had knelt to pray and found himself praying in an unknown tongue. Why did he have these experiences? I believe the answer may lie partly in his comment, "We were taught to believe in, and contend for, the Supernatural gifts of the Spirit."[1]

It has been twelve years since I attended either Sunday school or Relief Society, thanks to the block schedule and my calling in the Primary, but I cannot recall lessons about the need to seek spiritual gifts. Nor do I recall hearing sacrament meeting talks, stake conference addresses, or general conference sermons that urge us to desire, receive, and use spiritual gifts. I understand some of the reasons. First, we have all shuddered at manifestations of extreme, violent religious fundamentalism, which hears its own grotesque and violent voices as the voice of God. We might think, "If this is what happens to someone who seeks the Spirit, then better not to seek." Second, as the Mormon church has moved during the course of the twentieth century from being a despised and bizarre sect to being a solidly respectable, impressively well-financed, middle-class church, at least in the United States, excesses of enthusiasm leave us uncomfortable, make us suspicious, and seem more likely to

---

1. In Lavina Fielding Anderson, "In the Crucible: Early British Saints," *Ensign*, Dec. 1979, 52–53.

foment discord than to enrich the community life of the church. Third, the twentieth century (and now twenty-first) does not often impose upon us the sheer physical needs of the nineteenth century that made prayer the first, and sometimes only, resort when a Saint needed food, healing, knowledge, comfort, or protection. Fourth, the normative forces that tame and restrain charismatic manifestations may have acted differentially in the cases of men and women, making women particularly vulnerable to spoken or unspoken messages about appropriateness. To have a spiritual experience rejected as "just a hysterical woman" or even accepted but with cold politeness is chilling to further expressions.[2]

Of course, miracles still happen. In my own sacrament meeting within the last year one woman testified of seeing a vision of Christ on the cross and knowing he died for her. Our Primary president read from her missionary journal to the children during sharing time. In it, she reported, a woman received a visitation in a dream from a man named Abinadi who had a message for her. When she met the missionaries and saw the Arnold Freiberg painting of Abinadi in chains before King Noah from the Book of Mormon, she knew who he was.[3] A woman in her seventies, legally blind and a survivor of triple cancer, made a commitment to contribute a certain sum each month to support her nephew who was

2. This phenomenon is, of course, part of a larger devaluing of women's experience in our culture. Elaine Showalter, a literary critic, pointed out that women "are estranged from their own experience and unable to perceive its shape and authenticity, in part because they do not see it mirrored and given resonance in literature. ... They are expected to identify with masculine experience, which is presented as the human one, and have no faith in the validity of their own perceptions and experiences, rarely seeing them confirmed in literature, or accepted in criticism." Showalter, "Women and the Literary Curriculum," *College English* 32 (May 1971): 855–62. My thanks to Marnie Ebert Leavitt for bringing this quotation to my attention.

3. This example is almost comical since Freiberg, although not known for the modesty of his claims of artistic inspiration, never, to my knowledge, claimed a visionary basis for either King Noah or Abinadi.

on a mission. She won an amazing string of poetry contests for two years, supplying a virtually steady income in the sum she had promised. My husband, whose ancient Saab was not equal to the commute to BYU for his new job at the Museum of Art, prayed to find the kind of car he wanted at a price he could afford; two days later it was in the lot at $3,000 off the list price. My brother saw that his secretary was in such turmoil during a busy period in the office that she was incapable of dealing with the work effectively. As he talked kindly to her, a sudden, strong image came to him. "Did you almost drown as a child?" he asks her. "I see you in a whirl-pool." She stared at him in amazement. She *had* almost drowned as a child when she was almost sucked into a canal culvert; but she had never told anyone and only her mother, who had rescued her, knew about it. Ever afterward, that drowning experience would come back when she was feeling overwhelmed. My brother helped her visualize herself as big enough and powerful enough to break out of the whirlpool and pull herself out of the canal. The change in her personality and her work capacity was miraculous. At one point when C. S. Lewis's wife was dying of bone cancer, her de-calcified thigh bone "began to regenerate, to rebuild itself, to find some source of available calcium and regrow into a healthy femur." At the same time, Lewis began suffering from osteoporosis. On another occasion, when Joy was in such "terrible pain … that she really felt that she could not stand it any longer, [Lewis] prayed that he might be permitted to … accept the pain. … At once, he began to experience indescribable agony in his legs and, for a while, [Joy] was relieved of her pain."[4]

So I am not suggesting that spiritual experiences do not occur or that we do not seek them. However, I am suggesting that we perhaps seek them less often and less intensely than we might and

---

4. Douglas H. Gresham, *Lenten Lands: My Childhood with Joy Davidman and C. S. Lewis* (New York: Macmillan Publishing, 1988), 80–81.

that our spiritual lives are impoverished as a result. You probably know John Bunyan as the author of that wonderful spiritual allegory, *Pilgrim's Progress*. He also wrote a little spiritual autobiography called *Grace Abounding*, which chronicles his long and desperate search for God through a thicket of doubts and despair that seemed to grow up anew before him daily. He did not understand how the Atonement could apply to such a wretched sinner as himself. For some time, he had felt that the promises of the scriptures did not apply to him

> ... but now there was no time to wait: the avenger of blood was too close upon me.
>
> Now I caught at any word, even though I feared I had no right to it, and even leaped into the bosom of that promise that I feared shut its heart against me. ... In my great agony, I would floun[der] toward the promise as the horses in the mire do toward sound ground. ... I tried to take the words as God had laid them down without trying to explain away a single syllable of them. I began to realize that God had a bigger mouth to speak with than I had a heart to understand. ... Two or three times I had such an amazing understanding of the divine grace of God that I could hardly bear up under it. It was so out of measure that if it had stayed upon me, I do think it would have made me incapable for business.[5]

One sentence in particular struck me: "God had a bigger mouth to speak with than I had a heart to understand." I have the feeling that God has more to give us than we have capacity to receive. At one point when I had been reflecting very seriously on how to pray for genuine contact with the Spirit, an image came to me. I was in a cell, dragging a three-legged stool over to the barred window, balancing precariously on the stool and clinging to the bars with one hand while I reached out through them to a kindly benefactor who

---

5. John Bunyan, *Grace Abounding to the Chief of Sinners*, modern English version of Moody Bible Institute of Chicago (Chicago: Moody Press, 1959), 86–87.

stood outside, holding toward me a ripe apple, bursting with juice and bringing with it all the fresh, crisp scents of autumn. With great effort, we both stretched as far as we could. The apple exchanged hands. I sank back to the stool and gratefully ate the apple, savoring every bite. For days I lingered over that apple. I saved the core. Even when it was brown and shriveled, the scent of harvest clung to it. Finally, reluctantly, I acknowledged that it was a memory. Painfully I dragged my stool to the window again. There stood the benefactor, patiently waiting, eager to give me yet another apple. We went through the whole process again. And I did not notice that there were no walls in my cell except the wall that held the window. I could walk to the left or to the right and find myself in an orchard of trees, each laden and glowing with apples—scarlet, gold, russet, and green—ready to fall into my palm at the slightest pressure, ready to eat by lifting it to my lips. My own experience thus taught me that we have created a climate of scarcity in spiritual experience that contradicts the Savior's wish. We insist on getting our nourishment through a narrow window when he has created a world without walls.

That first generation of LDS converts struggled to find words to express the witness of the Spirit to them, using terms like these: "The sublimity and grandeur in the contemplation of the work of God ... would at times completely overshadow me and cast into momentary forgetfulness [my] many vain amusements." "Relief and peace and the gentle whisperings of the spirit of God ..." "I gazed with wonder ... and listened with delight." My "heart was full to overflowing." "It ran through me like lightning. It roused every feeling of my mind. ... Something seemed to bear upon my mind, like a clear calmness." "A bright light burst on my mind. Many passages of Scripture came plain and clear to my mind." A missionary "unfolded new principle after new principle, glory after glory, until my Soul was fed with fatness." "I have sometimes ...

been so filled with the love of God and felt such a sense of his favour as had made me rejoice abundantly."[6]

Many of the remarkable spiritual experiences of early members of the church spring from both their backgrounds in other religious traditions and their seriousness in asking for spiritual gifts. What if we were more open to other forms of spiritual communication besides those usually reported in testimony meetings?

Here is a second experience that was a revelation to me. It came under somewhat unconventional circumstances and took a perhaps unusual form; but it came with an unmistakable spiritual force and authority that I could not deny. In 1981, a group of fifty-six women from across the nation met at Nauvoo, Illinois, in a private celebration of sisterhood. We called ourselves a Pilgrimage. The energy generated by that gathering was so intense that we spontaneously decided to sponsor regional pilgrimages. They include the annual *Exponent* retreat in New England and its spin-off Provo Canyon retreat, a bi-annual Midwest Pilgrimage, and an annual Salt Lake City Pilgrimage. At the 1983 Salt Lake Pilgrimage, one of the small-group sessions was a guided imagery about friendship. During it, I received what I have come to regard as a personal revelation of comfort and consolation to heal the pain I was feeling over what I saw as the church's increasing rejection, in many ways and on many levels, of its women and its intellectuals. I never afterwards talked about what happened except infrequently, and never in detail, with a few of my closest friends.

In the fall of 1991, Paul and I were invited to address the Midwest Pilgrimage, an invitation we were delighted to accept. Before we left, while I was preparing my address for the Midwest Pilgrimage sacrament meeting on Sunday morning, I had a strong impulse

---

6. The speakers are, in order, Gilbert Belnap, Ebenezer Robinson, Ira Carter, and Mary Fielding Smith in Lavina Fielding Anderson, "Kirtland's Resolute Saints," *Ensign*, Jan. 1979, 51–55.

to include my 1983 Pilgrimage experience and started to look for my journal, but stopped, feeling that it might not be appropriate. During the testimony meeting on Sunday, September 15, 1991, I again had a strong prompting to share this experience. I resisted, since the focus of that sweet and spiritual meeting had not been, even indirectly, on feminist issues and I did not want to introduce what might be a discordant note.

After the closing song and closing prayer, however, when half a dozen women left to meet travel schedules and home obligations, Lynn Matthews Anderson said, "I feel that somebody here still needs to talk. I remember how I felt once when the meeting closed and I hadn't said what was in my heart; and I'm still here to listen if somebody else has something to say." Everyone else stayed. Two other women spoke, sharing personal feelings and experiences in the same trusting and supportive way that earlier women had spoken. By then the prompting was so urgent that I stood up and said, "I'm the one who has something to say, Lynn." I then related the vision.

The next day, when I was home, I went back to my journal and reread the original account for the first time in eight years. I was expecting considerable difference between the way I recorded it initially and the way I told it. It has been my experience that revelation adds layers of deeper meaning as events, understanding, and needs bring us to new stages of our spiritual journey. This revelation had been an extremely significant spiritual event to me, often present in my mind. In the eight years of my own development and changing conditions, I expected to find extensive reinterpretations and was amazed to discover only minor differences.[7] Here is the text of that vision:

---

7. These differences were: (1) Due, no doubt, to the imagery guidance, I had visualized specific, not generic, fruits; (2) I now recall the feelings of the first gardener as including appreciation of the tree's beauty; and (3) I recorded only the tears of grief; yet the most powerful emotions I took away from that experience were gratitude that my need for reassurance was met so directly, joy at the accompanying

I saw a two-fruited tree. One of the fruits was like oranges or peaches—brightly colored, glowing on the branches, tender, juicy, but delicate and perishable. The other fruit was hidden under the leaves, slow-growing and encased in a tough protective shell, like walnuts. The tree needed nothing from its gardeners. The sun and the rain came dependably and predictably. The soil was rich and fertile, the season progressed normally, and the fruit came to ripeness. But the tree needed a gardener to pick the fruit. It was ripe, ripe to the point of being overready, and then overripe. The gardener responsible for that section of the garden admired the tree. He thought it was beautiful, ornamental, and decorative. But the gardener was not going to pick the fruit. He was busy and impatient with the tree. Oranges had to be wrapped in tissue and put in cold storage or else made into marmalade or juice. Peaches bruised too easily and had to be preserved. It was just too much trouble to pick the fruit.

He walked away from the tree; and the fruit, unwanted, unneeded, began to fall to the ground. I felt devastated by grief at the waste and wept in sorrow. But the fruit was not wasted. It decayed quickly, sank easily into the earth, and nourished the tree. Meanwhile, high up—not easily accessible like the first fruit—the second walnut-like fruit continued to grow in black bitter hulls. After the freezing season, when the cold made the second fruit sweet and firm, the head gardener came himself with his high ladder. He searched every branch carefully, plucked the fruit gently, and put each piece in his bucket rejoicing, because they were all precious, every one. I wept again, but this time my tears were tears of joy.

It was a prophetic experience in many ways. It applied not only to the broad work and gifts of women, but also to *Dialogue: A Journal of Mormon Thought* where I was associate editor and to the broader search for truth and understanding of our history and doctrine, to the

---

peace of the vision, and total acceptance. I have included these three changes in quoting this account from my 1983 journal.

entire range of Mormon scholarship, symposia, and publications.[8] I could tell the rightness of the whole pattern, and I felt utterly at peace about the future. Yes, it would be hard. Yes, there would be rejection. But yes, oh yes, I concluded, ultimately it will be all right.

I feel that gratitude still. Probably never a week goes by when I don't think of that vision—sometimes with irony when something else goes "plop" and squishes underfoot, sometimes with an immense feeling of being sustained by the hands of divine love. I have no question that the tree is sound and healthy. I hear the rustle of its tender leaves unfurling when seasons of sunshine come. I feel its immense patience during the iron-cold freezing seasons. A growing tree makes no sound, but its silent roots can rend the very stones, and it knows in itself how to bring its fruit to ripeness.

I have no interpretation to offer with this revelation besides what I have already said: that it spoke comfort to me on the pressure points of the church's feminists and intellectuals. It was very personal to me, but it was not exclusively to me. I was not the tree, the fruit, or the gardener. I was an observer—a witness. I feel great peace about sharing this experience after the silence of years; but I do not have a specific interpretation to offer with it. Perhaps that is a gift reserved for someone else.

But in addition to the comfort that it may bring others, I want to make a specific point. I would not expect an exercise in guided

---

8. I would now add among the losses and crippling waste, the institutional church's rejection of the gifts of our LGBTI brothers and sisters. The First Presidency announced on April 5, 2019, two "adjustments"—already a long-overdue retreat from "doctrine" and even "policy." The first adjustment was no longer labeling as "apostate" legally married homosexual couples who therefore required disciplinary action, although they were still demeaned as guilty of "grave transgression." Second, it no longer excluded their children under age eighteen from church ordinances. These steps are a much-needed retreat from the calamitous 2015 gay-exclusion policy. Needless to say, it is not enough to compensate for a century's labeling as perversion, punishment, and shaming so severe that an untold number of these fellow Saints have died at their own hand.

imagery to be either the setting or the stimulus for a profoundly comforting personal revelation. But it was. I wonder what other treasures are waiting to be recognized, what other messages are coming from the mouth of God to a heart too small to hear, what other trees are bearing their harvest on the other side of a wall I could walk around at any moment.

Do we fear to ask because we think such things are inappropriate or greedy? Thanks to the handy computerized scripture program, I was able to learn in something under twenty seconds that the phrase, "Ask and ye shall receive," or a variation of it, occurs thirty-three times in the scriptures. That's a lot of encouragement. In fact, the scripture that triggered Joseph Smith's first vision is to us all: "God ... giveth to *all* men [and women] liberally, and upbraideth not" (James 1:5–7). God is pleased at our requests. Joel pronounced a prophecy that Peter quoted on the day of Pentecost: "In the last days, saith God, I will pour out of my Spirit upon all flesh: and your sons and your daughters shall prophesy" (Acts 2:16–17). Moses cried out in the congregation of Israel: "Would God that all the Lord's people were prophets, and that the Lord would put his spirit upon them!" (Num. 11:29). God not only promises spiritual gifts but promises a great diversity of gifts and, furthermore, promises them to "every man [and woman]" (Rom. 12:3; see also 1 Cor. 12, 14).

I hope that our comfort and trust can increase to the point that we can both seek and share spiritual experiences beyond the conventional and "correlated." Two paired scriptures seem relevant to this topic. The first is from a sermon of Alma's:

> It is given unto many to know the mysteries of God; nevertheless they are laid under a strict command that they shall not impart only according to the portion of his word which he doth grant unto the [human family], according to the heed and diligence which they give unto him.

... And therefore, [they] that will not harden [their] heart[s], to [them] is given ... to know the mysteries of God until [they] know them in full.

And they that will harden their hearts, to them is given the lesser portion of the word until they know nothing concerning his mysteries; and then they are taken captive by the devil, and led by his will down to destruction. Now this is what is meant by the chains of hell. (Alma 12:9–11)

And the second is the voice of the Lord speaking to Joseph Smith: "If thou shalt ask, thou shalt receive revelation upon revelation, knowledge upon knowledge, that thou mayest know the mysteries and peaceable things—that which bringeth joy, that which bringeth life eternal" (D&C 42:61). May we, with John Bunyan, "realize that God ha[s] a bigger mouth to speak with" than we have "a heart to understand" and let "the divine grace of God expand our hearts."

10

Covenants and Contracts

I delivered this address at the New England Sunstone Symposium in Boston, Massachusetts, on November 19, 1994, and also at private LDS-oriented study groups in Utah and southern California.

My title comes from a comment my husband, Paul, made as he dealt with his sadness in the aftermath of the September 1993 excommunications. "To me," he said, "the church has always been like a family. It's always been a place where I could feel accepted, where I belonged. And now I realize that I can't rely on that the way I did before."

I think he was articulating something that many of us have sensed for years—sometimes merely as a vague uneasiness and sometimes as a strong sense of alienation. As members, we belong to the Church of Jesus Christ of Latter-day Saints. We feel it belongs to us. These are attachments and identifications that go much deeper than preference or affiliation. We have covenantal feelings about it. But covenants can be made only with God, individually, one at a time, even though the church validates those covenants, provides the setting in which they occur, and creates the rites by which we make and renew them. This overlap can confuse us. Sometimes we think we are making our covenants *to* the church because we are making them *in* the church and *with* other church members. As a result, sometimes we can live our whole lives without realizing that the church makes no covenant in return. Rather, it makes contracts with us, sometimes explicit but mostly implied, and these contracts can be canceled, without arbitration or negotiation, for any number of "bad" behaviors.

Michael Quinn has talked about being a "DNA Mormon" and David Knowlton, an anthropologist, about being an "ethnic Mormon," but Jan Shipps, a Methodist historian, talks about the end of Mormons as a people and the beginnings of Mormonism as a sect. When Mormons are a people, you can't stop being one any more than a Jew can stop being a Jew. But when Mormonism is a sect, you can stop being one in the same way that you stop being a Republican, a Kiwanis, and a Methodist to become a Democrat, a Jaycee, and an Episcopalian. When Jan began studying Mormonism more than twenty years ago, she was called a "gentile," which is an ethnic designation. Now she is a "nonmember." The member/nonmember dichotomy means the church is something you can join and un-join. It is also, I might add, something you can be un-joined from, fired from, dumped out of.

In this essay, I want to examine some of the contracts we currently operate under, explore a scriptural view of covenantal relationships between members and leaders, examine the dynamic of obedience to authority, and then make some suggestions for how we can facilitate personal change.

What do I mean by a contract? I mean those tapes we run in our minds in which blessings are linked to performance. In the March 1994 *Ensign*, an article on children with behavioral disorders includes the following statement from a mother: "We often hear that if we attend the temple, read the scriptures, pray, and have family home evening, we will have peace in our homes. We are doing all these things, and I know that they are important and that we are blessed for doing them, yet we do not have peace. I have spent most of my life as a mother crying."[1]

---

1. As quoted in Jan U. Pinborough, "'Lead Me, Guide Me,'" *Ensign*, Mar. 1994, 50.

Think about the contracts you have based much of your life on: If you keep church standards, your wayward friends will secretly admire and respect you. Your mission will be the best two years of your life. If you marry in the temple, your spouse will be faithful and your marriage happy. You will grow spiritually from every calling. The scriptures will always be a source of comfort and inspiration. Your leaders will always be inspired in their decisions.

All of these statements are true on some level; we all wish they were always true on all levels and at all times. But the reality of the road through mortality is more complicated than the pretty simplicity of these maps. Perhaps if the maps were more complex—more realistic—fewer of us would set out on the journey. Yet every now and then we meet someone for whom reality matches the maps in the way it doesn't for us—and then other agonizing questions begin: Did we get the wrong map? Are we following it incorrectly? Sometimes the answer to these questions is "Yes," but often energy that we could better spend dealing with the situation gets drained away in self-recrimination. All too often, others are only too willing to add to the chorus of accusations. After all, if our map doesn't work for us, perhaps theirs will stop working for them, too; and that thought is simply too fearsome for some to contemplate.

Let me develop three specific situations in which the difference between covenants and contracts can be particularly lethal: (1) the role of the temple in Mormon spiritual life, (2) how contracting enables judgementalness, and (3) the need for more covenantal relationships between leaders and members.

The focus of the temple is a system of covenants we make with God. In my view, this focus has shifted dramatically in recent times, from our covenants with God to a contract with the gatekeepers of the temple. Entrance has always been conditional on worthiness, but there's a real difference between feeling that worthiness is a quality of your relationship with the Lord and feeling that worthiness is a question of agreeing with, or at least not alarming, your interviewer.

For example, one friend has been without a temple recommend for more than two years. His stake president took it away in a fit of anger when my friend would not obey him and disband a quarterly group that came together to discuss Mormon history and sociology. Over a year later, the stake president sent a third party to say "just go through the usual channels of the bishop's interview, then come see me. If your bishop feels okay, I'll feel okay." It sounds to me as if the stake president may be conceding, without saying so, that he acted hastily, that the issue isn't worth it, or that his conscience is uneasy with keeping this man and his wife from the temple. But my friend isn't sure how he feels about this invitation. A convert and the only member of the church in his family, he has always loved the temple and is an ardent genealogist, but he wonders why the stake president didn't talk with him directly. He wonders if he's being set up in some way. "I always thought that the temple was a blessing that was available to you if you were worthy," he said. "Now I see it's something that the leaders can use to club you with or blackmail you with. I don't think I want to put myself in that position again." My friend decided not to attempt further to renew his temple recommend and soon moved out of the stake.[2]

---

2. To his surprise, in 2006, he received a letter from his former stake president explaining that he had been strongly impressed, during a priesthood lesson based on Gordon B. Hinckley's October 2005 conference address, that he needed to ask my friend's forgiveness. He acknowledged: "I said things that probably made you feel bad. ... For that I am truly sorry. For expressing things in anger/frustration, I am truly sorry. For not listening more to you and expressing my feelings with love and understanding, I am truly sorry. For not being more patient, I am truly sorry." He expressed the hope that, on the other side of the veil, they could "embrace as brothers." My friend responded warmly to this communication and did some soul searching as well, examining his own response and feeling prompted to apologize where he also erred. That moment helped a new friendship develop, and trust has

In other words, the covenant relationship with God that has always been a source of spirituality and joy for my friend has shifted to an uneasy contract relationship with his stake president in which what this member offers as his worthiness can be rejected as insufficient by the stake president who can quite literally refuse to sign on the dotted line if my friend's opinions don't match his.

As a second example, a 1994 LDS seminary video, in teaching the principle of repentance, focuses on a young woman being interviewed before her temple marriage. In the context of her joy and anticipation, she confesses what was presumably an episode of unchastity (it's not explicit) with an earlier boyfriend. The bishop, showing no emotion, tells her that she has not faced the "eternal consequences" of her actions and that she is not worthy to go to the temple. When she dissolves in tears of shock and humiliation, he tells her, "Part of repentance is knowing that our actions have offended the Lord. … I want to help you clear this up so you can go [to the temple]."[3] He does not ask if she has repented, if she feels forgiven, or how *she* thinks the Lord feels about her. When she protests that the episode is far in the past and that unchastity has never been part of her relationship with her current fiancé, he brushes it aside as irrelevant. The bishop talks about the young woman's relationship with God, but the dominant relationship in this video is his relationship with her. Clearly, the bishop feels that the Lord is offended, and the bishop will tell her when she may feel worthy to go to the temple. He is stern and aloof. When she weeps, he does not try to comfort her, either by word or gesture. He watches her impassively. And the young woman accepts without question this

been restored. Now living hundreds of miles apart where ecclesiastical authority is no longer an issue between them, they are Facebook friends, comment and congratulate each other on their various accomplishments in life, and occasionally argue politics. Copy in my possession, quoted by permission.

3. "Godly Sorrow Leads to Repentance," presentation 16, *New Testament Media*, Seminary curriculum enrichment, ca. 1994.

identification of what God may be thinking and feeling with what the bishop obviously thinks and feels.

When Paul and I watched this video with our fourteen-year-old son, who started seminary in the fall, I was so upset I turned it off and exclaimed, "I think we need to talk about this!" Paul, who was calmer, interposed a question to Christian, "What do you think the main message of this video is?" Christian responded immediately, "You should lie to the bishop." Paul and I burst out laughing. Christian is an absolutely truthful boy. He has never, to my knowledge, lied to us about anything nor has he lied to anyone else that I know of in his entire life. But if he saw so easily and quickly through the coercive propaganda of this video, I think that it will probably do less damage to the teenagers of the church than I feared.

But on another level, it will do more. Telling the truth is a matter of personal integrity and relational trust. As brothers and sisters in the gospel, as members and leaders, we should be bound together in a supportive web of covenantal relationships that accommodate the whole person in love, respect, and trust. When these covenantal aspects are replaced by contracts which demand performance and revoke privileges for noncompliance and in which children learn that the best way to function within this system is to lie, it permanently damages the fabric of our community.

The role of the temple recommend as coercion is the first of my concerns about rampant contractualism. The second is that contracts give us a license to judge each other.

Covenants encourage a high standard of performance for ourselves and an attitude of acceptance and unconditional love toward others. Contracts, in contrast, establish an attitude of separation from others and encourage harsh judgments of others.

Where are the limits on our love? Who merits our loyalty?

The scriptures say, "And the eye cannot say unto the hand, I have no need of thee: nor again the head to the feet, I have no need of you" (1 Cor. 12:21). But Elder Neal A. Maxwell, speaking of "critics" at October 1993 general conference, said dismissively, "We need them not," although he corrected it in the *Ensign* version to "We heed them not," and Michael Quinn reports that Elder Boyd K. Packer, in interviewing him to be hired at BYU, told him: "I have a hard time with historians because they idolize the truth. The truth is not uplifting; it destroys."[4]

Yes, over and over, we hear the message within the church that some of us are more worthy, more valuable, more righteous than others—not on the basis of faith, which is difficult to measure, or even works, but on the basis of circumstances, like a divorce, or even appearances. The same *Ensign* article on children with behavioral disorders which I have already mentioned, contains a virtual catalogue of judgements perceived by the mothers of these children:

> Sometimes, when my son has caused a problem in the neighborhood, I sit in my house waiting for my neighbors to come to my door to complain. I feel barricaded in my home. I don't want to answer the phone or the door.

> People don't really say it, ... but more and more they seem to feel that we are bad people. They don't want their children associating with our child.

What's the contract here? If you have problems with your children, it's because you're a bad person.

> My husband doesn't want to admit that our son has a serious problem. He will not talk about it or let me talk to our son's teachers. He says if I could just treat our son differently, he would not have behavior problems.[5]

---

4. Associated Press, "Speaker Found Truth and 'Rest Is History,'" *Salt Lake Tribune*, Aug. 20, 1994, E-1, E-3.

5. In Pinborough, "'Lead Me, Guide Me,'" 50–51.

What's the contract here? It's that parenting is the mother's responsibility. And meanwhile, the contract is a license to judge.

The third example of the differences between covenants and contracts shows up in the relationship of leaders to members. The fine print on this contract says, "When the prophet speaks, the thinking is over. Leaders are always more inspired than members. Do what you're told and you'll be blessed. If a leader tell you to jump, just ask how high. If he tells you to do something that is wrong, do it anyway, because he'll be the one who is held accountable, not you."

There are a lot of problems with this particular contract. A conspicuous one is that free agency is inalienable from primal intelligence. Perhaps at other councils in other heavens, other Heavenly Parents and their spirit offspring voted in another way and came up with another plan of salvation. Perhaps free agency is not a fact in all universes, but it is a fact in ours. Surely it's occurred to most of us that at least part of the plan of salvation has currently been replaced by a program of conformity and that at least some parts of that program look a lot like the plan we voted against.

Our Heavenly Parents became gods because they learned how to balance the maximum of freedom with the maximum of love. We will become gods ourselves by learning the same balance. Contracts based on a mistaken assumption of leader infallibility are not acceptable substitutes. Leaders and members alike collude in placing leaders under the terrible burden of infallibility. Unable to make or admit a mistake, needing a certain answer to every question, responsible for knowing the right answer to every question, leaders quickly realize that infallibility is easy if only they can eliminate questions altogether. We let them do it. We help them do it.

One friend pointed out, "It's almost as if some leaders don't have faith in the gospel. They act as if they don't believe in repentance, don't believe in progression, don't believe in the grace of Christ, don't believe that they will be forgiven for making mistakes. Maybe that's why they seem so unforgiving."

This contract says: "I will give you perfect instructions. In return, you will render me perfect obedience. And we will both be perfectly happy." The only problem is that it's perfectly impossible.

In contrast to a contractual approach to religious life, I prefer to dwell on the beautiful scriptural models of covenantal relationships filled with the joy, compassion, and trust that should exist between members and leaders. Since the early 1980s, I have begun each new year by rereading the Book of Mormon. It takes about six weeks and gets the year off to a good start. This year was no exception; and the concentrated study, particularly in light of my changed circumstances since the last time I read it, was particularly powerful.

In the often-quoted discourse of Alma at the waters of Mormon he exhorts the people to "mourn with those that mourn; ... and comfort those that stand in need of comfort, and to stand as witnesses of God at all times and in all things, and in all places ... even until death" (Mosiah 17:9). Less frequently quoted and never, to my knowledge, in the context of leader/member responsibilities are the subsequent verses in which Alma describes how a Christian community is supposed to behave. "And thus [the people] should impart of their substance of their own free will and good desires towards God, and to those priests that stood in need, yea, and to every needy, naked soul" (Mosiah 18:28).

Who needs charity? "Every needy, naked soul." "Needy" and "naked" describe most of us in at least some aspects of our lives—in our incompleteness, in our limitations, in our terrible vulnerability, misery, wretchedness, and inadequacy. It is the blessing and mercy of God that we are not all naked and needy in the same ways and at the same times but rather that in some areas we have an abundance; and out of that abundance we can supply the needs and cover the nakedness of another human soul.

But—and this is the second message of this scripture to me—this description of the "needy, naked soul" applies also to the "priests" of this Nephite congregation—at times as needy, at times as naked—as any member. Our baptismal covenant binds us, in my opinion, to "impart of our substance of our own free will and good desires" to our leaders as well as to each other. Substance doesn't just mean money. It is the all that we have consecrated on the altar—not only teaching Sunbeams, faithfully home teaching, or energetically singing hymns during sacrament meeting, but also the fruits of our hands and our minds that we have produced without assignment, unbidden, and even, sometimes, unwanted.

I think of David Knowlton, a sociologist with a specialty in Latin America, explaining why the church is a target for terrorism and why its American missionaries are subject to assassination in Latin America. This was a gift he had to offer as a scholar, an academic, and a former South American missionary. His gift was not only rejected but he was fired from Brigham Young University. Yet the bombings continued—three in Colombia in January 1994 alone.[6]

The church is acknowledging indirectly the scope of this problem. An interview in the same March 1994 *Ensign* quoted the area presidency, admitting that "our greatest challenge is violence and terrorism." They don't even mention the attacks in Colombia or Chile. Instead they acknowledge bombings in Peru and Bolivia, admit that there are no more North American missionaries in those countries, and add that of the seven mission presidents in this area released in 1993, five were replaced by Latin Americans.[7] These

6. David C. Knowlton, interviewed on *Utah 1992*, Channel 4 by Chris Vanocur and Paul Murphy, August 16, 1992; my follow-up conversations with David, especially October 29, 1992, March 17, 1993, May 13, 1993, December 1, 1993. An official statement, "BYU Announces Decisions on Faculty Appeals," Nov. 30, 1993, reported that Knowlton would not be teaching after the termination of the academic year. Notes in my possession on all of the above sources.

7. "Conversation with the South America North Area Presidency [Elders Jay E. Jensen, Julio E. Davila, and Eduardo Ayala]," *Ensign*, Mar. 1994, 79.

were some of the same recommendations David offered. He also explained why denials that the church has a political component will have absolutely no effect, yet such statements continue to be issued. I'm glad David offered his gift on the altar. I mourn that it was so costly for him.

The second covenantal scripture between leaders and members is Doctrine and Covenants 88, a beautiful and powerful covenant between leaders and members that is, again, almost never quoted.

The president, the revelation specifies, is supposed to enter the house of God "first," not because it is correct priesthood protocol—in the words of the revelation—but so he (and I believe she) may

> … offer himself in prayer upon his knees before God, in token or remembrance of the everlasting covenant.
>
> And when any shall come in after him or her, let the teacher arise, and, with uplifted hands to heaven, yea, even directly, salute him or her with these words:
>
> Art thou a brother or a sister? I salute you in the name of the Lord Jesus Christ, in token or remembrance of the everlasting covenant, in which covenant I receive you to fellowship, in a determination that is fixed, immovable, and unchangeable, to be your friend and sibling through the grace of God in the bonds of love, to walk in all the commandments of God blameless, in thanksgiving, forever and ever. Amen.
>
> And he or she who is found unworthy of this salutation shall not have place among you; for ye shall not suffer that mine house shall be polluted … (D&C 88:130–33; edited for inclusive language)

Are leaders on the local and general levels making such a covenant, if only in their hearts, with members of the church? I know that many, many do; but I also know that some do not. They have been quick to judge some members as pollutants in the Lord's house. They have made haste to cast them out.

Nor have they always offered themselves on their knees to God.

Rather they have offered themselves to other leaders. I have talked with individuals who have reason to believe that during disciplinary councils when the leaders have retired to consult and to pray about a decision, they have instead called an area president to report on the council and receive instructions about the verdict. Against policy, against scripture, against the published statements of the Council of the First Presidency and the Quorum of the Twelve, directed verdicts are sometimes imposed upon members of the church by leaders who feel they are doing their duty, not to God but to their file leaders.

And this brings me to my next topic: the issue of obedience to authority. Probably most of you are familiar with the famous Stanley Milgram experiments of the early 1960s in which one subject, the "teacher," administered electrical shocks of increasing intensity when the "learner" made mistakes in memorizing word pairs. The "teacher" who read the word pairs and administered the shocks was, of course, the real subject. According to Milgram: "It is the extreme willingness of adults to go to almost any lengths on the command of an authority that constitutes the chief finding of the study and the fact most urgently demanding explanation."[8]

Milgram demolishes the argument that Nazis staffing prison camps were sadistic lunatics, the fringe of society. "Ordinary people, simply doing their jobs, and without any particular hostility on their part, can become agents in a terrible destructive process. ... Relatively few people have the resources needed to resist authority."[9]

The most gripping part of his analysis for me was his description of the six factors which influence the teacher to keep on obeying. First are such low-level social factors as a desire to cooperate and embarrassment at breaking off the experiment.

---

8. Stanley Milgram, *Obedience to Authority* (New York: J. Norton Publishing, 1978), 5. He describes the experiment on pp. 3–5.
9. Ibid., 6.

Second is the redirection of moral agency. Human beings can, and apparently do, shield themselves from the moral meaning of their actions by becoming absorbed in the task's "narrow technical aspects." Milgram describes how the teachers would "[read] the word pairs with exquisite articulation and [press] the switches with great care." He then makes this extremely important statement:

> The [teacher] entrusts the broader tasks of setting goals and assessing morality to the experimental authority. ... He divests himself of responsibility by attributing all initiative to the experimenter, a legitimate authority. He sees himself not as a person acting in a morally accountable way but as the agent of external authority. ... The disappearance of a sense of responsibility is the most far-reaching consequence of submission to authority. ... He does not respond with a moral sentiment to the actions he performs. Rather, his moral concern now shifts to a consideration of how well he is living up to the expectations that the authority has of him. In wartime, a soldier does not ask whether it is good or bad to bomb a hamlet; he does not experience shame or guilt in the destruction of a village: rather he feels pride or shame depending on how well he has performed the mission assigned to him. ... The individuals involved ... experience a sense of morality to the degree in which all of their actions are governed by orders from higher authority. ... Responsibility invariably shifts upward in the mind of the subordinate.[10]

I think with great sadness of my stake president, Marlin Miller, a loyal foot soldier in the church's army. He took action against me because Elder Loren C. Dunn, then the area president, gave him a copy of my article in the spring 1993 issue of *Dialogue: A Journal of Mormon Thought*, which chronicles about 130 impact points between the church and its intellectuals. He expressed "concerns" about this article. I do not believe President Miller saw himself as

---

10. Ibid., 7–8, 188.

morally free. I believe he saw Elder Dunn as bearing the moral responsibility. Was Elder Dunn a morally free agent? I don't believe so. I think he was, like my stake president, trying to be a good technician in carrying out someone else's moral decision.

Paul Toscano's stake president, Kerry Heinz, admitted to him that the "fair implication" of his discussion with Elder Boyd Packer—in which no instructions were given and no verdict was directed, at least, not explicitly—was that Elder Packer wanted Paul excommunicated. Was President Heinz a morally free agent from that point on? I don't believe so, whatever technical "freedom" he may have had to act.

Milgram also describes a variation of the experiment in which there were two teachers, one who read the words and one who administered the shocks. The reader always felt that the full responsibility was borne by the one who administered the shocks. "This may illustrate a dangerously typical situation in [a] complex society," observed Milgram—or, I would add, in a lengthy hierarchical chain. "It is psychologically easy to ignore responsibility when one is only an intermediate link in a chain of evil action but is far from the final consequences of the action. Even Eichmann was sickened when he toured the concentration camps, but to participate in mass murder he had only to sit at a desk and shuffle papers."[11] I have talked about my stake president and my area president, but how many times do we collude with evil in our own lives, saying, "It's not my job" or "they know better than I"?

The third factor Milgram identified that permitted the experiment to continue is what he calls "counter-anthropomorphism," or "attributing an impersonal quality to forces that are essentially human." Thus, when the experimenter said, "The experiment requires that you continue," the teacher did not say, "The experiment can't

---

11. Ibid., 11.

require anything. It's a thing. Who designed this experiment? And why does he or she need this?"[12] The "Experiment" had become a great, impersonal force that overrode his individual agency. We needn't take the time to run back over the many contractual elements that work only because "the church" has acquired the same kind of impersonal imperative as "the Experiment."

The fourth factor is the context. Many atrocities in war are justified because it is for a "noble cause." The laboratory setting conferred legitimacy upon the experiment; it invoked the participants' trust in "science."[13] We, too, use the church context to justify and explain away troubling areas. Accustomed to obedience and deference to authority, we accept much in a religious context that we would question or protest in a professional context.

Milgram also points out a fifth factor, even though it was not part of his experiment. This was "the intense devaluation of the victim, prior to action against him."[14] A decade of anti-Jewish propaganda in Germany preceded the concentration camps. We can see the same pattern in our community. The rhetoric of denunciation and suspicion from leaders of the church about devalued groups has intensified since about 1975. Elder Packer's attack on gays, feminists, and intellectuals in May 1993 is only different in explicitness, not in kind from his earlier statements and those of others. Their net effect is to create categories into which people can be placed and, once there, can be seen as expendable, undesirable, even worthy of eradication. Milgram found in his experiment that, even without any attempt to devalue the learner by the experimenter, the teacher spontaneously blamed the victim. "He was so stupid and stubborn he deserved to get shocked" was a common comment. "Once having acted against the victim," Milgram continues, "these subjects found it necessary to

12. Ibid., 8–9.
13. Ibid., 9.
14. Ibid.

view him as an unworthy individual, whose punishment was made inevitable by his own deficiencies of intellect and character."[15]

This process is called demonizing, and it has been busily at work in the cases of the September Six, David Knowlton and Cecilia Farr, David Wright, Michael Barrett, and Janice Allred. Rumors have come back to me that the "real" reason for all of the disciplinary actions is transgression, usually sexual. Some general authorities have asserted, "You don't know the whole story," to individuals who have questioned them, thus implying that there are hidden moral vices that justify the firings and the disciplinary councils. Local leaders have said the same thing.

The sixth factor Milgram identified is that of silent protest but outward compliance. Because teachers "were totally convinced of the wrongness of what they were doing," they somehow felt better, even though they continued to press the switches and administer the shocks. Milgram calls this "merely indulgence in a consoling psychological mechanism. Tyrannies are perpetuated by diffident men [and women] who do not possess the courage to act out their beliefs."[16]

Milgram's summary is a grim one: Far more dangerous than rage or episodes of sadism is "our capacity to abandon our humanity, indeed, the inevitability that we do so, as we merge our unique personality into larger institutional structures. This is a fatal flaw nature has designed into us, and which in the long run gives our species only a modest chance of survival."[17]

I am in no way claiming that the church is even close to the Nazi party, that excommunications are anywhere near the literal equivalent of massacres, or that spiritual abuse dominates the church. On the contrary, the overwhelming majority of wards and stakes are places of affection and affiliation, of nurture and spiritual

---

15. Ibid., 10.
16. Ibid.
17. Ibid., 188; paraphrased for gender-inclusive language.

nourishment. That same March *Ensign* contains news reports of the outpouring of neighborliness that responded to an earthquake in California and fires in Australia. These stories show the church at its shining best, and this side is utterly real. Yes, the silencing, demonizing, reprisals, and intimidations are also real, but they are the natural and inevitable consequence of a partially dysfunctional system in massive denial. I believe that they are all precursors to change, and that we can help bring change about.

The first thing we know about change is that change is hard. A few weeks after the excommunication, my husband, Paul, gave me a cartoon showing two prisoners hanging in chains from a dungeon wall. "Well," says one to the other, "so much for working within the system."

When I was an editor at the *Ensign*, I heard Elder Packer quoted as saying humorously, "Change in the church comes in two ways— slowly and not at all." I agree, but I think there is a third way as well. The church also makes progress by leaps and bounds—when it shoots itself in the foot and hurtles backward, sometimes spinning around so that it accidentally moves forward. So when things go terribly wrong, let us rejoice. We're on schedule and making progress. And change starts with us.

I have seven suggestions for how we can live with integrity and help the church develop more honesty, more respect for individuals, more love for each other, and more channels for the Spirit.

First, we can develop more faith. We truly do make our covenants with God, and it is to God that we must answer for them. He does not honor covenants, even those made and sealed by priesthood authority, unless they are ratified by the Holy Spirit of Promise. How much less does he honor contracts and backscratching arrangements and *quid pro quos* worked out privately with human beings. When God becomes as real to us as our bishop, when the Savior has a personality as tangible to us as our stake president's, then we can say with "Peter and the other apostles ... We ought to obey God rather than men" (Acts 5:29).

Second, we can grow a backbone. We can refuse to act against our conscience, and we can refuse to be silent when others do evil, particularly when they harm others who are vulnerable to them because of priesthood authority. We are here to learn to distinguish between good and evil. That means we are failing in our mortal mission each time we dodge a decision, pass the buck, or slough off the responsibility to choose and then abide by the consequences of those choices. We need to move beyond our fear and into love in exercising our freedom. The Lord is endlessly merciful during this learning process—much more merciful and accepting of our errors than we usually are of ourselves and of others. Remember Jacob's inspiring encouragement: "O then, my beloved people, come unto the Lord, the Holy One ... Behold, the way for us is narrow, but it lieth in a straight course before us, and the keeper of the gate is the Holy One of Israel; and he employeth no servant there" (2 Ne. 9:41; paraphrased for gender-inclusive language).

Third, I think it is important that we not mistake the medium for the message, the vessel for the content, the church for the gospel. The gospel is eternal, and human souls are eternal. The church is temporary. The church is a wonderful vessel for bearing the gospel and perfecting the Saints, but it is not a perfect vessel. It has a few chips out of the base. It's distinctly lopsided when it comes to women. Sometimes the gospel seems to stream out through cracks as fast as it's filled up. But the gospel is the water of life. Sand takes shapes as readily as water does, and it pours just as well; but it does not quench thirst. We need to stop mistaking sand for water, stones for bread, serpents for fish. How? Our spirits know if we've received refreshment or fatigue. We need to say so—certainly to ourselves and hopefully to others.

Fourth, I think we must learn to affirm covenant relationships with people even when they break contracts. Many people have done this for me. Being excommunicated places me suddenly on the other side of a barrier—sometimes a line, sometimes a gulf. My family, Paul's family, and many, many friends and even strangers have reached across that barrier to me to say, "You are still my sister, my friend." I cannot express my gratitude for those who have made that contact. Separating sheep from goats is a job Jesus reserves for himself. Our job is to be good undershepherds, caring for the whole flock, until he comes.

Fifth, we can learn to disagree without ceasing to love. I think that those of us who find ourselves with dissenting opinions need to set an example of how to handle dissent. We need to manifest patience, tolerance, and good will. We need to appreciate those who disagree with us as much as we appreciate those who agree with us. Both acts can be immensely supportive. Out of the hundreds of calls and letters of support I received, all of which were balm to my bruises, I also received letters from a handful of people who took issue with my public stand against ecclesiastical abuse. "I hope you can forgive me for not believing you are doing the right thing," wrote one friend, "since I so admire you for doing what you believe is the right thing." I deeply respected her candid ambiguity. Ambiguity is okay. In fact, we can avoid it only at the cost of shrinking inside a world view so deliberately simplified that we remain children.

Sixth, even though we are excluded and shunned in many ways—not all of them involving formal discipline—we can remain attached to the church by offering the testimony of presence.[18] Without anger, without accusation, and without apology, I want to bear the testimony of presence in my ward and my church. I want us to gather, not out of fear or anger, but as an act of faith. We have faith that the gospel can not only withstand intellectual inquiry but

---

18. I am indebted for this concept to Sharon Conrey Turnbull, who addressed the Circle of Love service on the concept of a "ministry of presence," Apr. 2, 1994, Salt Lake City, Utah. See my own essay on this topic in Chapter 4.

be enhanced by it. We believe that the God we worship rejoices in the gifts of our minds as well as the gifts of our spirits and the service of our hands. Continuing to affirm that faith is a great strength we can give each other. It is especially important to affirm it as other portions of our church deny it.

In our own moments of sadness and frustration, may we remember that the glory of Mormonism is its joyous affirmation of eternal human worth. As Mormons we believe that Jesus Christ himself thought we were worth entering into this mortal, fallen world to save. For us, the end of his atoning sacrifice is not just as creatures cleansed from the dust and blood of this world but as kings and queens, priests and priestesses, gods and goddesses worthy to stand in the presence of God and praise him because we know him and are known by him.

11

The Spiritual Power of Gratitude

On September 15, 1991, I delivered these remarks at Pilgrimage which, that year, met in Kirtland, Ohio, and where, thanks to the courtesy of the Reorganized Church of Jesus Christ of Latter Day Saints (now Community of Christ), we held a devotional in their stately House of the Lord, which LDS members call the Kirtland temple.

Kirtland is a place of spiritual power, of spiritual empowerment from its very beginning; but women had an ambiguous share in it. Linda King Newell's well-researched article on women's exercise of spiritual gifts probes the dichotomy between women's contributions and their confinement:

> The women of the church had worked to build the temple and they attended public gatherings there, but they were not allowed to participate in the promised endowment. George A. Smith, reminiscing later as a member of the First Presidency, recalled that some of the women were "right huffy" as a consequence.
>
> Perhaps the women compensated through the exercise of [the spiritual gift of] tongues, though it was an accepted practice in public meetings for both men and women. One woman, Prescendia Huntington, told of a fast meeting in the temple "during which a Brother McCarter rose and sang a song of Zion in tongues; I arose and sang simultaneously with him the same tune and words,

beginning and ending each verse in perfect unison, without varying a word. It was just as though we had sung it together a thousand times." Mary Fielding Smith, writing to her sister Mercy, described another meeting in the temple: "Many spake in tongues and others prophesied and interpreted. … Some of the sisters while engaged in conversing in tongues their countenances beaming with joy, clasped each other's hands … in the most affectionate manner. … A brite light shone across the house [temple] and rested upon some of the congregation."

About twenty years after, Wilford Woodruff, the future third president of the church, reminisced with Elizabeth Ann Whitney and Eliza R. Snow about "the days of Kirtland" and heard again Elizabeth's gift of singing in tongues in the "pure language which Adam & Eve made use of in the garden of Eden." This gift, Woodruff recorded, "was obtained while in Kirtland through the promise of Joseph [Smith]. He told her if she would rise upon her feet (while in the meeting) she should have the pure Language. She done so and immediately commenced singing in that language. It was as near heavenly music as any thing I ever herd."

Kirtland was also where the "blessing meetings" were instituted. These were evening gatherings where Joseph Smith's father as patriarch to the church pronounced prophecies and blessings upon the heads of the faithful. Sometimes several families assembled for the occasion. These gatherings were especially significant to the women; they relished them and left many detailed accounts. Caroline Barnes Crosby wrote of her and her husband, Jonathan, receiving their patriarchal blessings: "These blessings cheered and rejoiced our hearts exceedingly. I truly felt humble before the Lord. … They led me to search into my heart, to see if there was any sin concealed there, and if so, to repent, and ask God to make me clean, and pure, in very deed. … Mother [Lucy Mack] Smith was in the room. She added her blessing or confirmed what we had already received."

Sarah Studevant Leavitt remembered a spiritual blessing of another sort during this period. Sarah, praying to the Lord for her seriously ill daughter, Louisa, saw an angel who told her to get the girl out of bed, lay "hands upon her head in the name of Jesus Christ and administer to her and she should recover." Sarah awakened her husband and told him to prepare Louisa for the blessing. Though it was near midnight and she was weak, Louisa arose from her bed and Sarah administered to her. Louisa was soon "up and about."

Sarah's experience may be the first recorded instance in the church of a healing blessing by a woman.[1]

Kirtland, then, was a time of great spiritual empowerment for women. The first matriarchal blessings, the first healing blessings by women, an unprecedented outpouring of prophecy and comfort through the gift of tongues, and the visitation of angels.

So I think it is appropriate to think about spiritual power and how to develop it. There's no question that we need it. The Apostle Paul could have been speaking of our day when he said: "Wherefore, take unto you the whole armour of God, that ye may be able to withstand in the evil day, and having done all, *to stand*" (Eph. 6:13; emphasis mine). He then continues by enumerating the pieces of armour that God has provided for his people—the breastplate of righteousness, the shield of faith, the sword of the Spirit, and so forth. But an important part of the scripture comes before that verse, because to understand the power to stand, it seems to me that we must understand a little about weakness:

> Put on the whole armour of God, that ye may be able to stand against the wiles of the devil.
>
> For we wrestle not against flesh and blood, but against principalities, against powers, against the rulers of the darkness of this world, against spiritual wickedness in high places. (Eph. 6:11–12)

---

1. Linda King Newell, "Gifts of the Spirit: Women's Share," in *Sisters in Spirit: Mormon Women in Historical and Cultural Perspective,* ed. Maureen Ursenbach Beecher and Lavina Fielding Anderson (Urbana: University of Illinois Press, 1987), 111–50, quotation on 112–14.

This is a pretty scary list. What buckles your knees? What washes your courage away? Running out of money? Getting sick? Getting divorced? Getting married? Not getting married? Something terrible happening to a child? Doing something stupid? Doing something sinful? Looking different from everybody else? Some of these fears are irrational, some are psychological, and some are physical. But they are all real. Just because you tell yourself that it's stupid to be afraid doesn't make the terrible weakness of fear go away. Even if you tell yourself it's natural to be afraid, it still won't go away.

It's interesting, though, that the scriptures have a great deal to say about fear. Over a hundred times in the standard works, the Lord tells us, "Fear not." He tells us not to be afraid of poverty, of embarrassment, of death. The Psalmist says, "The Lord is my light and my salvation; whom shall I fear? The Lord is the strength of my life; of whom shall I be afraid?" (27:1). "Be of good courage, and [the Lord] shall strengthen your heart, all ye that hope in the Lord" (31:24). "Look unto me in every thought," Christ told the early Saints in New York. "Doubt not, fear not" (D&C 6:36). "If you are prepared," he counseled them in Kirtland, "ye shall not fear" (D&C 38:30). "There is no fear in love," says the apostle John, "but perfect love casteth out fear" (1 John 4:18). And to the uncertain young bishop Timothy, Paul sent these encouraging words: "God hath not given us the spirit of fear; but of power, and of love, and of a sound mind" (1 Tim. 1:7).

Even without these assurances and promises, I don't imagine anyone would want to cling to fears. They don't feel good. But how can we cast them aside and lay hold of the promise of power? I'm with those who say that you have to face your fear and name it: old age, illness, being unloved, unemployment. But beyond that, we need something more. We can put a lot of energy into trying to chase darkness out of a room, to sweep it out, to shove it through the door, to stuff it into a sack—but the best way is still to turn on a light. In the presence of light, darkness simply disappears. And if what John tells us is true, the answer to increasing our power and casting out our fear is to increase our love.

It may seem like a very roundabout way of dealing with the fear of not having enough money to pay the rent—to increase our love for the Savior. It's true that the connection between the two events is not through logic but through the world of transcendent reality that simply expunges fear. Those of you who have experienced it will know what I mean. For those who aren't sure, let me run through some examples.

I was coming back from a meeting several years ago with four friends. One was very troubled over the decision whether to have another child. She had four children under the age of seven and felt that she was going crazy. Her husband was immersed in his career and could give her very little help. They had just moved into a new ward and she felt no sustaining friendships from the other women there. They had never practiced birth control as a matter of faith and obedience to what was then the church's intrusive and rigid pronatalism, but my friend—I'll call her Ellen—really didn't think she could handle any more children.

All of us were extremely sympathetic, and the other three proffered advice readily. "For heaven's sake, four is enough. Get your tubes tied!" Or "What if you just waited a year? Surely this isn't a decision that has to be made right now?" Or "Tell Jerry that if he wants any more children, he'll have to help take care of them." And so on. I didn't say too much. I was unmarried and didn't know how much stress another child might be. But I was dissatisfied with the discussion, which was increasing Ellen's distress. It seemed to me that we were somehow missing the real point. I was driving, so I arranged to drop her off last. When we were alone, I asked her what kinds of answers she'd received to her prayers on the topic.

"I haven't been praying," she said miserably. "I'm afraid of what the answer might be."

As we talked further, she spoke with real longing of the closeness she'd felt to the Lord in earlier years. She and Jerry had married with no financial resources and spent their first five years as poverty-stricken students dealing with the births of four children. She told me story after story of answered prayers, of healings, of people who unknowingly came to their aid when they literally didn't have enough food for their children, of feeling God leading them lovingly through jungles of obstacles. Her voice was alight with love and rejoicing as she remembered these experiences. It seemed to me that almost any decision—not just another baby—would have been equally painful for Ellen at this point because that feeling of being loved had disappeared somewhere.

And yet I felt it strongly. I took her hands and said, "Heavenly Father loves you. He loves you now. I can tell you that."

She called me the next morning and said that she had had a wonderful experience during the night that had confirmed what I had said and had reaffirmed all of those old feelings. With that foundation of unconditional love once more solid beneath her, she was able to talk more openly with her husband; they decided to wait a couple of years before making the decision about another baby. Ellen's fears had clouded the power of love and blocked its manifestations in her life.

That sense of being surrounded and uplifted by divine love is the truest source of spiritual power I know. That love does not promise to spare us from hard decisions nor our loved ones from pain. Instead, it promises us that we are not alone at times when we may feel loneliest, that even the most difficult decisions do not confront us in the absence of a counselor, and that we are cherished as individuals—not for what we have done or not done, not for what we may do or for good intentions, but simply for ourselves—as Lavina, as Catherine, as Rebecca, as Eliza. This kind of exquisite, total reassurance is also totally irrational. Experiencing it, remembering it, believing in it, and choosing to make it a spiritual reality that transcends our physical reality is an act of spiritual power. It is this reality that the Psalmist expresses:

> Whither shall I go from thy spirit? Or whither shall I flee from thy presence?
>
> If I ascend up into heaven, thou art there: if I make my bed in hell, behold, thou art there.
>
> If I take the wings of the morning, and dwell in the uttermost parts of the sea; even there shall thy hand lead me, and thy right hand shall hold me.
>
> If I say, Surely the darkness shall cover me; even the night shall be light about me.
>
> Yea, the darkness hideth not from thee; but the night shineth as the day; the darkness and the light are both alike to thee. (139:7–12)

How can we increase this sense of love? How can we tap into this spiritual power and more closely approach our Savior? There are many helpful ways, and we know what they are: repenting of our sins, feasting on the scriptures, praying, bearing testimony, temple worship, fasting, partaking of the sacrament, serving others, and cultivating the gift of the Holy Ghost. These are all important, necessary, and wonderful stepping stones on the path of spiritual power. There is much to say about all of them, but I'd like to share with you a few thoughts on the spiritual power of gratitude.

The Lord doesn't very often curse, but the scriptures contain probably the most comprehensive and devastating curse ever pronounced against a people or an individual in Deuteronomy 28:

> Cursed shalt thou be in the city, and cursed shalt thou be in the field.
>
> Cursed shall be thy basket and thy store.
>
> Cursed shall be the fruit of thy body, and the fruit of thy land. ...
>
> Cursed shalt thou be when thou comest in, and cursed shalt thou be when thou goest out.

The Lord shall make the pestilence cleave unto thee. ... The Lord shall smite thee with a consumption, and with a fever. ...

... [The] heaven that is over thy head shall be brass, and the earth that is under thee shall be iron.

The Lord shall make the rain of thy land powder and dust. ...

The Lord shall cause thee to be smitten before thine enemies: thou shalt go out one way against them, and flee seven ways before them. ...

Thou shalt betroth a wife, and another man shall lie with her: thou shalt build an house, and thou shalt not dwell therein: thou shalt plant a vineyard, and shalt not gather the grapes thereof.

Thine ox shall be slain before thine eyes, ... thy sheep shall be given unto thine enemies . ...

Thy sons and thy daughters shall be given unto another people, and thine eyes shall look, and fail with longing for them all the day long: and there shall be no might in thine hand. (Deut. 28:16–19, 21–25, 30–32)

And do you know what the children of Israel had done to merit this curse? Yes, disobedience, but more than that: "Because thou servedst not the Lord thy God with joyfulness, and with gladness of heart, for the abundance of all things" (v. 47).

There's a parallel scripture in the Doctrine and Covenants in which the Lord almost casually tosses off a comment about what really makes him angry: "And in nothing doth man [or woman] offend God, or against none is his wrath kindled, save those who confess not his hand in all things, and obey not his commandments" (57:21). Well, there we go again. Not just obedience, but joyful obedience. Gratitude in all things.

That's easy enough when you're healthy, happy, surrounded by loyal friends and a loving family, but what if you're not? You remember what Job says after he has just lost all of his flocks, herds, sons, and daughters? His comment on this overwhelming calamity is instructive. He says: "The Lord gave, and the Lord hath taken away; blessed be the name of the Lord" (1:23). I remember reading that passage several times and thinking, "What is going on here? Is Job crazy? Doesn't he care? Or is he afraid that God will smite him if he says what's really on his mind?" Now I think that, despite the perplexity and pain, Job could still praise God because he knew and trusted the speaker.

I remember being struck by Alma 57—a real catalogue of disasters in which Helaman is reporting to Moroni how the war is going in the south. They have to "sleep" on their swords (and I imagine he meant this literally) to repel night attacks, the army is stretched to the breaking point trying to keep prisoners under control at the same time, the prisoners escape when the Nephites try to herd them to Zarahemla and the guards barely make it back in time to help turn a lethal attack, hundreds of them are killed, and many of Helaman's stripling warriors faint because of loss of blood. What is Helaman's comment on this state of affairs? "I was filled with exceeding joy because of the goodness of God in preserving us, that we might not all perish; yea, and I trust that the souls of them who have been slain have entered into the rest of their God" (v. 36). Well might one ask where the cause for rejoicing is in all this? Precisely in acknowledging the Lord's hand and knowing that his love—which is eternal—is much more important than circumstances, which are always temporary.

I find this concept remarkably powerful. Gratitude is a means of controlling our inner weather. Our foundation, which is Christ, the unshakable rock, can withstand the storms that come as long as we don't open our doors and windows to them. By being grateful, we insure two things: that the Lord can teach us whatever we need to know for our exaltation—*whatever* we need to know, and some of the lessons will hurt; and he can turn any circumstance to our blessing. It can become a vehicle which speaks his love for us. We won't miss it by pouting, or being angry, or self-pitying. We will have the power to stand steadfast.

I'd like to give two examples of how this process works, one from the life of two Dutch Protestant women and the other from the life of a Mormon convert.

The Dutchwomen are Corrie and Betsie Ten Boom, two sisters who helped hide Jews in their home during World War II. When they were betrayed and sent to the concentration camps, they were able to smuggle a little New Testament into Ravensbruck. When they are shoved into their crowded, stinking barracks where up to seven women have to crowd onto bunks stacked in tiers five and six high, the final indignity is that their moldy straw is crawling with fleas. Corrie and Betsie had always been scrupulously clean, and this vermin was abhorrent to them. Corrie tells the story:

> "Here! And here's another one!" I wailed. "Betsie, how can we live in such a place!"
>
> "Show us. Show us how." It was said so matter of factly it took me a second to realize she was praying. More and more the distinction between prayer and the rest of life seemed to be vanishing for Betsie.
>
> "Corrie!" she said excitedly. "He's given us the answer! Before we asked, as He always does! In the Bible this morning. Where was it? Read that part again!"
>
> I glanced down the long dim aisle to make sure no guard was in sight, then drew the Bible from its pouch. … "Here it is: 'Comfort the frightened, help the weak, be patient with everyone. See that none of you repays evil for evil, but always seek to do good to one another and to all. … Rejoice always, pray constantly, give thanks in all circumstances; for this is the will of God in Christ Jesus—'"
>
> "That's it, Corrie! That's his answer. 'Give thanks in all circumstances!' That's what we can do. We can start right now to thank God for every single thing about this new barracks!"
>
> I stared at her, then around me at the dark, foul-aired room.
>
> "Such as?" I said.
>
> "Such as being assigned here together."
>
> I bit my lip. "Oh yes, Lord Jesus!"

"Such as what you're holding in your hands."

I looked down at the Bible. "Yes! Thank you, dear Lord, that there was no inspection when we entered here! Thank you for all the women, here in this room, who will meet you in these pages."

"Yes," said Betsie. "Thank you for the very crowding here. Since we're packed so close, that many more will hear!" She looked at me expectantly. "Corrie!" she prodded.

"Oh, all right. Thank you for the jammed, crammed, stuffed, packed, suffocating crowds."

"Thank you," Betsie went on serenely, "for the fleas and for—"

The fleas! This was too much. "Betsie, there's no way even God can make me grateful for a flea."

"'Give thanks in *all* circumstances,'" she quoted. "It doesn't say, 'in pleasant circumstances.' Fleas are part of this place where God has put us."

And so we stood between piers of bunks and gave thanks for fleas. But this time I was sure Betsie was wrong.[2]

But as events turned out, it was Betsie who was right. Both Corrie and Betsie were diligent missionaries, constantly bearing testimony to God, bringing the hope of Christ to women trapped in that dreadful place. Betsie was too sick to go out with the brigades of women workers into the forest, so she was assigned to knit stockings for German soldiers. Because there were so many women, Betsie was in a group that had to work in the barracks instead of the work room.

> She was a lightning knitter who completed her quota ... long before noon. She kept our Bible with her and spent hours each [afternoon] reading aloud from it, moving from [sleeping] platform to platform.
>
> One evening I got back to the barracks late. ... Betsie was waiting for me, as always, so that we could wait through the food line together. Her eyes were twinkling.

---

2. Corrie Ten Boom, with John and Elizabeth Sherrill, *The Hiding Place* (New York: Bantam Books, 1971), 197–99.

"You're looking extraordinarily pleased with yourself," I told her.

"You know we've never understood why we had so much freedom in the big room," she said. "Well—I've found out."

That afternoon, … there'd been confusion in her knitting group about sock sizes and they'd asked the supervisor to come and settle it.

"But she wouldn't. She wouldn't step through the door and neither would the guards. And you know why?" Betsie could not keep the triumph from her voice: "Because of the fleas! That's what she said, 'That place is crawling with fleas!'"

My mind rushed back to our first hour in this place. I remembered Betsie's bowed head, remembered her thanks to God for creatures I could see no use for.[3]

We're often in such circumstances, aren't we? A long-term blessing comes wrapped up as a package of short-term inconvenience and tribulation. Exercising the principle of gratitude is an extraordinary recipe for simplicity and serenity. By acknowledging the hand of the Lord in all things, not just those that suit our temporary convenience, we allow all of them to become blessings to us. And I love the fact that the Lord accepts incredulous and even grudging acknowledgment of his hand. We don't have to be hypocritical or pump up fake enthusiasm for the fleas in our lives. We just have to acknowledge them and give thanks.

The second example is the remarkable experience of a woman named Elizabeth Francis Yates, the mother of Louise Yates Robinson, who became the seventh general president of the LDS Relief Society. There's a sweetness and serenity about her short autobiography that moves me, and the vital core of that serenity was the quality of gratitude. She was raised in a very Victorian home, married young, and had four daughters. She was too polite to refuse a tract offered by a Mormon missionary on the street and began to read it one rainy afternoon. She exclaimed aloud when she finished, "Praise

---

3. Ibid., 208–209.

the Lord, I have found the right way at last." When she attended her first Mormon meeting and heard a sermon on Joseph Smith's divine mission, she recalls, "To say that I was thrilled with Joy but feebly expressed my feelings at that time. I could see no other way but to repent of my sins and to be baptized. I knew my people would bitterly oppose it when they knew it, and that my former friends would treat me coldly but it was worse than I ever thought."

She was baptized one icy December midnight in 1851. "When I looked down in the dark water I felt as though I could not possibly go in it, but a Voice seemed to say 'there is no other way.' It seemed after that that everything had changed. The scales had fallen from my eyes and the gospel plan was glorious, and I covenanted with My Heavenly Father that however dark the clouds may be, if friends turned to be foes that by His help I would serve Him. And I have tried in my faltering way to do so. ... After years of fasting and prayers, and many tears, the Lord opened the way for me to come to Zion. I prayed earnestly to God to help me in the long tedious journey that was before me, that I may not murmur on the way or complain if a lion should be in my path. And he answered my prayers, for ... my heart was filled with gratitude all the way."[4]

The details that let us see the full magnitude of her achievement are not in her history but in a biographical sketch by her son. When she joined the church, her widowed mother disowned her. Her husband left her and the children, hoping that economic necessity would break her spirit; but she scraped by, working long exhausting hours in a mill. Then he came back and took the four children away. A mother then had no legal rights over her children. On that voyage to Zion, she was so ill crossing the ocean that fellow passengers thought she would die. She had to walk the entire

---

4. Lavina Fielding Anderson, "Elizabeth Francis Yates: Trial by Heartbreak," *Ensign*, July 1979, 62–63.

distance from Florence, Nebraska, to Salt Lake City. She remarried and bore nine more children, six of whom died before her.

She never gave up longing for her daughters in England and eventually learned that the two youngest children had died very soon after the separation. The oldest daughter, Susan, ran away at age eleven and lived with a Mormon family. A missionary returning to Utah mentioned "Susie Williams" to Sister Yates in Scipio, and they were reunited. The father had taken the last daughter with him to Michigan; but by placing advertisements in newspapers, they were able to find her. She came to Utah and lived with her mother for the rest of her life.

Think of what had happened to that woman—enough to break her heart with sorrow or harden it with anger—but she ends her sketch with these words: "I can say that I have seen the hand of the Lord over his people on land and sea. I have seen times when it required faith to believe that our enemies would not triumph over us ... I can say ... that I was young and now I am old, but I have never seen the righteous forsaken."[5]

We will have trials of our own. Adversity will wring our hearts and try us to the very core if it has not already done so. But we are also surrounded by delight, beauty, and celebration. Gratitude is truly the alchemist's metal, transmitting affliction into blessing and blessing into rejoicing. It is to me truly the great miracle of God's love for us that "all things work together for good to them that love God" (Rom. 9:28). May we have grateful hearts. May we look beyond the gifts to the Giver and thereby find the spiritual power to be among our associates a never-failing well of refreshment and comfort.

---

5. Ibid.

12

Loving the Questions

I delivered this sermon at the Salt Lake Sunstone Symposium, August 11, 1995, in conjunction with Harry Fox's sermon, "Three Difficult Words for Us to Learn: Ask, Receive, and Give." It was published in Sunstone, *June–July 1998, 110–13.*

After three days, they found [Jesus] in the temple, sitting in the midst of the doctors, both hearing them, and asking them questions. …

And when they saw him, they were amazed: and his mother said unto him, Son, why hast thou thus dealt with us? behold, thy father and I have sought thee sorrowing.

And he said unto them, How is it that ye sought me? wist ye not that I must be about my Father's business? (Luke 2:46–49)

I think it is significant that the first recorded action of Jesus in mortality was to ask questions. What were those questions? I wish we knew. Furthermore, the first recorded words addressed to Jesus in mortality were a question—the question of Mary; and the first scriptural words recorded from Jesus in mortality were also a question.

I want to talk about questions. The search for truth is a delicious, deliberate, and sometimes dangerous dance between questions and answers. It is a willingness to entertain questions, as though they were "angels unawares" (Heb. 13:2), to journey with the questions, to live with the questions, to love the questions, and sometimes to die with and for and in the questions, only to be reborn in new questions.

Jesus was a question-asker. His questions still ring in our minds and stir our hearts after two thousand years, compelling our attention and challenging our complacency. Think of the new avenues of communication and the many voyages of self-discovery triggered by the Savior's penetrating questions:

- What manner of [person] ought ye to be? (3 Ne. 27:27)
- What do you want me to do to thee? (Luke 18:41)
- Where is your treasure? (Matt. 6:21)
- Who is my neighbor? (Luke 10:29)
- Could ye not watch with me one hour? (Matt. 26:40)
- Who is the greatest among you? (Matt. 23:11)
- Which of you is without sin? (John 8:7)
- For if ye only love them which love you, what reward have ye? (Luke 6:32)
- How oft shall I forgive my brother [or sister]? (Matt. 18:21)
- Whom do ye say that I am? (Matt. 16:15)
- What shall it profit you if you gain the whole world but lose your soul? (Mark 8:36)

One of the reasons that these are such great questions is that they have powerful answers, simple answers, clear answers; and yet, at the same time, they invite—almost compel—us to ask further questions. Take, for instance, that simple, narrative-based question, "Could ye not watch with me one hour?" The answer to that question was obvious. No. The apostles were slumped sideways and snoring. The question was rhetorical. It is a question, on one level, designed to produce guilt and shame because of obvious failure and inadequacy. We have plenty of questions like this already: "Why aren't you a better wife? a more faithful home teacher? less slothful in service?" Or like this one: "So you're right but everybody else is wrong?" and that really terrific question, "What's the matter with your testimony?"

It is rare for us to phrase the question "Do you love me?" to all but a cherished handful of intimates. It reveals our raw vulnerability and insecurity. We more frequently ask for respect or validation. But during the increasing rigidity of the 1990s, with terrifying frequency, the answer has been, "I can't love you unless the church loves you." And during this decade, the answer of the church is, "This is a court of love. Of course we love you. In the name of love, we cast you out." In the minds of all of us, this should lead us to deeper questions: How is that possible? What kind of love is this? How can we get the church to love us? What is love purchased at such a price worth? And how can we continue to love the church?

On one level, all of us are here with questions. I know it, because Sunstone is about this question: What does it mean to offer God our minds as well as our hearts—to put the fruits of our intellects and skills at the service of our faith? But we have other questions: What does God want me to do with my life? What does discipleship mean? How can we be in the world but not of the world? How can we love if we cannot serve, and how can we find ways to serve? What do I do with brothers and sisters who ask different questions or who ask no questions? Does God respect my questions as much as he respects someone else's answers? And there are deeper questions still: What does it mean to be God? Who is he, or she, or they? What makes me feel like their son or daughter?

I've said that questions are dangerous. Certainly one of the questions we ask is: Do we have to ask questions like this? Do we have to ask questions at all? Isn't it more comfortable to lean on our certainties or on the certitude of others? Hugh Nibley asked, "Are you ashamed of getting the right answer, just because it's the same as everyone else's?" Jesus healed the epileptic son, but didn't he also ask the father, "Do you have faith that I can heal him?" The father answered, "Lord, I believe. Help thou mine unbelief" (Mark 9:24). Jesus accepted the father's answer, but what if he really wanted a different answer? John Donne, in his Third Satire, writes in cautious paradox: "To adore, or scorne an image, or protest / May all be bad; doubt wisely; in strange way / to stand inquiring right, is not to stray; / to sleep, or runne wrong, is." I remember Elouise Bell, an English professor at BYU, saying, "I don't apologize for my doubts. I'm not particularly proud of them either." Isn't it just as dangerous to have only questions and no answers as it is to have all the answers and recognize none of the questions?

These aren't questions to supply easy answers to. These are questions that we need to live with, to lie down with and rise up with, to take with on our journey, sometimes to wrestle with as Jacob wrestled with the angel, and sometimes to dance with.

I think of metaphors for questions. Questions can be treasures, the pearl of great price to be carried in the bosom and protected from thieves, as the faint and flickering light from a candle in a windy place that will show us our path one step ahead while we take that step in faith, trusting that, if we continue our journey through the weary night, the sun will rise in the morning, drowning the light of our candle in the glorious light of full day.

A question can be a companion on our journey, just as Paul was accompanied on his journey to Damascus by his question, "Who art thou, Lord?" (Acts 22:8). He received an immediate answer and then spent the rest of his life working out what that answer meant as he shared the glad message with others.

A question can be like a child that we carry within our bodies. We protect it and nurture it as it grows. We have faith that the kicks and swelling and heartburn will turn into a baby with fingers and toes and flawless curling ears. We carry the question in hope, but questions like this make us weary. They give us backaches and headaches. Not infrequently, they make us sick to our stomachs. And they never stay little and contained. They lead to birth, sometime rending and tearing as they come forth and take on a life of their own.

Asking questions requires courage. It requires a willingness to open oneself to incertitude, to doubt, to disparagement, and to discouragement. It is being willing to die to the old self, sometimes to die little deaths daily, in the confidence that change does not mean to lose oneself but to find oneself. Helen Keller said with sublime confidence: "I cannot understand why anyone should fear death. Life here is more cruel than death—life divides and estranges, while death, which at heart is life eternal, reunites and reconciles. I believe that when the eyes within my physical eyes shall open upon the world to come, I shall simply be consciously living in the country of my heart."[1]

One of the great questions that Christianity poses is its paradox that we save our lives only in losing them. I think we're uncomfortable with this paradox—which is, no doubt, its purpose. I think we're meant to struggle with Pilate's question, "What is truth?" (John 18:38). I think sometimes we hope that if we never ask ourselves that question, we will never have to ask ourselves the next question, which is: "Is this particular concept a piece of the truth?" and then the third question, "And if it is true, how does it call me to live my life?"

I think there is no question that Mormonism, which, in our sacred narrative, began with the humble question of Joseph Smith in the Sacred Grove, which provides a glamorous and glowing list of new questions to be asked, and which provides some of the most soul-wrenching and soul-satisfying answers imaginable in human terms, does not currently welcome many questions. What can be our response? If we can give up questions, then I think there is no doubt whatsoever that we will have more comfortable lives. But I think most of us have already passed that point. We have already begun the terrifying and satisfying journey of asking questions. And

---

1. Helen Keller, *My Religion* (1927; New York: Swedenborg Foundation, 1986 printing), 110.

I really don't think it's possible to go back. We can't unask questions. We can't unknow what we know. We can't uneat the fruit.

We are launched on Eve's quest for the knowledge of good and evil. We have asked her question, "Is there no other way?" I hope that we will also be able to affirm her answer—that passing through sorrow is better because it allows us to know good from evil. Not easier, not safer, nor more comfortable—but better. That means, I think, that we have to recognize the questions that fear asks and answer them with courage.

Audre Lorde, in a poem called "We Were Never Meant to Survive," got my undivided attention, not by minimizing the fear but by casting it in the most intense and ultimate of terms. In this poem, she speaks of

> ... learning to be afraid
> with our mother's milk ...
>
> And when we speak we are afraid
> our words will not be heard nor welcomed
> But when we are silent
> we are still afraid.
> So it is better to
> speak remembering
> We were never
> meant to survive.[2]

We need to remember that we have taken upon us the name of a leader whose speaking led him straight to the cross. Caiphas must have breathed a sigh of relief when he heard the thud of the hammer on the nails, thinking, "Well, that's that. We certainly silenced *him*." But Paul gave us the view from eternity when he reminded us that Christ will "put down all rule and all authority and power" and "put

---

2. Audre Lorde, "Meditation 587," *Singing the Living Tradition* (Boston: Beacon Press/Unitarian Universalist Association, 1993), n.p.

all enemies under his feet," for "the last enemy that shall be destroyed is death." It was because Paul knew that end that he could say, by the "rejoicing which I have in Christ Jesus our Lord, [I stand] in jeopardy every hour" and "I die daily" (1 Cor. 15:24–26, 30–31).

Father Leo Booth, who describes himself as both a recovering alcoholic and a recovering priest, has written a powerful book about religious addiction called *When God Becomes a Drug*. Right at the top of his list of the symptoms of religious addiction he places the

> inability to think, doubt, or question information or authority. This is the primary symptom of any dysfunctional belief system, for if you cannot question or examine what you are taught, if you cannot doubt or challenge authority, you … miss the messages and miracles God places in your life because you literally do not know how to recognize them.
>
> In refusing to think or question, you hand over responsibility for your beliefs, finances, relationships, employment, and destiny to a clergyman or other so-called [spiritual] master. You are usually told that not thinking, doubting, or questioning is a sign of faith. … Faith is said to mean unquestioning obedience. This is how religious abusers control; it is how ministers and leaders are able to financially or sexually abuse their followers. …
>
> If you are not permitted to think for yourself, to question, you stop your spiritual growth because you do not know how to see the ways God is working with you and through you. When you use your critical faculties to analyze, interpret, explore, and question, you discover new shades of meaning and greater richness in God's truth. Questioning and exploring [are means] of having a dialogue with God. To refuse to doubt, think about, or question what you are told is to miss an opportunity to talk with God.[3]

I never thought that one of the consequences of being excommunicated would be that I would stop being afraid. To be more precise,

---

3. Leo Booth, *When God Becomes a Drug: Breaking the Chains of Religious Addiction and Abuse* (New York: G. P. Putnam's Sons, 1991), 60–61.

I never thought that one of the consequences of being excommunicated would be the revelation of how afraid I had been—how much in love with legalisms and rules and restrictions I had been, how quickly and willingly I drew lines to exclude others, how easily I ranked others by righteousness, how much of my own life was governed by rules: what I ate and drank and wore, what I could say and how, what I couldn't say. I was a Pharisee supreme, judging others by how they spoke, walked, dressed, spent their money, acted on their political beliefs, prayed, and thought.

There is nothing like being judged to show the dark side of judgement. I tell people that nothing in my personal and family life has changed because of the excommunication—and from one perspective, that's the literal truth. We still have family prayer, read scriptures daily, sing hymns together nightly, go to church weekly, spend our time and money in good causes, and find people who need our service. I had wondered if excommunication would mean a greater interest in smoking and drinking, if I would give myself permission to try the marijuana brownies that I denied myself as a student at BYU. None of those things happened.

But an immense internal change has occurred. The fear is gone; and with it is the burden of the rules and regulations and restrictions. It simply slipped off my back like the burden that Christian, in *Pilgrim's Progress*, dropped at the feet of Christ as he passed through the wicket gate of baptism. I no longer feel any need to evaluate my own righteousness or, more importantly, the righteousness of others according to the rules. It's not that I have given it up as an act of will. It has been lifted from me by a merciful hand. Was I afraid, all those years, that only a rule stood between me and moral chaos? How could I have had so little faith? And how could I have had so little love that the first thing I wanted to know about someone else was their righteousness checklist instead of their stories and their hearts? There's an immense freedom in listening for understanding instead of listening to evaluate, judge, prescribe remedies, and fix in various ways. I can't think of the difference without feeling my heart brim with praise and gratitude to God.

I believe that an essential and important part of goodness—of being right with God—is asking questions. I think we cannot save ourselves without asking questions. I think we are totally useless at saving others without asking questions. And I believe this because, without asking questions, we will never approach the Savior to ask the terrible and tremendous question of faith: "Good master, what must I do to be saved?" You remember that the Savior responded first with a question: "What says the law?" But that question was just to clear the ground, so to speak, for the real answer came next, "Come, follow me" (Luke 18:18–22). We cannot get real answers unless we ask real questions. Or as Wilson Mizner says, "I respect faith, but doubt is what gets you an education."

The most intense and urgent invitations to ask questions come from the Savior himself. Paul warns people to shun "fables and endless genealogies, which minister questions" (1 Tim. 1:4), but Jesus urges, begs, commands, promises:

> Draw near unto me and I will draw near unto you; seek me diligently and ye shall find me; ask, and ye shall receive; knock, and it shall be opened unto you.
>
> Whatsoever ye ask the Father in my name it shall be given unto you, that is expedient for you. (D&C 88:62–64)

It is to those who "confessed they were strangers and pilgrims on the earth" that the Savior promised to "reason with you, and ... speak unto you" (D&C 45:13, 15)

I think of all the anxious warnings that we receive not to delve into the mysteries. What exactly are these mysteries? Alma identified the resurrection of the dead as a mystery (Alma 40:3), and Paul explained to the Corinthians that the change that will come "in the twinkling of an eye" upon the righteous living "at the last trump" is "a mystery" (1 Cor. 15: 51–52). Jesus himself in explicating the parable of the sower to his apostles, explained that the reason he was doing so was because "unto you it is given to know the mysteries of the kingdom of God" (Luke 8:18). When Joseph Smith and Sidney Rigdon saw their vision of the three degrees of glory, they described it as "the mysteries of his kingdom" (D&C 76:114–115). The Melchizedek Priesthood, we are told, "administereth the gospel and holdeth the key of the mysteries of the kingdom, even the key of the knowledge of God" (D&C 84:19–20).

In what sense are they mysteries? True, we can't make these processes happen from our own knowledge. They are mysteries in that we don't understand how they work. I agree that there are many layers to our understanding, but even little children can explain the parable of the sower. Missionaries have no trouble making the logic of the three degrees of glory apparent to investigators. The ordinances of baptism and the laying on of hands are the first steps into membership, not the culminating steps of salvation. Even the endowment is urged for the many, not reserved for a privileged fraction.

And, perhaps more importantly, it is not the scriptures that forbid us to search the mysteries. The scriptures propel and lure and coax us toward mysteries. The Doctrine and Covenant promises, "And if thou wilt inquire, thou shalt know mysteries which are great and marvelous; therefore thou shalt exercise thy gift, that thou mayest find out mysteries" (6:11). The Savior urges: "Ask that you may know the mysteries of God, … according to your faith shall it be done unto you" (D&C 8:10–11). "If thou shalt ask, thou shalt receive revelation upon revelation, knowledge upon knowledge, that thou mayest know the mysteries and peaceable things—that which bringeth joy, that which bringeth life eternal" (D&C 42:61). "Unto him that keepeth my commandments I will give the mysteries of my kingdom, and the same shall be in him a well of living water, springing up unto everlasting life" (D&C 63:23).

But what exactly are these mysteries? I think that the mysteries may lie not in technical questions of how the resurrection will be performed or who may visit whom in the kingdoms of glory but rather what Paul calls "the mystery of Christ," "the fellowship of the mystery ... to the intent that ... the principalities and powers in heavenly places might be known by the church" (Eph. 3:4, 9; Col. 4:3). He refers to the "great mystery" of the union of "Christ and the church" (Eph. 5:32), the "mystery of faith" (1 Tim. 3:9), the "mystery of godliness" (1 Tim. 3:16). In Doctrine and Covenants 107:19 "the mysteries of the kingdom of heaven" seem to be defined as: "to have the heavens opened unto them, ... and to enjoy the communion and presence of God the Father, and Jesus the mediator of the new covenant." Perhaps the clearest definition of this central mystery is Paul's statement to the Colossians that "the riches of the glory of this mystery ... is Christ in you" (Col. 1:27). Now that is a mystery: within our limited, sinful, ignorant, mortal selves resides the purity, the power, the unfailing love, the immortality, and the glory of Christ himself. Think of the questions that mystery contains and engenders!

If the mystery is Christ in us, then our journey is one of discovery, of learning to love ourselves, to love the questions that show us new sides of ourselves, that lead us toward the divine within ourselves and others. I hope that we will love these questions, live with them, struggle with them, dance with them, rejoice in them, weep over them, stretch ourselves to the cracking point with them, measure ourselves against them, and be filled to the brim with them:

> That Christ may dwell in [our] hearts by faith; that [we], being rooted and grounded in love,
>
> May be able to comprehend with all saints what is the breadth, and length, and depth, and height;
>
> And to know the love of Christ, which passeth knowledge, that [we] might be filled with all the fulness of God. (Eph. 3:17–19)

In the name of Christ, I invoke upon us the hunger of Eve in the garden and the clear vision of Anna in the temple who saw the Anointed One in the face of a helpless baby. May we ask our questions with faith, and courage, and above all, with that love which is the fullness of God.

13

In the Garden God Has Planted

EXPLORATIONS TOWARD A MATURING FAITH

*I delivered this address as part of the "Pillars of My Faith" panel
at the Sunstone Symposium in Salt Lake City on August 23,
1990. It was published in* Sunstone, *Oct. 1996, 24–27.*

When I was teaching freshman English at the University of Washington in about 1969, I had a very bright Chinese–American student who uncharacteristically missed two classes in a row. When he showed up for the third class, I asked where he'd been. "I was in my room," Garry said. "I couldn't think of a good reason to come out."

I spent the rest of the afternoon with him just talking, trying to understand why this bright, competent, hitherto motivated young man was suffering an existential crisis of enormous proportions. He had experienced no triggering trauma, but he had been overwhelmed by the meaninglessness of life. He literally could not find any good reason to continue living, though he was not particularly suicidal. As we talked, I caught a glimpse of his universe, a black hole that pulled into it all sparks of awareness, remorselessly extinguishing them one by one. I sensed the crippling and crushing that happens as someone looks out into the universe and sees, not the face of a loving Father and Mother, but only blackness whirling toward oblivion.

And I wondered about myself. Why, despite my glib graduate school discussions of angst and existential despair, had I never ever taken either seriously? Why, even as I saw Garry's universe, did I sense, beneath my feet and at my back, as solid as granite, a loving and attentive presence? Whatever I identify as my consciousness is anchored in and shared with a consciousness of God—inseparably connected with that attentive, loving presence. I cannot remember a time when this has not been so. My patriarchal blessing, bestowed upon me at age eleven, told me, "You have received a testimony of [the gospel], knowing within your heart that God lives, that Jesus is the Christ and the Savior of all mankind." I do know. I accept that gift of faith as pure grace.

I grew up in a devout and loving home with five brothers and sisters on farms in southern Idaho and central Washington. Ours was a household of faith and miracles: miracles of healing, miracles of protection, miracles of adverse weather controlled. Ours was also a household committed to the LDS Church. My father was a bishop twice and built two chapels. My mother taught Primary for forty-five years. Both were returned missionaries. All of us children married in the temple; my two brothers and I went on missions; as of 2020, my three sisters have served at least two missions each with their husbands.

Furthermore, I had the immense good fortune to be persecuted for my religion when I was growing up. My family moved from a solidly Mormon community in Idaho when I was about twelve to the Columbia Basin in Washington, where the construction of the Grand Coulee Dam had made it possible to bring thousands of acres under cultivation. One side effect was to upset the existing agricultural base of dryland farming, much of it by families who had been in the area for more than a generation. The only church in town to that point had been a comfortable little Congregational church. Since many of the new farmers came from Mormon areas of Idaho and Utah, the economic differences coincided with religious differences. The Congregational minister responded by preaching openly anti-Mormon sermons that were, for a time, quite popular with his parishioners. The natural problems of integrating newcomers with old and well-established families were thus exacerbated by religious suspicions.

I'll have to admit that the persecution amounted only to mild social ostracism and very mild name-calling ("carrot-snappers," for Mormons). Our school was too little to turn up its nose at the husky Mormon athletes, and you didn't have to have a date to go anywhere except to the junior prom. Thus, with very little inconvenience or distress to me, I chose Mormonism and its values as my own, solidifying my already solid Mormon identity and bonding culturally with my own community. The most important predictive fact about me then was that I was a Mormon. It explained me, summarized me, justified me. As I grew into consciousness of myself as a person, it was as a *Mormon* person, identified wholly with what I perceived to be the major values and norms of the Church.

My mission in France, graduating (twice) from BYU, and spending seven and a half years on the staff of the *Ensign* were all experiences that both deepened and challenged my simple one-to-one identification with the church. I still am a Mormon, a committed believing Mormon. I never considered marrying anyone but an active Mormon, and Paul's own strong testimony and devout family were both attractions. He has been in a bishopric and on the high council, from which he resigned to teach our son's Primary class. We pay tithing. We have temple recommends. We attend church weekly, have daily devotionals of hymn-singing and scripture reading, hold a more formal weekly family home evening, and pray as a family at every meal and individually. I subscribe to and read all of the church magazines. I have taught Primary since age fourteen, with only a few gaps, and currently teach Sunbeams (three-year-olds) and run a den of Cub Scouts. I have been a visiting teacher since age nineteen. We feel deeply blessed with a loving family life, stimulating work, good friends, and good health. We acknowledge the Lord's hand in these blessings.

In short, there are many ways in which the word "Mormon" summarizes the most important things about me. But "Mormon" is not the only adjective I would use today. Others are "intellectual" and "feminist."[1] These are aspects of myself that the church does not approve, reinforce, and encourage. Instead, the message that I hear is one of denial, repression, and suspicion.

Intellectually, the church, through BYU, gave me what I consider to be a first-rate education and reinforced a powerful hunger for learning; but I now find the official attitude toward scholarship in general and Mormon studies in particular to be quite dismaying.

As a woman, I feel deeply alienated from the structure of the church. Theologically, it offers a vision of godhood that includes the feminine principle in the form of a Mother in Heaven who is, like the Father in Heaven, divine. But as a practical matter, the church defines women primarily as child-rearers and husband-nurturers, steers women into supportive roles organizationally, uses their labor to operate important programs but withholds from them the final financial and managerial authority it grants to men, and gives men an apparently preferential relationship with God through their ordination to the priesthood.

I know many other intellectuals and feminists, with whom I share much, who have become disaffected and disappointed with the church. Some have "drifted away," as the saying is. Others have marched out, slamming the door behind them. Neither is a viable choice for me. God does not speak to me only through the church nor does God speak to me in everything the church says; but I still hear that divine voice in many of the church's messages. I accept the

---

1. My awareness of the cruelty and exclusion practiced institutionally against LGBTI members came later; but I was shocked at its depth and immediately took the position of "ally."

beauty of its community, the authority of its ordinances, its shaping of the vessel from which we may drink the waters of life.

Over the years, as I have found my own identity taking shape in a different pattern than the one the church prescribes for women, I have also found my understanding of God developing in some non-correlated ways. Two aspects of God's character that I am searching to understand most keenly right now are diversity and free agency.

First, diversity. Last week, I stood in a little meadow below our cabin, in the mountains east of Salt Lake City, up to my waist in green plants. Slowly, I rotated in a circle, looking at what was growing within a three-foot radius. I counted twenty-three different varieties, none of them trees or shrubs, none of them flowering, all of them a different shade of green. To perceive each of those aspects of color, texture, and shape without being able to name them, describe them, or probably even remember them accurately, was an exhilarating revelation of how highly God values diversity in even little things.

God doesn't plant lawns. He plants meadows. But we belong to a church that, right now, values lawns—their sameness, their conformity, the ease with which they can all be cut to the same height, watered on schedule, and replaced by new turf if necessary. (And against which it is easy to spot dandelions.) All organizations are limited in their ability to handle diversity, but our church seems particularly limited right now in its ability to cherish and nurture individuals as individuals—as wild geraniums, and catnip, and western coneflowers, and yarrow—not as identical blades of grass in a uniformly green lawn.

When Joseph Smith said he taught his people correct principles and let them govern themselves, I've usually assumed that this must be God's method, too. Now, I'm not so sure. I think rather that he expects us to identify those correct principles out of the floods and torrents of raw experience with which he drenches us daily—experiences of good and evil and every gradation in-between. Some of those principles will make us more like him. Others will take us far from him. Our choices relentlessly reveal the true desires of our hearts, no matter what our lips may say. When we find principles that work for us—principles that teach us "the manner of happiness" (2. Ne. 5:27)—then we naturally try to share them with others. When a group of us share the same principles, we have a community. The church teaches many of those principles, but I no longer believe that it teaches all of them nor do I believe that the church is the only place we should seek them.

I now believe, at this stage of life, in the fundamental holiness of diversity. One of the results of this discovery (along with the humbling revelation of how easily I, myself, drift toward conformity) is an evolution in my understanding of revelation and how it comes. Revelation is not an orderly, linear process. It can be a sunburst of insights, a glimmer of comprehension, the rethinking with understanding of long-past events, the testing of a beloved principle in an unforeseen crucible. But most important of all, it's *our* experience. Even if it begins with instructions from elsewhere, it must become our experience before it becomes our revelation.

The second principle, free agency, is even more fundamental than diversity, since diversity could not exist without it. As I grew up, I learned in Sunday school and seminary that free agency was a kind of true-false quiz or, at best, a multiple choice test—the freedom to make right choices as defined by the rulebooks in the hands of our teachers. I no longer believe in this view of freedom. We are far from understanding the absolute and deadly seriousness with which God regards our free agency. Contemplate, if you will, his profound reluctance to tamper with it, no matter what is at stake, his terrible patience as we make choices—sometimes stupid, sometimes irresponsible, sometimes downright dangerous. I believe that he suffers with us as we learn the consequences of some choices—suffers so profoundly that only the atonement could preserve for us the continued ability to choose. Other decisions he celebrates with us.

Jesus did not say, "Read my mind." He said, "Come, follow me." That divine invitation sets us in motion. Freedom is a dance that we enter into, understanding only as we move that each gesture flings grace or grief to the far reaches of the universe. It is a dance with life, with death, and ultimately with the light that fills the immensities of space where no space exists without kingdom.

Well, these are discoveries that I am just now making. They are far from the final word in the divine dialogue that I hope will last for the rest of my life. We belong to a church that, for the time being, enforces and rewards conformity, hierarchy, and obedience. I think that this direction is an experiment—the result of choices perhaps instigated by some leaders but in which we have cooperated. It happens to be an experiment which tacitly encourages adults to remain dependent and which exacts a particularly high price from its women. I think God is watching it with loving attentiveness and with a terrible patience.

Patience is hard, but I plan to still be here when the church stops experimenting with lawns and refocuses on the garden which the Lord has planted. The glory of the church, realized in many shining ways even now, is its ability to foster conditions in which richly loving relationships can thrive—with each other, with God. And ultimately it is these relationships that are our defense against the darkness of despair. Then shall the Lord "comfort Zion … and he will make her wilderness like Eden, and her desert like the garden of the Lord. Joy and gladness shall be found therein, thanksgiving and the voice of melody" (2 Ne. 8:3).

14

The Grammar of Inequity

A version of this essay was first presented at the Mormon Women's Forum, November 30, 1988, Salt Lake City. With revisions made in November 1998 and March 1990, it was published in Women and Authority: Re-Emerging Mormon Feminism, *ed. Maxine Hanks (Salt Lake City: Signature Books, 1992), 215–30.*

The thoughtful and subtle philosopher Montaigne once remarked: "Most of the grounds of the world's troubles are matters of grammar."[1]

Now this is not just one of those terribly clever French writers being cute. He was expressing a principle that I, as a writer and editor, have come to see as a fact of our universe. The way we arrange words is determined by and, in turn, determines the way we arrange our reality. The labels we apply to people determine, in large measure, our relationships with them; but our relationships also reshape those categories and labels.

This essay explores some of the strengths of deliberately choosing to relate to our world with gender-inclusive language in three areas crucial to our religious life—our scriptures, our hymns, and our prayers. I recognize that not everyone is comfortable with analyzing how we speak nor with altering traditional forms of speech. This discomfort becomes particularly acute in the discussion on

---

1. Michel Montaigne, in *The Viking Book of Aphorisms* (New York: Dorset Press for Viking Books, 1962), 155.

prayer where I double the stakes: I urge not only the use of inclusive language, but also replacing the formal language of prayer with everyday speech. I make this double plea because I feel that one shift in understanding—including Mother in Heaven—cannot occur without the other—praying in the most familiar and direct ways we can.

Why am I urging this program of grammatical reform? Inclusive speech is not only ethically right but has profound spiritual consequences. How we read the scriptures and how we pray shapes our relationship with our divine parents. It is a truism to say that we speak in ways that are familiar to us, but it is a painful thing to realize that the familiar speech of our religious experience excludes women. The mother tongue belongs to the fathers. For Latter-day Saints, familiar religious speech is the language of the King James and Joseph Smith translations of the Bible, the Doctrine and Covenants, the Book of Mormon, and the Pearl of Great Price. The scriptures are profoundly exclusionary. It is an agonizing paradox; but to the degree we love and use the language of the scriptures, we also love and use the language of exclusion.

Yet this is not my view of God. I feel to the very depths of my soul that the Savior's mission was to women as well as to men, that our theology embraces a divine couple, that the place of our Mother in Heaven is as secure as that of our Father in Heaven, and that a full understanding of godhood will eventually include an understanding of her powers and responsibilities. I feel that women must be fully included in the gospel of Jesus Christ, not because the scriptural texts fully include them nor because our theology perfectly includes them but because any other pattern does violence to the fabric of the universe, distorting and misshaping the image of God toward which I strive, however imperfectly. When language becomes a veil, masking and disguising God, then it is imperative, as a matter of spiritual health, that language change. I think that the process, though arduous, will be accompanied by joy.

I had the instructive experience some time ago of reading through an entire conference issue of the *Ensign* (Nov. 1988) looking specifically for messages of inclusion and exclusion. I would not particularly recommend this exercise, except as a research project, since it narrows one's focus. Nor is it the way I usually read conference addresses. However, I enjoyed spending this concentrated time with the conference texts, discovering points of agreement, feeling called to repentance by some talks, comforted by others, and being astonished by still others.

But with my particular focus in mind, I looked for references to women and made lists. I excluded scriptural quotations because women are comparatively rare in the scriptures. In the interests of fairness, I also excluded references to Jesus and Joseph Smith. This particular conference happened to be the October 1988 conference, in which Richard G. Scott was sustained as an apostle. I excluded references to him that were ritual expressions of welcome to the Quorum of the Twelve and references to President Ezra Taft Benson that were expressions of support, appreciation for his presence, and so forth.

Here are the results of what I found:

1. Except in the priesthood session, all talks were addressed equally to both men and women.

2. When speakers quoted named individuals who were not scriptural personages, they quoted thirty-one men and five women.

3. In examples and stories, thirty involved men only, nine involved women only, and seventeen involved men and women.

4. Twenty men were named and two women.

Yes, the results were fairly lopsided. So what else is new? And furthermore, expressions of ritual indignation about the imbalance are actually pretty boring. Far more interesting are some additional observations:

One is that Michaelene P. Grassli, the Primary general president, spoke in the Sunday afternoon session with general authorities on both sides. This is definite progress. This new custom is a trend which I'm happy to applaud, along with the continued presence of the women organizational leaders on the stand.[2]

Another cheering item is that about half of the general authorities who referred to their wives called them by their names. I also consider this to be a helpful, hopeful trend since a name is an individual expression of personhood whereas "wife" (like "husband") is a role that is automatically created by marriage.

Even more significant in the good news department were the evident, serious, concentrated efforts of the men who spoke to use inclusive language in their remarks. For example:

1. In Elder Neal A. Maxwell's eloquent address, he said: "Why do some crush and break the tender hearts of spouses and children through insensitivity and even infidelity?" and called them "pathetic men or women." The reference to "breaking the tender hearts," of course, echoes the language of Jacob's strong denunciation of adulterous husbands in the Book of Mormon ("ye have broken the hearts of your tender wives," Jac. 2:35). Elder Maxwell has correctly noted that either spouse can commit adultery with the same devastating effects (p. 33).

2. Elder David Haight rephrased a quotation from Laurel Thatcher Ulrich that had originally applied only to women so that it also included men: "'I suppose every Mormon [man and] woman [have] measured [themselves] at one time or another against [their] pioneer ancestors'" (brackets his). Elder Haight also added a masculine example to parallel Laurel's feminine one. "Could I leave my wife and children without food or means to support themselves while I responded to a call to serve a mission abroad, or take these same innocent ones, dependent solely upon me for their survival, into hostile territory to set up housekeeping and provide a livelihood for them?

---

2. Two women from the general auxiliary presidencies now (as of 2020) speak as a matter of routine and at least another also offers a prayer.

Or, were I a woman, [and here he's quoting Laurel's example], Could I crush my best china to add glitter to a temple, bid loving farewell to a missionary husband as I lay in a wagon bed with fever and chills, leave all that I possessed and walk across the plains to an arid wilderness?" (82–83). Yes, we all know that the "best china" sacrifice is a myth, since there was plenty of already broken china to hand. Also most pioneer women could probably not accurately be described as "solely dependent" and, in fact, usually managed to support those same husbands on missions while putting food on the table for their children at home—but it's quite obvious that a sincere effort to apply a principle of inclusiveness prompted Elder Haight's effort.

3. President Thomas S. Monson, in speaking at the priesthood session, referred to athletic teams of "young men and young women" (44)

4. President Howard W. Hunter reminded his listeners that "God knows and loves us all. We are, every one of us, his daughters and his sons" (60). This language is particularly noteworthy because it specifies daughters and sons, rather than the more usual phrase "children of God" and also puts daughters first.

5. Elder Richard G. Scott, in referring to the dedication of the Mexico City temple, mentions the presence of "many of the men and women leaders of Mexico and Central America" (76), a deliberate and inclusive specification instead of the more usual reference just to "leaders."

In short, I feel confident in affirming a sensitivity and courtesy on the part of general authorities that manifests itself in real efforts to use more gender-inclusive language and to include women more visibly in the public rituals of general conference. Why, then, did I end up feeling those all-too-familiar and all-too-awful feelings of grief as I read the thoughtful and kindly messages of these sensitive and decent men?[3]

---

3. Beginning in October 2018, the awkward pre-conference "women's meeting" was smoothed out by making both the women's and the priesthood sessions

The answer is that it has very little to do either with them or with me. The mechanisms of patriarchy are embedded deep in our culture and our language. I have long been dismayed at what the church "does" to women, but I have been short-sighted. The church did not invent the mechanisms of patriarchy nor shape the grammar of inequity. The sources of oppression seep through the bedrock of our culture itself. That insight has brought me feelings of understanding and even forgiveness that are very healing.

However, it has not brought me acceptance. Inequity is wrong—ethically and morally wrong. If the wrong runs to bedrock, then correcting it cannot be done quickly and easily, but it must be done. I am not qualified to discuss political and economic strata in that bedrock, but I do want to explore the sedimentary accretions of its grammar.

I am going to use President Benson's powerful closing address (1988) as an example. I do so with some hesitation, since I am aware of the danger of making a person "an offender for a word," in the terms of Isaiah's rebuke of those whom he calls "the scorners" (Isa. 29:20–21). Not in a critical spirit, then, but to demonstrate the terrible irony that "feasting" on the words of the scriptures is a diet deficient in inclusiveness, let's look at that address. He speaks to "my beloved brethren and sisters," and refers to "offspring of a loving God," children of God, members, parents, leaders, teachers, and families, all in gender-neutral language. But he also refers to "the agency of man" and "all mankind," and says (1) "God reveals His will to all men," (2) "I testify that it is time for every man to set in order his own house. ... It is time for the unbeliever to learn for himself that this work is true," and (3) "In due time all men will gain a resurrection" (87). Although he appropriately uses masculine references about the apostles Christ chose and about the president

held on the Saturday night of general conference weekend into meetings that alternate annually—priesthood in the spring and women in autumn. At the April 2019 conference, two women spoke and two prayed.

of the church, there is no contextual reason for exclusionary language in the settings of the quotations I have just cited.

I am not, as I said, accusing President Benson of insensitivity or discourtesy to women. I am simply using his address to point out how deeply and strongly traditions of usage grip our language. Yet I believe that we cannot correctly understand either the God we worship or our own ultimate potential as gods as relationships of male-female inequity. If I am correct, then we must change those traditions and foster a new language of inclusion. But how? We will not find a complete answer to this dilemma in the scriptures, nor in our history, nor in our theology, although we can find support for an inclusionary position in all three. I believe that we must find the answer first in our own hearts, then turn outward with questions— not questions like "Why are things the way they are?" or "How can we make *them* or *it* change?" but "How can I behave so that my actions mirror the truth of what I feel in my heart?"

What are the implications of approaching our scriptures, our hymns, and our prayers with language that reflects our deepest convictions about the relationships that should exist among men and women and about our even more important relationship with God?

READING THE SCRIPTURES INCLUSIVELY

An obvious beginning is to read the scriptures with inclusionary language. This is quite a bit easier than we might think. Our son, Christian, was, as I recall, about four and a half when I realized how adept he had become. Our bedtime story involved a rabbit in red overalls, and I said something like, "See the bunny? He's looking for something to eat." Christian, absorbed in the picture, commented absentmindedly, "Or she." At age eight, Christian has no trouble editing John 3:3 at normal reading speed to emerge as: "Verily, verily, I say unto thee, Except a man [or woman] be born again, he [or she] cannot see the kingdom of God." Inclusionary language has already become, to a large extent, the familiar speech of our son, and we hope that he will learn to correct exclusionary language with the same reflex that he corrects incorrect grammar.

I might add that Christian is getting into the spirit of the thing at age nine (1989) and is lobbying to include children. Now, if a nine-year-old can successfully negotiate the grammar of this passage—"Except a man or a woman or a child be born of the water and of the Spirit, he or she cannot enter into the kingdom of God"—I think the rest of us just might be able to stumble along in his or her footsteps.

In addition to the very real psychological impact for women of consciously including themselves and for men of consciously including women, there are some theological advantages. Think, if you will, of Christ as the "Son of Man—and Woman."[4]

Let us become editors—all of us. Let us shape our daily experience so that inclusionary language becomes our common speech.

SINGING OUR HYMNS IN A NEW VOICE

My husband, Paul, who has received probably more attention and appreciation for his hymn texts in the new (1985) hymnal than anything else he has done in a list of quite considerable achievements, has observed wryly that more Mormons get their theology from the hymnal than from the scriptures. As a former English major, I would also observe that most Mormons get their poetry there as well. It is unfortunate, then, that our current hymnal, the first in two decades, made no visible effort to modify or reduce exclusionary language in its texts.[5]

---

4. Elder Bruce R. McConkie rather awkwardly dodged this problem by announcing that the phrase meant "Man of Holiness."

5. The Church Music Department invited submissions for a new hymnal, deadline July 2019. Many hopes are riding on this long overdue update, but the actual selection remains to be seen. Even more problematic is that the opportunities for congregational singing have been sharply curtailed by the 2018 policy reducing the

It is more difficult to change words in many hymns than in the scriptures, however, since there are requirements of rhythm and, even more difficult, of rhyme to consider. Frankly, our family editings are not overly concerned with creating smooth alternative readings to the hymns; but our growing ability to spot and correct exclusive language as we sing along has enlivened many an otherwise lackluster meeting. This month in our ward, we've been singing, "Know This, That Every Soul Is Free" (No. 240), which includes those truly shattering lines: "Freedom and reason make us men; / Take these away, what are we then? / Mere animals ..." As I recall, I sang "make us persons," Paul sang "make us human," and Christian sang "make us homo sapiens." Christian then continued with gusto, "Take these away, what are we then? / Meerschweinchen ..." (He had just learned the German word for "guinea pig" and was delighted to find such a good place to use it.) I think this memory may even replace that memorable Sunday when we all disgraced ourselves with giggles over a line that talked about how "faith buoys us up" and Paul triumphantly sang "boys and girls us up."

Many uses of "man" or "men" in a hymn yield gracefully to such monosyllables as "we," "us," "all," or "souls," as: "Gently raise the sacred strain, / For the Sabbath's come again / That we may rest ..." (no. 146). Or the line from "It Came upon the Midnight Clear": "Peace on the earth, good will to all ..." (no. 207); "And praises sing to God the King, and peace to us on earth" (no. 208). I confess that I haven't found a graceful solution to the last line of "I Believe in Christ" which concludes: "When on this earth he comes again / To rule among the sons of men" (no. 134). Usually we just

three-hour block meeting schedule to two hours and specifying that the Relief Society/priesthood hour should eliminate hymns and the opening prayer. The "practice hymn," which offered a brief exposure to singing in Sunday school was eliminated decades ago. Our ward has taken a step toward countering this trend by devoting one sacrament meeting (so far) to asking selected members to briefly share the special significance a hymn has to them; the congregation then sings one verse of it.

go for broke and recklessly cram in, "To rule among the sons and daughters of men and women."

I'd suggest experimenting with your own singing to find gender-inclusive language that you feel comfortable with. I loved Kelli Frame's report of her glorious experience in singing "A Mighty Fortress Is Our God" with feminine pronouns ("She overcometh all / She saveth from the fall …").[6] At my most recent women's scripture study group, I tried singing it with inclusive pronouns: "They overcome it all / They save us from the fall/ Their might and power are great. / They all things did create / And they shall reign forevermore." It truly felt glorious!

ENCOUNTERING OUR HEAVENLY PARENTS IN PRAYER

A third area in which our language benefits from thoughtful reshaping toward a more inclusive reality is in our prayers. Here, I think grammar offers a single-stone solution to two hard-to-kill birds: the impediment of formal language and the fact that our public prayers are addressed only to God the Father.

I am not, at this point, urging that we pray to Mother in Heaven. I hope the time will come when we can address both of our divine parents in our public petitions;[7] but for the moment, I propose a first step toward that solution. I think that the real obstacle to including our Mother in Heaven in public prayers is not

---

6. Kelli Frame, "From the Editor," *Mormon Women's Forum* [Newsletter], 1 (Oct. 1989): 1.

7. Gordon B. Hinckley forbade such prayers on the basis that Jesus prayed only to his Father. He delivered this statement at the women's annual meeting in September 1991, which then preceded general conference by a week; he had first made the same statement to the semi-annual conference of Regional Representatives, as an example of the "small beginnings of apostasy" to which they should be "alert." Gordon B. Hinckley, "Cornerstones of Accountability," address to Regional Representatives, April 5, 1991, photocopy of typescript in my possession; published version in Gordon B. Hinckley, "Daughters of God," *Ensign*, Nov. 1991, churchofjesuschrist.org/study/Ensign/1991/11.

theological as much as it is grammatical. We've all worked hard to master the intimate pronouns and verb forms of seventeenth-century England. We have a real intellectual and emotional investment in the grammar of such prayer phrases as: "We thank thee that thou hast preserved us and ask that thou wilt watch over us." Again, after putting in thirty or forty years, we hear such language as familiar speech. There is a shock in hearing, "We thank you for preserving us and pray that you will watch over us."

I am firmly convinced, however, that we have confused reverence with grammatical familiarity and, as with inclusive language in the scriptures, it's simply a matter of saying the new words over and over until we get used to them. I suggest that we start praying privately in our own normal speech, using *you* and *your*. It will make these prayers more intimate, more natural, and more loving. It is a pleasant coincidence in our language that *you* is both a singular and a plural pronoun. I think that once we make the grammatical adjustment of hearing the ambiguous *you*, we can then tackle the theological problem of how many people it refers to.

There is, however, a political problem. (There usually is with grammatical points.) The church has a policy on the language of public prayer. Those seventeenth-century pronouns and verb forms have become shibboleths of ecclesiastical respectability that are hard to displace. When I worked on the *Ensign* staff, we prepared a special issue on prayer in January 1976. It included a message by Elder Bruce R. McConkie, "Why the Lord Ordained Prayer," that included ten points he thought essential in understanding prayer. In addition to such points as "ask for temporal and spiritual blessings," and "use both agency and prayer," he also insisted, "Follow the formalities of prayer."

> Our Father is glorified and exalted; he is an omnipotent being. We are as the dust of the earth in comparison, and yet we are his children with access, through prayer, to his presence. ...

We approach Deity in the spirit of awe, reverence, and worship. We speak in hushed and solemn tones. We listen for his answer. We are at our best in prayer. We are in the divine presence.

Almost by instinct, therefore, we do such things as bow our heads and close our eyes; fold our arms, or kneel, or fall on our faces. We use the sacred language of prayer (that of the King James Version of the Bible)—thee, thou, thine, not you and your.[8]

This argument deserves some serious consideration. I do not question that Elder McConkie was absolutely sincere in what he said or that this description represents his experience. However, I honestly cannot say that my best prayers have always been uttered in "hushed and solemn tones." Many of my best prayers have been uttered when I've been all but speechless with fury, or weeping with pain, or near bursting with delight. I know, because these are the prayers when I feel instantaneous and profound contact—not always answers, but unquestionably a fully understanding listener.

Nor do I believe that we "instinctively" assume the posture of prayer. I may hold the world's record for length of term as a Sunbeam (three-year-olds) teacher, and I can state authoritatively that there is *nothing* instinctive about folding one's arms. Assuming this posture requires endless coaching. Likewise, I don't think we instinctively use the "sacred language" of prayer. I think we instinctively try to use the most meaningful language we have, but people who are floundering around trying to decide between "wilt" and "wouldst" are not having a worshipful experience. They are having a confusing experience and, if the prayer is offered in public, probably an embarrassing one as well.

8. Bruce R. McConkie, "Why the Lord Ordained Prayer," *Ensign* 6 (Jan. 1976): 7–12; the quotation is on p. 12. This position is not just a historical one but a very current one. The home teachers' message for February 1990, "Pray Always," delivered by my visiting teachers along with the visiting teachers' message for the same month, concluded its remarks on prayer with: "We can show greater respect to Deity by using Thee instead of you, Thou instead of your, and Thine instead of yours" (typescript in my possession).

For that same issue of the *Ensign* in January 1976, the staff commissioned an article by Don E. Norton Jr., a BYU professor of English, called "The Language of Formal Prayer." It begins by quoting Joseph Fielding Smith's guilt-producing statement that the rise of modern translations of the scriptures that use "the popular language of the day, has, in the opinion of the writer and his brethren, been a great loss in the building of faith and spirituality in the minds and hearts of the people."[9] From that point, the article is well-written and engaging. It explains the rules for using *thou, thee, thy, thine* and their accompanying verb forms and provides several useful quizzes to check knowledge and skill levels as the article progresses.

I remember liking the article very much in 1976; now, I'm rather shocked at myself. It is not that the article's quality has deteriorated in the meantime but that my feelings about how we should relate to God have changed. I recognize now that, even in 1976, I was maintaining a rather complex double standard in my prayer speech. As a missionary a decade earlier in France, I had learned appropriate Mormon prayers which, as a matter of linguistic convention, use the intimate pronouns, *tu-toi*. These are, like their English counterparts of *thee* and *thine*, the only pronouns in French for singular *you*. French, again like English, uses the plural "you" (*vous*) on "formal" occasions whether one individual or several is being addressed. Missionaries were forbidden to *tu-toi* anybody except little children "as a matter of propriety"; but normal French-speakers *tu-toi* lovers, relatives, youngsters, chums, pets—and God. (German and Spanish have similar conventions.)

Clearly, if the church were being consistent about addressing God in the most exalted and formal speech available to them, French members and missionaries would have been counseled to use *vous*.

---

9. Don E. Norton Jr., "The Language of Formal Prayer," *Ensign* 6 (Jan. 1976): 44–47; the quotation is on p. 44.

They weren't, I believe, because the issue was not one of formality at all. The issue was one of having a special language—and in English, a now difficult, abstruse, and abnormal one—reserved for God. I am pleased that this is one cultural manifestation of Mormonism we have failed to export.

As I gained more familiarity and fluency in French, I began using French for my private prayers. I still remember how tender, how affectionate, how close it made me feel to God. Naturally I asked myself why my own language did not have quite this effect. As the daughter of two conscientious and thoroughly orthodox Latter-day Saints, I literally cannot recall ever having heard God addressed as *you* up to that point. I maintained the habit of praying in French for a full fifteen years after my mission because I cherished its intimacy.

The church has been attached to the King James Version of the Bible since its founding; but as Philip Barlow's careful and convincing study establishes, that attachment is largely a historic accident—a combination of tradition and the personal preference, bolstered by the persuasive but illogical arguments, of J. Reuben Clark Jr.[10]

Similarly, the attachment of any special reverence or respect to *thee* and *thou* is based on historical ignorance, a reading backward into a perfectly ordinary grammatical construction of a magical meaning. I commend Roger Terry's excellent two-part article to those interested in more detail.[11]

My point is simple. There is nothing inherently "sacred" about

---

10. Philip L. Barlow, "Why the King James Version?: From the Common to the Official Bible of Mormonism," *Dialogue: A Journal of Mormon Thought* 22 (Summer 1989): 19–43.

11. Roger Terry, "Authority and Priesthood in the LDS Church, Part 1: Definitions and Development," *Dialogue: A Journal of Mormon Thought* 51, 1 (Spring 2018): 1–37, and "Part 2: Ordinances, Quorums, Nonpriesthood Authority, Presiding, Priestesses, and Priesthood Bans," ibid., 51, 2 (Summer 2018): 1–41. In his nuanced discussion of priesthood, he painstakingly unpacks the many ways vocabulary is assigned to, analogized from, and expanded to serve frequently confusing authoritative functions.

obsolete though charming language. The eloquence and beauty of the King James Version deserve our study and love for those qualities—but not because they help us communicate better with God. God does not listen more approvingly to "Wilt thou bless us?" than to "Please bless us." In fact, he probably does not even have to listen more attentively, given his merciful promise to listen to the prayers of our hearts. That being so, requiring children, young people, and converts to make their petitions to the Lord in a fragmentary and foreign formal language reminds me uncomfortably of the situation the Savior condemned during his mortal ministry: "Woe to you. ... You shut the kingdom of heaven in [people's] faces. You yourselves do not enter, nor will you let those enter who are trying to" (Matt. 23:13, New International Version).

At home, we use the Revised Standard Version, the New International Version, the Phillips translation, and *Good News for Modern Man* (or *Persons*). These editions do not use inclusionary language but, as I've mentioned, we're handling that quite nicely on our own. Our intention is simple: we want Christian to understand the scriptures, to seek information from them, and to think about them. We want them to speak directly to him, to convey the spiritual experiences of others, and to be models of and catalysts for his personal spiritual experiences. We don't want the scriptures to lie in a category completely apart from all of his other learning experiences. And, I might mention, Paul and I desire the same results for ourselves.

I think other people will enjoy the same experience. When Paul gave a Christmas Sunday school lesson a few years ago, he read the Luke nativity from the J. B. Phillips version and had several people come up and say, "That was so beautiful! Did you write it?" I suggest that reading the scriptures in an accessible translation will bring a freshness and immediacy to their message that we quite desperately need. From there, it is an equally logical and rewarding step to make them gender-inclusive.

A related grammatical point is the argument that *man* is a generic which includes *women* as part of "all mankind." I concede that the term has, in fact, been so used and still is. But I don't buy the argument. Rather, I see *man* as a categorical noun, the existence of which implies a correspondent: man/woman. Other examples are husband/wife, parent/child, teacher/student, and master/slave. Correspondence is not the same as inclusion. The category of *husband* predicts but does not include the category of *wife* any more than the category of *child* includes the category of *parent*.

It is an unfortunate historical and social fact that most of these categories connote hierarchy—subservience and superiority. Precisely for that reason, then, I think we should be both scrupulous and courteous in acknowledging the real existence of each category. If one category cannot exist without the other, then both deserve to be named. I think that it is much more graceful and practical to simply acknowledge that English contains both parallel terms and inclusive terms: brotherhood/sisterhood/siblinghood, mankind/womankind/humankind, husband/wife/spouse, son/daughter/child. If we want to communicate gender, then let's use the marvelously specific tools our language gives us. If we want to communicate inclusion, then let's not use confusing gender-laden nouns which we must afterwards explain.

For example, a well-meaning attempt at being inclusive painted one unwary general authority into this corner:

"This is my work and my glory—to bring to pass the immortality and eternal life of man." (Moses 1:39)

The word *man* as used above is generic. It includes man and woman, for, as Paul said, "Neither is the man without the woman, neither the woman without the man, in the Lord." (1 Cor. 11:11).[12]

---

12. Gordon B. Hinckley, "Our Responsibility to Our Young Women," *Ensign* 18 (Sept. 1988): 8–11. Address to Regional Representatives. The quotation is on p. 10.

I fully respect the speaker's intentions, but how could it possibly have escaped his notice that *man* could hardly have been so unquestionably inclusive if he had to use both *man* (definitely male in Paul's example) as well as *woman* to define it? I anticipate the inevitable, though probably delayed, day when we will be able to read that scripture as "to bring about the immortality and eternal life of people"—or "souls," or "human beings."

Reading the scriptures inclusively, singing hymns inclusively, and praying with inclusive language are quiet grammatical revolutions that will reshape our reality to make it more truly a partnering—an equal honoring of maleness and femaleness. But it will be inadequate without an underlying commitment, which must be renewed often, to inclusiveness. We must accept the realities of the world we live in and forgive where we can understand; but we must never, never acquiesce in justifying it.

As I read through those often inspiring conference messages, wondering why I felt so sad, I received my answer when I came to the greeting of an apostle to Elder Richard G. Scott, the newest apostle: "Elder Scott, I would just like to add my welcome to the others that have been given to you as you assume this great position. You are joining a unique quorum. It is made up of very common men with a most uncommon calling. There is a spirit, a unity, a devotion in this body like none other you will ever experience. We are excited to have you and your great talent and abilities with us in our quorum. Welcome! Welcome! Welcome!" (73)

Then I knew the source of my sorrow. I will grieve before the Lord until those words can be spoken to a sister as well as to a brother, before the Holy Parents of us all, until we can fulfill in our society the promise of Paul: "There is neither Jew nor Greek, there is neither bond nor free, there is neither male nor female: for ye are all one in Christ Jesus" (Gal. 3:28).

15

Fear Training

I delivered these comments to VOICE: The Committee to Pro-
mote the Status of Women at Brigham Young University, an
association of women students at Brigham Young University,
Provo, Utah, on March 11, 1993, and later as part of a panel
sponsored by Mormon Women's Forum on June 2, 1993. The
following September my stake president excommunicated me.

My topic is fear and how fear is used as a mechanism of social control for both women and men in the church who are committed and active members.

I hasten to add the qualifiers that must be added to every such flat statement. Fear is not always necessarily a bad thing. Fear is not always used with conscious malice by those who employ it. Social control is not always necessarily a bad thing. Nor is the church the only institution that uses social control mechanisms. In fact, it's probably safe to say that the church is one of the more benign institutions that makes high demands of its members in a context that can also be highly supportive.

I ask you most earnestly to remember these qualifications as I work through the main idea. I mean them from the bottom of my heart. I realize that to focus on the purpose and use of fear in the church is to discuss an aspect of our institutional life that we not only want to deny but have, in fact, been carefully trained to deny.

That's what my title means: we are trained to be afraid under circumstances in which we are simultaneously trained to deny that there is anything to be afraid of.

I also ask you to recognize something else. I speak from a position of faith. I profoundly believe the gospel and accept its tenets as my personal joy and as the hope of humankind in this life. I love the Savior and bear reverent testimony to the power of his atonement in my life. I accept the prophetic mission of Joseph Smith and his successors. And I love the church. There is nothing like its wards when they are working as they should—as communities of affiliation, affection, and service.

This topic grows out of a year's worth of research. On August 23, 1991, two weeks after the Sunstone Symposium in Salt Lake City, the Council of the First Presidency and Quorum of the Twelve Apostles issued a statement warning members about "symposia ... that result in ridiculing sacred things or injuring the Church ... detracting from its mission, or jeopardizing the well-being of its members."[1] I, with many others, recognized the statement as directed toward the Sunstone Symposium, but I also did not believe that these dire events had actually happened. Certainly they had not occurred in the sessions I attended.

But I was also interested in the statement as yet another step in the bungling, awkward process by which the church was attempting to talk to its intellectuals. It is a dialogue, not between individuals or committees or representatives but one carried out in the media, with intellectuals approaching conference talks and public statements in the time-honored academic tradition of analysis and interpretation while the official response is faceless, anonymous, directed at no one in particular and at everyone in general, and phrased in lofty abstractions. I began thinking about the rest of that dialogue, prompted in large part by my heart-felt desire that the

---

1. "Statement," *Deseret News*, Aug. 31, 1991, B-1.

dialogue could lead toward mutual forgiveness and reconciliation. I did not like the polarization, the delight with which non-intellectuals or anti-intellectuals within the church exploited official statements, not to carry on a dialogue, but to attempt to intimidate and silence the intellectuals. I also did not like the cynicism of some intellectuals, And I was appalled at the amount of misunderstanding and suffering that was occurring.

I began documenting significant events, speeches, policies, and voices in that dialogue. I gave an oral presentation, first at the East Coast Sunstone Symposium in Washington, DC, and again at the Salt Lake Sunstone symposium in the summer of 1992.[2]

Items relevant to women during January–March 1993 include:

January 31, 1993. *Boston Globe Magazine* published a lengthy article about Laurel Thatcher Ulrich in which she recalled her enthusiasm at discovering the *Woman's Exponent*, the nineteenth-century Mormon women's newspaper. She commented, "These 19th century women were saying things in public that we were afraid to say in church in 1970. They were talking about women's rights in the name of the God of Zion. That was very exciting, and it made me realize that history had a purpose." History also had a personal claim. "I grew up with these images of sacrifice and not measuring up." The writer, Suzanne Gordon, observed: "History helped her to put the past in its proper place. Indeed, her very relationship to history seems to be a brilliant and canny way both to rebel against and yet stay connected to her own traditions."[3]

<hr/>

2. The examples were so numerous that they were sorted in one segment focused primarily on women, in "Landmarks for LDS Women: A Contemporary Chronology," *Mormon Women's Forum* [newsletter] 3, nos. 3–4 (Dec. 1992): 1–20. The second segment was published as "The LDS Intellectual Community and Church Leadership: A Contemporary Chronology," *Dialogue: A Journal of Mormon Thought* 26 (Spring 1993): 7–64. This essay was awarded *Dialogue's* Lowell L. Bennion Prize for Essays in Gospel Living.

3. Suzanne Gordon, "Herstory in the Making," *Boston Globe Magazine*, Jan. 31, 1993, 23–24, 33–39.

February 6, 1993. The *Salt Lake Tribune* published the report of Laurel Thatcher Ulrich's rejection as a potential speaker at BYU's women's conference in April by the Board of Trustees. They gave no reason and BYU officials also had no comment. Laurel says she is "not upset or outraged—just a little puzzled. I always enjoy speaking to young people in the church. ... And I think of myself as a good role model." She had earlier received a standing ovation from an audience of BYU honor students after receiving the Pulitzer Prize, and had lunch with Bruce Hafen and the Relief Society general board. Marie Cornwall, a professor of sociology at BYU, commented, "When they don't provide a reason, it shows a lack of respect to those of us who are trying to plan such events. ... It seems they don't value women scholars and that goes to the heart of what we are."[4] Laurel's Pulitzer Prize was, at the time of this decision, on exhibit at the Church Museum of History and Art in a show about the Relief Society's sesquicentennial. A sidebar to the article reported the truncating of Aileen Clyde's welcome to priesthood leaders at the women's fireside in September 1992 to eliminate an allusion to partnership. Aileen was second counselor in the Relief Society general presidency.

February 7, 1993. Gloria Steinem, speaking to a crowd of more than a thousand in the Foothill Village atrium in Salt Lake City, asked them to do one outrageous thing each day. "It might be as simple as saying, 'Pick it up yourself,'" she said. She also observed, "I'm sure the Mormon Church is responsible for making more feminists than I am." Students from BYU announced their intention to plan an alternative conference.[5] Although she was not identified in the story, the student who made this announcement was Kody Partridge, later one of the two LGBT couples whose successful lawsuit provided a brief

    4. Peggy Fletcher Stack, "LDS Pulitzer Prize Winner Puzzled by Rejection as Speaker at BYU," *Salt Lake Tribune*, Feb. 6, 1993, A-1.

    5. Norma Wagner, "Steinem Tells Crowd: Listen to Inner Self," *Salt Lake Tribune*, Feb. 3, 1993, B-1.

window for legal same-sex marriages in Utah before the US Supreme Court's ruling swept away prohibitions on such marriages nationwide.

February 22, 1993. I received from Elaine Jack an answer to my letter expressing dismay at the decision about Laurel and asking for a reconsideration. In it, Sister Jack expressed her high regard for Laurel and quoted a statement by Margaret Smoot issued for the BYU administration affirming respect for Laurel's "scholarship and achievements," noting that the speaker selection process is both "private" and the university's "right," and then making the following statement: "It is university policy to consult with Board of Trustee members and others as appropriate, but this decision was made by the university administration."[6] Thinking the newspaper reports might have been mistaken in identifying the decision as that of BYU administrators, I made some inquiries. My sources confirmed that the decision was made by the Board of Trustees. The administration may have accepted and implemented it, but the administration did not make it.

February 25, 1993. In a lengthy letter to me, one woman shared her belief that spiritual abuse occurs because men have "fears, deep seated fears, about women and power—spiritual power especially." Out of those fears, she believes, they act irrationally. She told her own story. She came to BYU as a student who loved the church; in some respects it was her family, her source of stability during her parents' divorce. Then her dorm mother instructed her to remove a poster of a popular musician from her room that she had purchased. To her, it represented a "special occasion" that she and her father had attended and enjoyed together." She declined; but a few weeks later, the dorm mother called all the women together, announced that one of their number had been possessed by evil spirits, and that

---

6. Elaine L. Jack, Letter to Lavina Fielding Anderson, Feb. 22, 1993. A California woman who wrote a similar inquiry received a letter that was virtually identical except for the addition of a paragraph inviting her to "share the above information with those sisters in your ward who may be disturbed by the decision." Elaine L. Jack, Letter to Irene M. Bates, Mar. 4, 1993; photocopy in my possession.

she had called in the elders to find the source of evil. They found this seventeen-year-old girl's poster and ordered her to remove it. This is what she says: "I told them I had prayed about this picture and that I felt it was not in any way wrong or immoral. ... They informed me that they had the priesthood and had a better understanding of these things than I did. At this point I reasoned that either I was right and they were wrong, or they were right and I was responsible for a girl being possessed by the devil. ... My confidence in my own communications with God crumbled. ... I could not be certain that I was right. I was a 17 year old woman and they were *two* men, who had the priesthood! They told me that I had to take the picture down and then they could save the girl. It was the final act of compliance. They wanted to see *me* take the picture down. I did, with tears rolling down my cheeks and with the feeling that my spiritual experience counted for nothing in the face of church authority. I obeyed. I complied. It was a wound that made me forever distrustful of authority."

For this young woman, the issue was who could have spiritual experience, and whose spiritual experiences could be accepted as authentic. She summarized, "There are no clear battle lines here. It is not women against men or men against women or power against individuals. It is many things. But fear is at the heart of it. ... It is the fear that creates an 'enemy.' I've been a victim of that fear. We feel we have so much to lose that we're willing to give up our very souls to be a part of the Mormon Church."

March 12, 1993. An ad hoc committee of BYU students, Lynne Whitesides (then president of the Mormon Women's Forum), and I organized a one-day conference on April 28, themed: "Spaces and Silences: An Enhanced Women's Conference."[7] This conference's announcement read:

---

7. This "Counterpoint Conference," sponsored by the Mormon Women's Forum, was sufficiently popular that it continued to meet in Salt Lake City until 2017. For at least its last decade, Janice Merrill Allred and Margaret Merrill Toscano, strong theological voices, shouldered the work of organizing the annual event.

Healthy human beings need both space and silence so they can discover their identity. Not enough smothers us. Too much isolates us. How much is enough? As one woman expressed it: "We live on a knife's edge. If we're 'good,' then we silence ourselves by not talking about the unpleasant realities of our lives, our questions, and our discomfort with things that feel wrong. If we're 'bad' and talk about these things anyway, we are ostracized and marginalized. We lose temple recommends, Church callings, opportunities to speak and serve." Right now, I feel that Mormon women have to deal with too much silence, not enough voice, too much space, not enough community.

Interestingly enough, one of the most frequent comments we conference organizers received during the planning period was, "Aren't you afraid?" In a way, that question is the most sorrowful aspect of this whole sorrowful situation. Why should we be afraid? What do we have to fear from our church, the institution into which we were baptized, whose meetings we attend, in whose temples we marry and worship, whose classes we teach, of whose divine origin we bear testimony? How can we say we're afraid of an institution that exists to bring us to Christ? How can we say we fear priesthood leaders who only want what is best for us? All of these goals and purposes are true. I know them. I believe them. But the fear is real, too.

First, women are afraid of losing their jobs if they're employed by the church. They're afraid of being seen as trouble-makers, of being passed over for promotions, of being derailed or shunted off into dead-end positions. Yes, men are, too. Please remember all of the qualifiers I mentioned at the beginning of my address. They're all still true.

Second, women are afraid of social stigma, of being ostracized in their wards, of being scolded by leaders, of having lessons pointedly directed at them, of being marginalized and silenced, or being denied opportunities to serve or to speak.

Third, women are afraid of what will happen to their children.

All of the mechanisms of marginalization and stigmatization that they fear for themselves can also operate against their children. Even if they can accept mistrust and suspicion for themselves, they are hesitant to make their children bear the same burden. Furthermore, women are afraid that their children will leave the church if they express negative feelings about the church. They do not want their children to jettison the church's good values, its ethic of service, and its expansive theology of personhood, no matter how they may feel about its restrictive social practices.

Fourth, women are afraid of losing their temple recommends, of not being able to see their children married, of not accompanying missionary sons and daughters to the temple. As a result, the meaning of the temple has changed. A friend of mine told me that she and her husband were brooding over the situation involving Laurel, racking their brains to think of some reason that might possibly explain her unsuitability. "Maybe Laurel doesn't happen to have a temple recommend right now," ventured the husband. Their twelve-year-old daughter, who was listening, looked puzzled and commented, "I thought you got a temple recommend so you could go to the temple, not so you could speak at BYU." This little anecdote captures a very thorny problem that lies close to the nub of the issue of social control.

The meaning of the temple has shifted, within the last ten years, I would say, from viewing temple worship as an opportunity to make and renew sacred covenants as part of our relationship with God to viewing the temple recommend itself as a sign that we are acceptable to God's representatives. A young woman who moved recently from my ward volunteered the comment in Relief Society that the two thrills of being endowed and of being married in the temple were important, but the greatest thrill of her life was when she completed the cycle of interviews and received her first recommend. "I held that piece of paper," she said, "that told me I was worthy." I flinched when she said that. I hope life will soon bring her the realization that worthiness is a description of the quality of her relationship to God, not the opinion of men who have temporary ecclesiastical responsibility for her.

Fifth, women are afraid of reflecting badly on their husbands. Men in high office must have "acceptable" wives who know how to behave "appropriately." Being married to the wrong woman can end those dreams for men. Nor do I believe that the men are just being power hungry. Like the women, they desire to serve; and it is deeply painful to see avenues of service shut to them.

Although the plight of women has become more visible, men likewise suffer comparative powerlessnessness in the face of ecclesiastical power and privilege. Like women, LDS men receive the message that there is only one right way or sufficient way to be a Mormon man in the church. This identity is closely linked with social performance, personal righteousness, individual spirituality, and gender roles. Personal happiness and social/spiritual success are promised to the man who will be the right kind of husband, the right kind of father, the right kind of priesthood holder, or the right kind of church worker.

But the church also makes men responsible for having the right kind of wife and producing the correct kind of children. Single men are excluded, marginalized in important ways, and restricted in their contributions—just as women are. Divorced men—like divorced women—frequently suffer from being stigmatized in their wards. The church's insistence that the husband, as priesthood holder, is the family's representative to and from the church strands part-member families in which the wife is the active member and leaves the active husband of an inactive wife with no one to "preside over."

Perhaps more insidiously, the message of the church to the married male is "preside, rule over, control. Make this family respectable." The 1992 official "The Family: A Proclamation to the World," ritualizes this role by assigning nurturing to "mothers" and the triple roles of presiding, providing, and protecting to "fathers," even while it simultaneously asserts that they "are obligated to help one another as equal partners."[8] The church structure promises men membership in ever more exclusive circles of acceptability and power—in elders' quorum presidencies, in bishoprics, in stake high councils and stake presidencies, as regional representatives or area authorities, as temple presidencies, and even as general authorities. But it also pressures men, along with being acceptable themselves, to keep their wives and children in line. What is the personal humiliation to men of this kind of conformity? Do such expectations function as a sort of complex initiation ritual, necessary for the individual male to become a member of a higher inner circle? What happens to a man who becomes an instrument of oppression to show that he is worthy of ruling over an expanded stewardship of the oppressed?

I have phrased this situation in the harshest possible terms. In a vast majority of cases, I know Mormon men are motivated by a desire for the rewards of service, not by a secret lust for power. From the presidencies of Howard W. Hunter to the present, loving and sacrificial fatherhood has been increasingly valorized, sought, and cherished. But in that other fraction of cases, I wonder how many men, acting out of good motives, try to suppress their wives and children as a way of keeping them safe? How many speak with the church's mouth, regardless of their personal feelings, to avoid embarrassment, to avoid the sympathy of other ward members who wonder, "How can he put up with her?", and to purchase respectability for themselves.

When a woman steps "out of line," what does it to do her husband?

---

8. After teetering on the verge of what seemed to be inevitable canonization for "The Family: A Proclamation to the World," the trend dipped sharply for April 2019 general conference speakers, only three of whom quoted it, contrasting, in some years, to fifteen or twenty. It remains to be see whether this diminished trend will be permanent.

If he chooses not to try to "control" her, neither can he "protect" her, and certainly he also bears to some extent the marginalization, ostracism, and stigmatizing that follows. Sharon Conrey Turnbull of Tennessee told me about trying to explain to the stake president an abusive situation in their ward. Sharon's husband, Jay, was present, and the stake president "became visibly agitated," she said. "He kept looking at my husband, trying to get him engaged in the conversation. It was really obvious to me that he was thinking, 'When are you going to step in and control this woman?'" Jay remained a silent and supportive witness, occupying the ill-mapped male territory of allowing a woman to speak for herself, with his permission and support, to other men.

Where are the models for the men who want to be free participants, not part of a chain of command? What are the options for men who want to be partners, not part of a priesthood pipeline? What will be the impact on the men of the church when they fully acknowledge the diminished status and restrictions imposed by patriarchy and hierarchy on their mothers, wives, sisters, and daughters? And then what will be the impact when they take the next step and realize what it has done to them?

But any institution or social group with boundaries needs to maintain those boundaries. Fear is not always bad. Maybe fear of getting pregnant isn't the best reason for avoiding premarital sex, but surely premarital sex is a greater ill than the fear? We all accept the fact that toddlers need to learn not to run out into the street. Does it matter whether they stay on the sidewalk because they fear getting scolded? What's really wrong with fear? Why, really, shouldn't the church intimidate women if it keeps them safer and prevents them from doing things that may destroy their happiness?

I can think of three reasons:

First, fear perverts our purest and highest motives. I'm not talking about members who hate the church, want to leave it, and secretly break as many rules as they can get away with. I'm talking about men and women who love the church, who willingly give it years of service, a significant share of their money, and a high degree of loyalty. It is their very loyalty and love—wonderful, positive qualities—that are perverted and betrayed by fear. You can only take a temple recommend from someone who has one, and you can punish someone by taking a recommend away only if she or he values the recommend.

Second, fear distorts the relationship of spiritual care and nurture that should exist between an ecclesiastical leader and a member. I have heard a number of experiences of students at BYU who have learned the hard way that the ecclesiastical endorsement is an instrument to coerce conformity, not a way of growing spiritually. Many students have been put in the brutal and abusive circumstance of having to choose between repentance and their education.[9]

Nor is the situation confined to BYU. I spoke to a woman earlier this week who recounted a devastating history of sexual, incestual, and physical abuse. When she found the church, embraced the gospel, and married a good man, she thought she was safe forever. She is in her third year of recuperating from ecclesiastical abuse so shredding and mauling to her that she literally lost her will to live for a time. She was not telling her story for revenge, out of anger, or even for her own sake. She said, "I just want someone to understand that some of us are being hurt who just can't afford to be hurt anymore." Where do you go when your priesthood leaders won't believe you or actively turn against you? There is no

---

9. Exposure in 2018–19 of abusive policies in dealing with rape, long-time discrimination of LGBTIs at BYU, and the recent relaxation of those punitive policies provide hope that such wisdom and respect for individuals and their agency will continue. Without acknowledging the poor publicity, *BYU Magazine* published an extensive description of the university's "unique" and "refocused" Honor Code. Peter B. Gardner, "Sitting Down in the Honor Code Office," *BYU Magazine*, Summer 2019, 10–11.

alternative. There is no back-up system. There is no ombudsman. There is no advocate.

Third, fear stunts our spiritual growth by making us morally dependent on another human being to determine what's right and what's wrong. The young woman in my ward is an example.

But am I making too much of this? Surely some of these members have just overreacted? Surely some of these ecclesiastical leaders have just been overzealous? Surely there's a way to sit down and work these things out? Yes, yes, and yes. But all of these questions and all of these yesses are also ways of saying, "There's nothing *really* to be afraid of."

Well, I'm afraid there is. In a hierarchical system where the power is very unevenly shared, where some parties always have more credibility than other parties, where claims of spiritual power can always be used to justify social and political demands for conformity, and given that it is the nature of "almost all men" (D&C 121:39) to abuse power once they have it, the system itself teaches women and men to think twice before they speak, to tailor their utterances anxiously to the audience, to maintain masks, and to live silently behind them.

When the church works well, it is beautiful, nurturing, support-ive, and growth-promoting. I believe that most of the time it does work well. But even one lapse is one too many and calls out for per-sonal and institutional correction. I think such lapses will continue as long as we give too-unlimited power and too little accountabil-ity to people who are, alas, all-too-limited. For me, the solution is not to create new hedges of rules about how power may be exer-cised, over whom, and by whom, but rather by sharing power more broadly among a free people.

One of my favorite scriptures is from Isaiah 58:4–9. It's in the con-text of fasting, but I think it has applicability in this context as well:

> Behold, ye fast for strife and debate, and to smite with the fist of wickedness: ye shall not fast as ye do this day, to make your voice to be heard on high.

... Is not this the fast that I have chosen? to loose the bands of wickedness, to undo the heavy burdens, and to let the oppressed go free, and that ye break every yoke?

Is it not to deal thy bread to the hungry, and that thou bring the poor that are cast out to thy house? when thou seest the naked, that thou cover [them]; and that thou hide not thyself from thine own flesh?

Then shall thy light break forth as the morning, and thine health shall spring forth speedily: and thy righteousness shall go before thee; the glory of the Lord shall be thy rearward.

Then shalt thou call, and the Lord shall answer; thou shalt cry, and he shall say, Here I am.

These are the voices that cannot be silenced. These are the voices that give me hope that, at some point, all voices will be heard.

16

"The Only Life You Save"

THE SEDUCTION OF SACRIFICE

On September 18, 1999, Counterpoint, an annual conference sponsored by the Mormon Women's Forum, honored me with its annual Eve Award, in recognition of my support of an expanded role for Mormon women. This address is printed here for the first time.

It's an honor to accept the Eve Award today on behalf of all women who have asked questions and have refused to be put off with easy answers, who have resolved in their hearts to find out and follow the will of God for them, and who have exercised leadership for themselves, their families, and their communities.

I'd like to begin with an illuminating little parable, which swam anonymously over the Internet:

> Sherlock Holmes and Dr. Watson went on a camping trip. After a good meal and singing around the campfire, they lay down for the night and went to sleep. Some hours later, Holmes awoke and nudged his faithful friend: "Watson, look up at the sky and tell me what you see."
>
> Watson looked and, after a minute, replied, "I see millions and millions of stars."
>
> "What does that tell you?" asked Holmes.
>
> Watson pondered for a minute, then answered. "Astronomically, it tells me that there are millions of galaxies and potentially billions

of planets. Astrologically, I observe that Saturn is in Leo. Horologically, I deduce that the time is approximately a quarter past three. Theologically, I can see that God is all powerful and that we are small and insignificant. Meteorologically, I suspect that we will have a beautiful day tomorrow. What does it tell you, Holmes?"

Holmes replied, "Watson, you idiot! Someone has stolen our tent!"

I believe in the stars in the gospel sky for Mormon women. I've seen them and been inspired by them. I try to follow them in living my life. But I think that Mormon women work so hard to see those stars—astronomically, astrologically, horologically, theologically, and meteorologically—that we've colluded in our own deprivation. I think we've been looking at the stars and drawing deductions from them, so to speak, about the patriarchal system we live and move within—trying to find a place, trying to work out accommodations with patriarchy, trying to make good marriages and to bring up children who respect themselves and respect the agency of others, but we've failed to notice the most important fact. Someone has stolen our tent. We wouldn't have to work so hard, bend ourselves around so many corners, and accommodate so many sharp edges if it weren't for the system.

This address is a status report on what I see happening with women in the Mormon church at the turn of the century. As one of my friends, Maryann MacMurray, optimistically said, "Progress is when things are getting worse more slowly." In that sense, we could, I suppose, call this a progress report. But it begins with some unpretty, unoptimistic, unpleasant observations.

My dear friend Irene Bates, who has brought me so many good things during the years of our enduring friendship, first introduced me to the poem, "Dream Work," by Mary Oliver, a British writer. Oliver describes the moment of "finally [knowing] what you had to do," accompanied by the need to surmount the hindrances of voices shouting "bad advice," your house beginning to "tremble," and the demands to "Mend my life!" It required courage to set out through the "wild night" with "sheets of clouds" and over a road filled with "fallen branches and stones." But by continuing,

> ... there was a new voice
> which you slowly
> recognized as your own,
> ... determined to save
> the only life you could save.

I believe that Mormon women need to make the same discovery: that the only life we can save despite our sacrifices is our own and that the only way we can save it is to trust the new voice within us. The context in which we must do it is a Mormon culture which, after a generation wakened to feminism—and that's our generation—reacted decisively to suppress feminism by making it clear to the next generation that they had to choose between feminism and following the prophet. After six years of Elaine Jack, Chieko Okazaki, and Aileen Clyde heading the Relief Society, we now have a hard-working but almost invisible presidency whose dominant message is gratitude for acting under priesthood direction and a president who wants Mormon women to come home from the mall and write their family histories.[1] When was the last time you heard a serious public discussion on the pros and cons of priesthood for Mormon women from someone who wasn't already excommunicated?[2] And except

---

1. Mary Ellen Smoot: "I would like to see women get out of the mall and away from the television, and start writing their own story, [and] research their past," she told a reporter as one of her presidency's three goals. The others were: (1) women "need to learn to be happy in the era of life we are in" and (2) Mormon women should "set that example [of happiness] for other women in the world" because "I don't see women in the world as happy women." Kirsten Sorenson, "Women's Leader Strives for Happiness: New LDS Relief Society President Hopes to Help Women Better Themselves," *(Ogden) Standard-Examiner*, Aug. 23, 1997, posted on the Internet, Aug. 27, 1997; printout in my possession.

2. Mary Ellen Smoot also stated: "I don't think our women want the priesthood. ... [And even if they do,] ... you cannot change the Savior's church." Ibid. In

for Janice Allred's faithful continuing witness to and exploration of the role of the Divine Mother in our identity and salvation, when was the last time you heard a serious public discussion about Mother in Heaven? The First Presidency has spoken, and the thinking may not have been done—indeed, in most cases, I feel that the thinking has not even begun—but the discussion is over. Yes, the excommunications and firings have stopped; but that's because, with the exception of a few courageous individuals, most of the targets have just hit the deck.

In this context, then, I want to talk about the dichotomy between sacrifice and selfishness that is usually presented to us as Mormon women. Mary Oliver talks about the voices calling us to "mend my life." These are seductive voices. They speak, not to our weaknesses, but to our strengths. They appeal to our love, to our desire to serve and lift, to our willingness to postpone our own needs, and to our desire to facilitate the achievements of others. Love and service are strengths, not weaknesses. We find true joy in exercising these gifts. But the central paradox of the matter for Mormon women is that we are allowed to have strengths only if we use them to benefit others—not because strength is beautiful in and of itself and not because there is value in *our* being strong. I think the central fact of discourse about women in the church is the built-in double message, the poison in the words of praise, the judgment in the words of appreciation.

Please understand that I am engaging in special pleading to make a point. I want us to focus on the missing tent for a few minutes,

this she was echoing church president Gordon B. Hinckley's official pronouncement on LDS women; see his comments in an interview with Mike Wallace, reprinted in "This Thing Was Not Done in a Corner," priesthood session, general conference, Oct. 5, 1996, Internet version in my possession. See also his statement to the *New York Times*: "I think we place women on a higher pedestal than any organization of which I know. And I think that the vast majority of our women would say so." Qtd. in Gustav Niebuhr, "A Mormon Church Leader Weighs Dissent and Growth," *New York Times*, July 4, 1994, 6, national edition.

not the stars. I do not think that men are evil, that no progress has been made toward equality for women, or that patriarchy is motivated by malice. I reject the dichotomy, so eloquently chronicled by Martha Sonntag Bradley, that positions feminism as the opponent of motherhood.[3] The work of parenthood is crucial work—and real work. It deserves top priority from both fathers and mothers. I do not devalue or diminish the choices of women in the employment vs. at-home motherhood debate that has polarized Mormon women shamefully for a generation. I think the fact that over 64 percent[4] of Utah women are working sends a commentary of its own about the economic circumstances of many women, nor do I respect as realistic the advice of the current Relief Society general presidency that women who need to work can do it from their homes thanks to modems, faxes, and computers.[5] While some women can and do work from home, what unconscious assumptions is Mary Ellen Smoot, mother of seven, married to an affluent real estate developer in Bountiful, making about the economic status of Mormon women, and what unconscious assumptions is she making about the

---

3. Martha Sonntag Bradley, panel presentation, "The Church, Gender, and Politics: From ERA to DOMA," Counterpoint Conference, Sept. 17, 1999. Notes in my possession.

4. This 1999 figure is two decades old but is still generally accurate. Rod Decker, *Utah Politics: The Elephant in the Room* (Salt Lake City: Signature Books, 2019), ch. 4, provides greater context: Utah compared to American statistics, women compared to men, labor-force participation, and pay scales. Beginning in the 1980s, Utah women's employment exceeded that of American women, a fact that has changed only in degree from then until the present. Decker also cites a 2018 study showing that "Utah had the second largest pay gap of any state"—70 percent of men's wages compared to 80 percent nationwide. See esp. pp. 99–101, 104–106.

5. Undated newspaper clipping in my possession. Compare with a similar statement by Wendell Ashton, President Gordon B. Hinckley's former missionary companion in the British Mission, who appeared on a call-in radio talk show. He attributed the problem of gangs largely to two working parents and suggested that parents arrange their work so that one of them can be home after school or, by using faxes and modems, do part of their work at home. *Religion on the Line*, KTKK Radio (630 AM), Salt Lake City, Apr. 9, 1995, hosted by Van Hale, audiocassette in my possession.

quality of care that children are receiving while theoretically coexisting with a home business?

To the extent that this church is a vehicle for the gospel of Jesus Christ, I think there is nothing to equal or surpass it. To the extent that it is a socially constructed patriarchy, I think it has a long reckoning chalked up against it. I think that, as an institution, it is afraid of its own women, that its men in general are selfish and lazy enough to prefer being served by women to being partners with them, that these men lack the moral imagination to envision true partnership, and that they are genuinely ignorant of the pain they are inflicting on the women in their lives and the pain in which they are consequently living themselves. I acknowledge with appreciation the exceptions, chief among them my own partner, Paul.

I have a few quotations and examples, all taken from recently published reports, that will give the gist of what I mean. You can consider them in the nature of those dot-to-dot pictures that children connect, searching for the next number, and then discovering at the end what they have drawn.

President Hinckley, in addition to repeatedly telling Mormon men to consider their wives and children as their "most important asset" or "investment"—(and we all know that assets are to be "managed")—also has a message to women. Please note this technique of what I call prescriptive praise. Under the guise of praise—which I think he means quite sincerely—he is actually providing a script for Mormon women and how they should act, with the clear subtext that they are deviant and unworthy if this description does not fit their lives. Please also note that it deals not only with matters of behavior but also with thought and feeling.

> ... the women of the Church ... love this Church, you accept its doctrine, you honor your place in its organization, you bring luster and strength and beauty to its congregations. How thankful we are to you. [By this simple choice of pronouns, President

Hinckley has created an us/them dichotomy with women as the Other.] How much you are loved, respected, and honored ….

You bring a measure of wholeness to us. You have great strength. With dignity and tremendous ability, you carry forward the remarkable programs of the Relief Society, the Young Women, and the Primary. You teach Sunday School. We walk at your side as your companions and your brethren with respect and love, with honor and great admiration. It was the Lord who designated that men in His Church should hold the priesthood. It was He who has given you your capabilities to round out this great and marvelous organization, which is the Church and kingdom of God. [Note how vague these capabilities are in comparison to the concrete possession of priesthood.] I bear testimony before the entire world of your worth, of your grace and goodness, of your remarkable abilities and tremendous contributions.[6]

In another place, he makes it painfully clear who the important person in the LDS marriage is—and it is not the woman:

It has been my responsibility to extend calls to scores of men, their wives, and their families to leave all behind and go into the mission field. … I have never had anyone turn down such a call. There have been a few who, when I have inquired concerning their circumstances, we have felt that they should not go. … But … a strange thing happens. Once a man has been talked with concerning such an assignment, … he never seems to get over it. Before long he is writing a letter or telephoning to say that he is ready to go.[7]

I checked the selections on leadership in *Teachings of Gordon B. Hinckley*. In a fairly extensive passage of about 183 words, he quoted eight individuals, all of them men. Of the nouns referring to persons, forty-six were masculine: man, men, son, father, boy, bishop, etc. A few such as leader, executive, or administrator, were

6. *Teachings of Gordon B. Hinckley* (Salt Lake City: Deseret Book, 1997), 697. This quotation is from his general conference address, Oct. 1996.

7. Ibid., 566–67.

technically gender-neutral; but, in the context, were also masculine. He quoted no women. Only three references to women appeared in these selections. The first acknowledged that both men and women supported the bishop. Second, he again counseled men to "treat your wives with kindness" because "you will never have a greater asset in all of this world." But this is my favorite: He described a conversation with a man who had been a counselor in a bishopric and a stake presidency, a mission president and a regional representative: "and he doesn't have a thing to do [now], except to sit home with his sick wife and ... tend her. He is almost destroyed because he has nothing to reach out to, no responsibility in this kingdom."[8] Maybe it's just me, but I had trouble visualizing a scenario in which a woman was being destroyed because "all" *she* was doing was nursing her sick husband. In other words, when it comes to leadership in the church, both men and women loyally support the bishop. Women are assets to their husbands, but taking care of a sick wife is a destructive activity unless it is balanced by a more interesting and fulfilling administrative calling.

Here's another example. Elder Boyd K. Packer pointed out that "the needs of men are seldom, if ever, discussed in priesthood quorums. Certainly they are not preoccupied with them. They discuss the gospel and the priesthood and the family!" He counseled women to "follow that pattern" and "not be preoccupied with the so-called needs of women," promising, "As you give first priority to your family and serve your organization [the Relief Society], every need shall be fulfilled, now, every neglect will be erased, every abuse will be corrected, now or in the eternities."[9] In other words, if you should be so unfortunate as to have needs, then the solution is to devote yourself to Relief Society. And if, after doing so, you should still be so unfortunate as to have needs, or be suffering

---

8. Ibid., 304–11.
9. Boyd K. Packer, "The Relief Society," *Ensign*, May 1998, 73.

abuse, or be enduring neglect, then it's still your fault because somehow you did it wrong.

Glen Lambert, a therapist specializing in drug addiction and recovery in Salt Lake City, has observed: Although Mormons abuse illegal substances at a lower rate than the national average, Utah chillingly "ranks in the top three in the nation in the use of every prescribed drug. There is strong evidence to suggest that we abuse legal substances like no other culture."[10]

Lisa Mountain, a therapist speaking at the 1999 Sunstone Symposium as a panelist on eating disorders, provided these appalling statistics: In Utah alone it is estimated that over 40,000 women are suffering with an eating disorder; the actual figure may be higher because so much shame and stigma is attached to eating disorders. Nationwide, 75 percent of American women "are dissatisfied with their appearance"; 50 percent of nine-year-old girls and 80 percent of ten-year-old girls have dieted. Fifty percent of American women are on a diet at any one time; 90–99 percent of these diets do not produce long-lasting weight loss. Young girls are more afraid of becoming fat than they are of nuclear war, cancer, or losing their parents. An estimated 25 percent of college women have an eating disorder. Anorexia nervosa has the highest mortality rate of any psychiatric diagnosis: up to 20 percent of those diagnosed with this disorder die from its effects.[11]

---

10. Glen Lambert, panelist on "Latter-day Addictions," Sunstone Symposium, July 1999, audiocassette SL99 #275 in my possession.

11. Lisa Mountain, panelist on "Latter-day Addictions," Sunstone Symposium, July 1999, audiocassette SL99 #275 in my possession. She continued that Mormonism can both ameliorate and exacerbate therapy for her Mormon clients. Some positive aspects include the support system offered by the strong family culture, personal peace from feeling that God will help them, and a sense of order and structure to mitigate the personal chaos they experience. Some negative aspects are expectations of high external achievement, perfectionism related to the idea of "be ye therefore perfect," and the church's need for control. The Word of Wisdom restrictions also play into the individual restrictions of the person with eating disorders. Sometimes

A Salt Lake newspaper reported in April that a dice game called "Bunko" (which I've never heard of)

> has caused such chaos in some neighborhoods that several Mormon bishops, mostly in Sandy and Murray, have ordered from the pulpit that women in their wards not part[icipat]e. It is not because the game could be considered gambling, which the church opposes. The problem: Bunko typically is played at a different member's home each month. The hostess is responsible for gifts for the winners and, apparently, the competition goes beyond the game. Some players are buying more expensive gifts than other players. Some have been trying to outdo the others on what is served for dinner, and reportedly, some women have gone into debt remodeling their homes to outclass their neighbors.[12]

Apparently no one challenged the bishops' self-imposed mandate to set these women straight and save them from themselves, which is distressing enough, since I think most bishops don't need any more encouragement to freely interfere in the lives of ward members. But at the same time, I'm so ashamed that Mormon women are wasting their time in such trifling, trivial, time-wasting activities, and in such juvenile competitions. Perhaps Mormon women really do deserve the patronage, the condescension, and the micromanagement with which they are often greeted by their leaders?

A question-and-answer about the use of the church's TempleReady computer program in the July *Ensign* elicits this advice from the Temple Department's managing director: "Make sure descriptions and

---

the woman with an eating disorder can use the disorder as "a silent protest" against being deprived of voice and participation by the church's patriarchal characteristics. The focus on appearance and the importance attached to being a "good example" can translate into looking and acting perfectly. Many of these issues are common in the national society but can be intensified in Mormon society.

12. Paul Rolly and JoAnn Jacobsen-Wells, "Bishops Debunk Tame Reputation of Bunko Games," *Salt Lake Tribune*, Apr. 14, 1999, B-1. They add, "The church's General Authorities obviously have bigger concerns. They have no official position on Bunko."

titles are not included to names submitted for ordinance work. For example ... *boy, girl, child, widow, Miss, Jr., Dr., Judge, Reverend [Rev.], Colonel [Col.] ... General [Gen.]* ... Because the identity of a woman can be derived from the name of her husband, the use of *Mrs.* is an exception."[13]

This same issue of the *Ensign* includes an anonymous account by a "single mother" (Name Withheld) whose thirteen-year-old daughter, Mandy, tells her she is pregnant. The first-person account focuses on the struggle of Mandy's mother to accept adoption as the best option for the baby. The mother participates in the counseling sessions with LDS Social Services, the school counselor, the bishop, and finally, slowly, accepts Mandy's decision, which she made "about midway through the pregnancy" to relinquish the child. I'm not saying that this is the wrong decision or that LDS Social Services acted improperly, although a spate of lawsuits in recent years have challenged exactly these points. I was wondering where Mandy's father was and where the father of Mandy's baby was. The article does not mention either one. This article has only one audience: Mormon women who are supporting their unwed daughters in keeping an illegitimate baby. This article was printed to hold up an example: there is one right way to react to your daughter's unwed pregnancy; and if you don't do it this way, you're wrong.[14]

Another story of exactly this type also appears in the same issue of the *Ensign*. Kandy Martin, a thirty-one-year-old single woman with four married sisters, enjoyed her numerous nieces and nephews and was even present at the birth of her niece Kayleigh, but "I felt awkward being the only single sibling and wasn't sure where I fit into our family picture or what I could offer as a single woman. I tried to have faith that someday the blessings of marriage and motherhood would be mine, but at times my faith wavered and I

---

13. Paul E. Koelliker, "Now That Members ...," *Ensign*, July 1999, 65–66.
14. Name Withheld, "But What Was Best for the Baby?" *Ensign*, July 1999, 62–63.

felt very alone." When Kayleigh asked her, "Are you a mommy?" Kandy felt "pain that seemed to shoot through my whole being." When Kayleigh followed up with, "Are you an aunt-mommy?" Kandy, in her own words, "[saw] my role a bit more clearly. ... I was like a mommy, and I was an important person in her life. ... I now understand that one does not have to be married or have children to be of value. There are many opportunities to influence the lives of others and to be touched by those who surround us."[15]

It's also clear who the target audience for this little essay is. It is women who have heard, all too clearly, the message that Kandy heard: that you do have to be married and have children to be of value, and that if you don't manage to do this on your own, you can achieve pseudo-worth by achieving pseudo-motherhood status. The order of the suggested indexing topics is alphabetical, but it ironically underscores the same message. The topics are, in this order, "family, motherhood, personal worth, singles."

I also note that I have yet to read an *Ensign* article by a single man describing "pain that seemed to shoot through his whole being" because he has not yet achieved fatherhood, or finding peace of mind in pseudo-fatherhood as an uncle or feeling himself of worth despite his obvious status as a spiritual and social cripple. I also haven't read any *Ensign* articles from unwed fathers who are dealing with nine months of suffering as a result of having impregnated a thirteen-year-old girl, from abusive husbands who are praying to hold their families together, from incestuous fathers who are striving to repair the damage they have caused, or from men who are "struggling" to find their role in the work-place. What's the matter? Doesn't guilt work on Mormon men? Or would such articles contradict President Boyd K. Packer's approving statement that men just don't spend any time talking about their so-called needs

---

15. Kandy Martin, "'Are You a Mommy?'" *Ensign*, July 1999, 28.

in quorum meetings and that women would be better off if they didn't either?

Certainly men are not immune from stigmatizing and punishment in the church. Just to make it clear that the new Mormon culture, characterized by "follow the prophet" and by "The Family: A Proclamation to the World," is an equal-opportunity abuser, a divorced man may not serve as a bishop for ten years after the divorce nor as a temple ordinance worker for five. A divorced man may not be hired to teach at BYU nor in the Church Education System as a seminary or institute teacher; if he is teaching at the time of the divorce, he is fired.[16]

And a final example comes from this same issue of the *Ensign*. The visiting teaching message, which is on charity as the pure love of Christ, prominently features the story of a woman whose father had been abusive to her (in unspecified ways) throughout her childhood. The woman had, not unnaturally, resented him "for many years." Reading the scriptures and "our prophets" convinced her that she was being hard-hearted, so for nearly two years she "prayed and fasted" to feel differently. During a meeting "on parenting," she experienced a great sensation of love for her father. After the meeting, she and her husband drove to her father's house. Her father was "very angry" when he saw her and slammed the door. She kept ringing until "he finally let me in but only because I wouldn't leave." She writes:

> I had no idea what I was going to say; I assumed it would be something like, "I forgive you for not being a very good dad." But I had it all wrong. As we sat together, I took his hand in mine, looked

---

16. Panel presentation: "The Patchwork Quilt: Blended Families," Robyn Davis, Craig W. Davis, Alan Rudd, Debra Rudd, Brad Collings, Kathy Collings, Sunstone Symposium, Salt Lake City, July 1999, audiocassette SL99 #273 in my possession. I understand that some, if not all, of these policies have been rescinded since 1999.

into his eyes, and said, "I want you to know I love you, and I am so glad you are my dad." The miracle was that I actually meant what I said! My anger and hurt had turned to love. ... His personality didn't change, [she was writing this "many years later"] but a loving Heavenly Father healed my heart.[17]

Again, this message is not wrong—much about it is right, including the sheer fact that the very topic appears in the *Ensign* at all—but it grossly oversimplifies reality and heavy-handedly scripts a response. I believe in the transforming power of charity, the pure love of Christ. I have experienced it. But because this message does not specify the kind of abuse that occurred, then any woman whose past includes anything from incest to neglect can read herself into it. The message does not acknowledge the genuine damage of abuse, the father's responsibility to change, or the fact that forgiveness is a complicated process that does not happen on demand and may, in fact, take a lot more work and a different kind of work than two years of fasting and prayer. Again, what this message communicates to women whose stories do not or cannot match this one is that they are failing spiritually.

And my final dot in this picture we're drawing is a story that comes from a Native American tradition—I'm afraid I don't know which one or even if it is genuinely Native American. I'm including it to underscore that Mormonism, even though it is not on the forefront of solving sexism, did not invent all of it. The friend who passed it on to me works with Young Women; she, in turn, received it from someone who didn't know her very well but was helpfully giving her the "Corn Husk Doll" as just the thing to give Mormon girls the message they needed.

A long time ago, the parents were so busy working, they needed

---

17. "Clothed in Charity," [Visiting teaching message], *Ensign*, July 1999, 55.

help watching their children. So they asked the Creator for help. The Creator made a doll from [a] cornhusk to watch the children.

The Corn Husk Doll played with the children. She taught the boys how to use their bows and arrows. The Doll showed the girls how to cook and sang songs to the little babies.

One day, a rain storm came. The Corn Husk Doll gathered the children into the long house. She told stories to the children.

After the rainstorm ended, the children and the Corn Husk Doll went outside to play. The Corn Husk Doll looked down at a puddle and saw her reflection. She saw that she was very beautiful.

The Corn Husk Doll went into the woods and picked flowers to put in her hair. She put beautifully colored shells on her dress.

The Corn Husk Doll forgot about the children. The parents had to watch their children and still try to get their work done. The parents called to the Creator. They told him that the Corn Husk Doll was not watching the children as … was her responsibility.

The Creator … asked the Corn Husk Doll what her responsibility was. The Corn Husk Doll answered that she was there to watch the children. Then the Creator asked her why she was not watching the children. She replied that she had to pick flowers for her hair and sew beautiful shells on her dress. With her beauty they should adore her, and she should not have to watch the children.

At that, the Creator took away Corn Husk Doll's face. That is why Corn Husk Dolls do not have a face, so they remember to watch the children as the Creator created them to do.[18]

There's a lot we could say about this story, but let me point out only what a constricting message it is for young girls to hear—that they were created for a purpose that serves the convenience of others, a purpose they were not consulted about and did not consent to (at least, in this life), that God will punish them if they neglect their duty by taking away whatever they value, and worst of all, that

18. [No author], "The Cornhusk Story," n.d., typescript, 1 p. Photocopy in my possession.

their beauty—which we may say symbolizes personality or individuality—is the very trait that will bring punishment and deprivation upon them. In a lesser form, we have seen this same message perpetrated in the last three Young Women general meetings, stressing that the primary responsibility of teenage girls is to serve their families. Examples included girls who were not just helping their mothers but taking over the functions of absent or dead mothers.

Are we going to see change anytime soon? Not with this First Presidency. In an interview commemorating the fifth anniversary of his ascension to the presidency, President Hinckley, in response to the question "What about the role of women?," responded, "What about it? It's wonderful."[19]

Even though Sheri Dew, as President Hinckley's biographer, worked hard to show that President and Sister Hinckley had a strong, companionable marriage and that he missed her when she was not traveling with him, a number of incidents gave another message: that his truly important relationships were with men. For example, President Hinckley told about seeing missionaries "enraptured" by President Harold B. Lee. "I have seen few things more touching than a strong young man embracing the President and then later with tear-moistened eyes saying, 'Never have I been so near to heaven.'"[20] He himself told a BYU audience: "I hope that I shall have the opportunity of embracing the Prophet Joseph Smith and of thanking him and of speaking of my love for him" (359). When President Hinckley was called into the First Presidency by President Spencer W. Kimball, he knew about the call for a week before it was announced, but he did not tell Sister Hinckley nor did

19. Transcript of interview with Gordon B. Hinckley published Saturday, Feb. 26, 2000, conducted Feb. 23 by Vern Anderson and Peggy Fletcher Stack; print-out of the transcript, posted on the *Tribune*'s website, in my possession.

20. Sheri Dew, *Go Forward with Faith: The Biography of Gordon B. Hinckley* (Salt Lake City: Deseret Book, 1996), 329. Additional references from this book are cited parenthetically in the text.

he attempt to get permission from President Kimball to do so. She found out in a "quick call" between the meeting of the joint council at which he was sustained and set apart and the press conference at which it was announced (381–83).

Although told as humorous experiences and—I believe—genuinely experienced as such by the Hinckley family, I did not find amusing a number of stories: When President Hinckley took his children to visit California for the first time in the 1950s, he drove them to the beach, then, five minutes later, announced: "'Okay, you've seen the ocean. Let's go'" (186). He typically called on Sister Hinckley to speak at stake, mission, and even regional conferences without advance warning (337), obviously communicating the expectation that she would speak briefly and without delivering a substantive message. On one of his numerous Asian tours, which lasted anywhere from four days to four weeks, he had still not decided, the night before departure, if she "was going to accompany him. When Marjorie finally asked if she should plan to leave with him the next morning, he responded with a hint of impatience, 'Do we have to decide that *right now?*'" (338) His daughters are described as "faithful *but* forthright" (526; emphasis mine), a different message than "faithful *and* forthright," and Dew quotes daughter Virginia Hinckley Pearce's introduction to a panel on which Marjorie Hinckley and the three daughters spoke at a BYU women's conference: "Our father is here, probably out of self-protection. We realize he can always jump up and bring the meeting to a close if we get out of control" (527). It's a revealing "joke."

This dot-to-dot picture that we've constructed shows, in my opinion, sacrifices that women are asked to make for the church and by the church that are unacceptable for three reasons: First, they are sacrifices that men are not asked to make. Sheer playground fairness and the Golden Rule provide a withering critique of this lopsided demand. Second, there is no feedback mechanism so that those asking women to make these sacrifices understand the cost, in terms of women's lived experience, that such sacrifices really require. And third, there is no on-going dialogue to see if the ends supposedly achieved by these means could be achieved in another way. In the endowment ceremony, when Eve asks, "Is there is no other way?" she is solemnly assured that there *is* no other way by a Distinguished Personage whose other name is the Father of Lies.

Let me add again all the qualifiers—yes, I know that the church does not have a monopoly on these problems, that many of them grow out of our larger American culture, that they are not necessarily driven by malice, and that many, many women find the actions they are thus persuaded to take acceptable, even a source of blessings. I also affirm that sacrifice is a true principle of the gospel, but I think that the voice calling us to sacrifice should be the voice of God, not the voice of a human being who benefits directly and materially from that sacrifice.

If we look at the model for all sacrifice—the atoning sacrifice of Jesus Christ—I think that he showed us how important sacrifice was. He also showed us the proper mode of sacrifice. His sacrifice consisted in doing for us what we couldn't do for ourselves; in this way, the oft-cited model of parenthood holds true. The baby can't feed her/himself, clean her/himself, or protect her/himself. The parents have to sacrifice their own comfort, time, and often their simple human need for sleep to meet the baby's needs.

But I think that sacrifice in the church and for the church frequently does not meet these criteria. All too often, it consists of someone in authority telling someone in a subordinate position to do something that the authority figure doesn't want to do himself, wouldn't do himself, and furthermore, can aggrievedly say that he shouldn't do himself. To take an obvious example, President Hinckley counsels women, both collectively with all members and specifically as women, to "get all the education you can. Education unlocks the door of opportunity for you and helps you to achieve in life something good and wonderful and worthwhile. Don't destroy your chances. Don't destroy your opportunities. Watch the little decisions in life that make the tremendous difference."[21] Simultaneously, married women with children are told never use their education except at home with their children unless they are forced into the workplace by the disappearance of their husbands.

I think this situation presents women with one of the cruellest of double-binds. It devalues their efforts to be obedient to the first instruction—efforts that usually require significant sacrifice both from their parents and themselves to acquire the education in the first place. Furthermore, in most fields, you can't drop out for fifteen years and then reenter as though you had just graduated from college; thus, the decision not to use the tools you have acquired with such effort amounts to the nullification of education for many women on the altar of motherhood or, in the case of unmarried or childless women, the constant undercutting of their professional achievement by reminding them that what they're doing is really not as important as what they should be doing.

I repeat, the seduction of sacrifice is that it appeals, not to our weaknesses but to our strengths—to our love, to our desire to serve, to our idealism, to our willingness to communicate an ultimate commitment to God. Yet I think these sacrifices often fail the test of whether we are doing what the person being sacrificed for cannot do for him/herself.

And I think the rhetoric of sacrificing for the church is an especially subtle trap. Who is the church? The prophet? The people in the ward? The pioneers who crossed the plains? We don't use the phrase anymore that they did in the nineteenth century: "a prisoner for conscience's sake" or sacrificing "for the gospel's sake." Nearly

---

21. Member meeting at Schenectady, New York, Oct. 17, 1998, "Messages of Inspiration from President Hinckley," *Church News*, Sept. 4, 1999, 2.

always, in the nineteenth century, sacrificing "for the gospel's sake" meant sacrificing comfort, reputation, family ties, and security for yourself. For your conscience. For your own soul. For the burning faith that this was truth, the precious pearl of great price, and that you had found it and that life would be meaningless without it, no matter how long you lived, if you gave it up. This hunger to sacrifice good things to achieve something better meets the criterion of a Christlike sacrifice: only you could make the sacrifice of "the world" to put yourself in a position, through the mercy of Christ, to receive truth and salvation.

I believe this point deserves some stress because true sacrifice also fulfills something that is so fundamental to the self that full self-actualization is impossible without it. This was certainly true of Christ, who, despite the enormity of the sacrifice asked of him, affirmed to Pilate: "To this end was I born, and for this cause came I into the world" (John 18:37). It is true of the athlete in training who gives up many other good activities and indulgences so small as a single potato chip to offer the very best she has within her and can, in biblical language, "rejoiceth as a strong [one] to run a race" (Ps. 19:5).

And this dynamic—that sacrifice expresses our deepest, best self—explains why any leader or any institution who asks us to sacrifice our conscience, our integrity, or our spiritual compass is asking something that verges on blasphemy. The sacrifice of conscience usually occurs in one of two ways. Let me give you extreme examples, since they're easier to follow: (1) The Mountain Meadows Massacre example. The leader describes a course of action which you, as a dutiful and righteous follower, are supposed to espouse. This internal dialogue then takes place: "Killing all those immigrants just doesn't seem right to me but it must be right because the leader says so; so I'll suppress my own feelings and obey the leader and on his head be the consequences." In many cases, the leader is only too glad to assure you that he is willing to take the consequences because he's so sure he's right; and even if he's not, he's following instructions received from his own file leader.

A subtle subset of this example is the secret unacknowledged temptation: "Killing those Arkansas immigrants probably is wrong, but I'm really mad at them anyway. Fortunately, Isaac Haight (stake president) says they're guilty of the blood of the prophets and it's my duty to kill them, so I'll tell my conscience I'm just doing my duty and not listen to it saying, 'You're just indulging in blood lust and shoving the consequences off on Haight.'"

The second way we are often asked to sacrifice our conscience is to pollute and deny the whisperings of the Holy Ghost. In this scenario, we tell ourselves: "My conscience is telling me something—maybe that it violates the Golden Rule to withhold priesthood from women or marriage from gays—but what if I'm wrong? What if this isn't a moral choice after all? What if I can't tell the voice of my conscience from the voice of sloth or anger or lust? Better not to listen to it at all." This method totally abrogates the only moral compass we have—just puts our heel on it and grinds it into the dirt. If we can't tell the difference between right and wrong for ourselves, how can we possibly tell whether the decision to turn our decision-making capability over to an authority is either right or wrong?

Now of course, cases of terrible self-delusion exist. We must check our conscience by reason, by inspiration, by the message of the scriptures, by trusted authorities, and by the most persuasive possible arguments of critics taking the opposite position. But when it comes right down to it, if we don't trust the whisperings of that internal voice, then we don't even have the basic equipment for making a moral choice.

Let me close with the inspiring words of Nelson Mandela, speaking at his presidential inauguration in 1994:

Our deepest fear is not that we are inadequate. Our deepest fear is that we are powerful beyond measure. It is our light, not our darkness, that most frightens us. We ask ourselves, "Who am I to be brilliant, gorgeous, talented, fabulous?" Actually, who are you not to be? You are a child of God. Your playing small does not serve the world. There is nothing enlightening about shrinking so that other people won't feel insecure around you. We are born to make manifest the glory of God that is within us.[22]

That is not a bad manifesto for all of us as we move out into the wild night, striding down the road littered with stones and fallen branches, seeing the burning stars above us, listening to the voice within us, and saving the only life we can save.

22. Qtd. by Don Corbett, panelist on "We Are Many Parts: We Are All One Body," Sunstone Symposium, July 1999, audiocassette #136 in my possession.

17

Women in the *General Handbook of Instructions*

I made this presentation at the Sunstone Symposium, Salt Lake City, on August 14, 1993. Six weeks later, my stake president excommunicated me. The handbook I describe and quote here—the version dated 1989—is a historical artifact that has since been revised at least twice. If I provide more current information than 1993, I cite the source of the update in the footnote. Also, the emphasis on secrecy has been largely dialed back, with one handbook for bishops, stake presidencies, and mission presidencies (which is still restricted), and a separate handbook for auxiliary and ward officers. This second handbook is available officially on-line and so, unofficially, is the leaders' handbook. (On January 30, 2020, the First Presidency announced that a new online handbook would replace Vols. 1 and 2 on February 19.) The implications of condensing Sunday meetings from three hours to two and the "home-centered, gospel-supported curriculum," effective January 2020, have yet to become fully apparent. The church's detachment from the Boy Scout program, the announcement of a children and youth program effective in 2020 that will be internationally uniform, the back-pedaling from seeing homosexuality as automatic grounds for excommunication, and the replacement of home and visiting teaching by a program of "ministering" are other markers of organizational change generated by the current (2020) LDS president, Russell M. Nelson.

My dear brothers, sisters, and friends, it's a pleasure to be with you at the crack of dawn on a pleasant summer Saturday morning to discuss a thrilling piece of writing like a procedures and policy manual. My interest in the *General Handbook of Instructions* stems from my larger interest in the differential treatment of men and women in the church. What, I wondered, would the handbook that describes church procedures and policy to male priesthood leaders communicate, both overtly and silently, about the place of women in the church?

Let me share with you my two general conclusions: First, women are virtually invisible in the handbooks except where sexuality or sealings are involved. Second, the important division is not between men and women but between male leaders and members, both male and female.

MENTIONS OF WOMEN

The invisibility of women begins on the first page of the handbook where it describes the distribution of the handbook. Those authorized to receive it include general authorities, general church department heads and auxiliary presidencies, directors of temporal affairs, regional representatives, temple presidents, stake presidents, bishops, mission presidents, district presidents, and branch presidents. The instruction sheet states: "Local Church officers could make a copy of the handbook available temporarily, as needed, to such leaders as high councilors, high priests group leaders, elders quorum presidents, stake mission presidents, ward mission leaders, executive secretaries, and clerks."[1] You were probably keeping a running tally in your head of who does not have a copy. Except for the general auxiliary presidencies, no woman is on the list. I believe that this list also conveys another message: that no woman *needs* to see a handbook.

---

1. *General Handbook of Instructions* (Salt Lake City: Church of Jesus Christ of Latter-day Saints, Mar. 1989), iii; hereafter cited parenthetically in the text by page number.

Granted, male members without these specific callings also are precluded from having the handbook; but I submit to you that there is an enormous emotional difference in impact on the two groups. A man may have already been or may confidently anticipate being one of these officers at some point in his life. It does not take extraordinary imagination to think that one day you might be a clerk—if you are a man. And certainly the other offices are not impossible either for men to imagine, although, in modesty, they may not take that step. But if you are a woman, the imaginative effort of thinking "Someday, I may be a bishop" is roughly equivalent to thinking, "Someday, I might be a horse." I use the hyperbole to make a point. Women have to become a different species to read themselves into the handbook in the way that, in my opinion, men can do with very little effort.

This point became clear to me only slowly as I read on and then back through the handbook. Probably like most readers, I filled in the sparse administrative language with memories of past bishops and stake presidents, with my father, twice a bishop, with my husband, who has served in both a bishopric and on the high council, with my brothers-in-law. "How would they behave in this situation?" I asked myself. "How would they interpret these instructions?" I also asked myself, "Could a woman do this job? How does this policy or this information impact women? Where would they fit in these instructions?"

When I reached the section on "Church Discipline" (section 10) I suddenly realized that I could see only men applying the instructions. The only role for women was to be the recipients of or to be acted upon by the policies, procedures, definitions, warnings, actions, and levels of discipline. As I tried to read myself into this section, there is no question which side of the desk I was on. Perhaps this was an inevitable reaction since my stake president, disturbed by my *Dialogue* article on ecclesiastical abuse, considers me unworthy of a temple recommend and has suggested that "other disciplinary actions may be necessary"[2] if I continue to document cases of ecclesiastical abuse. This realization, not surprisingly, affected my reading of the rest of the manual and, I might add, made it considerably less benign.

I do not, however, think this is a purely personal reaction. A woman, responding on an Internet site this spring, to the announcement of the newly stiffened missionary requirements, pointed out her feelings about the handbook's inaccessibility:

> It is a book that remains in the bishop's care. One cannot see it without asking his permission. One cannot photocopy pages and take them away to study. ... You [she was responding to a male participant] may have had access to this book and not understand what it might feel like to have a book that contains instructions about how you are to be dealt with, and not have it readily accessible so that you can understand the implications of what it is saying. ...
>
> If such rules are going to exist, they ought to be published in a place where we have access to them. If I were the parent of a disabled child, ... I would not want to spend a lot of time preparing them [sic] for missionary service, only to learn later that they will not be allowed to serve.
>
> ... I do know that it is not fun to be a woman and not know the rules by which you are going to be judged.[3]

I'm giving you my conclusion first because I think where I ended up emotionally is more important than where I ended up intellectually. Based solely on the handbook of instructions, the church could operate very nicely, organizationally and structurally, as an all-male organization. But now for specific references to women.

---

2. Marlin S. Miller, Letter to Lavina Fielding Anderson, June 3, 1993. In fact, he excommunicated me three months later. Although he cited as grounds both "conduct unbecoming a member" and "apostasy," it was more probably my refusal to accept his instructions to stop talking with members struggling to understand experiences of ecclesiastical and spiritual abuse.

3. Arta B. Johnson, Electronic transmission, Mormon-L, May 25, 1993.

I first checked the index. There are no references under "women" or "wives." The entry for "mothers" says, "See parents." "Sisters" refers the reader to "lady missionaries." There are no entries under "men" but under "husband" is the subentry, "call extended to wife." There are five entries for "fathers." "Relief Society president" has twelve entries; "bishop" has sixty-three.

The first two lengthy chapters are on "Church Administration" and "Meetings," complete with charts about who may call whom, who needs to sustain whom, and what releasing procedures are. These activities and functions are all male directed and male centered. A ward, I was interested to learn, must have "at least 300 members … and thirty active Melchizedek Priesthood holders" (1–5). In other words, the members are important, but one special tenth is essential.

Women may sing in Relief Society choirs for stake conferences (2–1), keep the sacrament tablecloths "clean and pressed" (5–4), and "offer prayers in Church meetings" (11–3). "Unmarried women ages twenty-one through thirty-nine may serve full-time missions for eighteen months" but "should not feel obligated and should not be urged unduly to serve full-time missions" (7–1).[4] "Auxiliary organizations may not have checking accounts or petty cash funds" although "Melchizedek Priesthood quorum funds and Scouting funds" must have their own checking accounts (9–3). The Relief Society president may attend stake and ward welfare services committee meetings with priesthood leaders. The Young Women's and the Primary president may attend an even smaller handful of meetings at which priesthood leaders are present. The general handbook's descriptions of these meetings do not include any mention of

---

4. Despite this official reluctance to encourage women missionaries, they accounted for 30 percent of the missionary force, according to Quentin L. Cook's April 2019 conference talk. See www.lds.org/general-conference/2019/04/43/Cook?lan=eng. This is the first time, to my knowledge, that the percentage of women's participation has been officially reported.

consultation, discussion, exchange, conferring, dialogue, or consensus. In other words, there is no indication of what a woman would do in such a meeting besides be there. The wife of a student ward's bishop should stay in the resident ward with her children (3–3). "Mature, qualified students, both men and women, should be given leadership opportunities in student stakes and wards" (3–3). New converts should be ordained to the Aaronic Priesthood soon after baptism; the explanation justifying this policy is one to which I wholeheartedly subscribe: "If they are worthy of baptism, they are worthy to hold the Aaronic Priesthood" (4–1). Clearly, women are so completely invisible at this point that the possible misreading of this sentence which I have just made did not enter the minds of the writers. Fathers are supposed to attend the ordinations of their sons; there is no mention of mothers (4–2). "Only those who hold the Melchizedek Priesthood should particiate [sic] in the ordinance of naming and blessing children" (5–1). Repeatedly, the duties and privileges of "worthy fathers" are stressed; worthy mothers are not mentioned once in the handbook.

Sexuality and sealings are sections that come closest to dealing directly with women, but the overall impression is highly negative because the policies exist to eliminate or resolve problems. For example, bishops are assigned the rather bizarre role of fashion controllers for brides, being instructed to "review … requirements for temple wedding dresses with each bride and her parents as early as possible in the planning stages." These dresses, by the way, should be white, long-sleeved, "modest in design and fabric, and be free of elaborate ornamentation." Pants and nondetachable trains are not permitted.[5]

Abortion is "one of the most revolting and sinful practices" of this

---

5. *Bulletin*, 1992–1, 2. These instructions replace those in *Handbook*, 6–3: "Brides may wear white wedding dresses in the temple if they have long sleeves and modest necklines. All sheer material should be lined. Gowns designed to be worn with long dress pants and dress pants are not acceptable in the temple."

day, but even in cases where it is permitted,[6] the language of decision-making assumes that a "couple" is involved and that the bishop
should be "consult[ed]" (11–4). Single women who conceive a child
through artificial insemination are "subject to Church discipline"
(11–4). Women "who voluntarily submit to abortions growing out
of their immoral conduct will not be called on full-time missions"
(7–1). Unwed mothers of at least age seventeen who choose to keep
their child "should be welcomed into Relief Society."[7]

The section on sealings is complicated and extensive (6–4 to
6–6). Gradually I recognized what it reminded me of: deeds trans-
ferring parcels of property from one owner to another. A time-only
wedding can be performed in a temple if the wife has been sealed to
a previous husband. She can be sealed to a deceased husband from
whom she is currently divorced only with the written consent of
her present husband, if any, and the surviving widow, if any, of the
deceased candidate. A woman sealed to a former husband may not
be sealed to a present husband without a cancellation of sealing. The
excommunication of a husband or wife "suspends but does not can-
cel their sealing." "A deceased woman sealed in life to one husband
may also be sealed to another man with whom she lived as a wife." "A
deceased couple who lived together as man and wife may be sealed
even though there may be no documentary evidence of marriage."[8]

---

6. These cases include conception as the result of incest or rape, when a medical authority certifies that the mother's life or health is jeopardized, or when the
unborn child is, in medical opinion, suffering from lethal birth defects.

7. *1991 Supplement to General Handbook of Instructions* (Salt Lake City:
Church of Jesus Christ of Latter-day Saints, 1991) 9. This policy establishes that
marriage is preferred, or if that is not "feasible," "placing the infant for adoption."
See Chap. 14 for an official example of pressure to place the baby for adoption.

8. The language of the handbook is determinedly male. Sacrament meeting
speakers are to speak in "a spirit of ... brotherhood" (2–5). Pronouns are universally male, even in a context that obviously can include women. For example, at
baptisms, the one performing the baptism should "call the person by his full name"
(5–3) and if an adult endowed member, not sealed as a child in a family, wishes to
be sealed to foster parents, "he must obtain permission" from the First Presidency

In short, explicit mentions of women are minimal. In most cases, they are not singled out for special treatment nor specifically excluded. They are simply erased by being stirred in with "all members," and this leads me to my second point: the leader/member dichotomy.

THE LEADER/MEMBER DICHOTOMY

The foreword to the handbook explains its purpose:

> This handbook has been prepared to guide priesthood officers so "that they themselves may be prepared, and that my people may be taught more perfectly, ... and know more perfectly concerning their duty, and the things which I require at their hands" (D&C 105:10). The instructions in this handbook should guide servants of the Lord in directing the Church and helping to strengthen families. (xi)

Duty, direction, requirement, instruction—Strengthening families sounds almost like an afterthought. I had anticipated subconsciously, I suppose, that at least part of the leaders' task would be defined as testifying of Christ's love, of the atonement's power to change lives, and of helping people to grow. I found nothing remotely similar. In fact, the picture that forms from these pages of what leaders do is rather unpleasantly intrusive and aggressive. Bishops instruct, direct, conduct "searching" or "detailed" interviews, report (endlessly) to the stake president, make assignments, issue callings, make sure that two people are present to open tithing envelopes, and ensure that Christmas decorations are not flammable. I looked in vain for any instructions to love the members, to listen to them, to try to understand them, to consult with them about their needs and desires, to respect their agency, to enjoy their diversity, and to be guided by the Spirit.

(6–6). The section on disciplinary councils, or church courts, states: "All references to transgressors are in the masculine gender, but include the feminine" (10–1). Encouragingly, the Oct. 1991 supplement, in speaking of preparation for a patriarchal blessing, says, "The member may fast if he or she chooses" and speaks of an "unwed parent" as "him or her." I consider these steps toward inclusiveness to be important.

The omission of any reminder to the bishop or stake president of the role of the Holy Ghost was particularly startling. Such instructions appear literally only three times. First, "Members should be guided by the Holy Spirit to answer for themselves personal questions about wearing the garment."[9] It seems to me that encouraging members to be guided by the Spirit could be profitably applied to many, many areas in addition to this one. Second, "Decisions on Church discipline are within the discretion and authority of bishops and stake presidents as they prayerfully seek guidance from the Lord" (10–9). Again, it seems to me that local leaders could be encouraged to "prayerfully seek guidance" on many, many topics where only a dry, administrative guideline is given. Even in the section on counseling, church members are told to "make a diligent effort, including earnest prayer, to find solutions and answers themselves"—which definitely isn't bad, as far as it goes; but it continues: "If they need help, they are to consult freely with their bishops and receive from them the counsel they need" (11–2). The assumption is that the bishop unquestionably has the needed counsel.[10]

The handbook is to be destroyed once a new edition replaces it.

9. Compare "Instructions for Priesthood Leaders on Temple and Family History Work," n.d., 1: "Members should seek the guidance of the Holy Spirit to answer for themselves any personal questions about wearing the garment." Lengthy instructions about various styles and colors of garments for endowed members in the military conclude: "Bishops normally should not attempt to interpret this information for members. Rather, endowed persons, having read it or had it read to them, should decide for themselves what to do under the circumstances." "Instructions for Priesthood Leaders on Military Relations," 1990, 3.

10. The tone of the handbook is directive, even peremptory. It is extremely rare that the reason for a policy is given. I found only three explanations: "Local leaders should discourage" adopted children from trying to identify their biological parents "to protect the rights of the adoptive parents" (6–7), and artificial insemination using any but the husband's semen is discouraged because it "may seriously disrupt family harmony" (11–4). See also the policy forbidding wards and stakes to use the official church logo on locally produced materials because "improper use of the Church logo hampers the Church's efforts to register it as the official Church trademark." *Bulletin 1992–2*, 2.

(p. xi) Why? Well, obviously, such a policy has a non-sinister function. You don't have old handbooks cluttering up the office. But it also means that there is no sense of history, no sense of change over time except personal memory, no documentation that things were different in the past and, consequently, will almost certainly be different in the future. The explicit instruction to "destroy," coupled with the spelled-out list of who may have a manual, also suggests urgency and danger, as though something terrible will happen if other people have access to handbooks.[11]

But there's a more optimistic way of looking at this issue. Perhaps the secrecy itself will eventually backfire. If members of the church do not know these rules, they can reasonably protest being held accountable to them; and ultimately, if they have no voice in shaping the policies that impact so heavily on their spiritual lives, it seems to me that they can point out that they have bound themselves by no covenant to accept them.

THE LARGER PROBLEM

But I was disheartened by reading through this handbook with its assumptions of the need to control, its minute legalistic job descriptions and meeting formats, its lists of rules and regulations, and especially by its unconscious assumptions of the superiority of leaders and the inferiority of members. I want to concentrate on this last point. I see this assumption in the handbook as part of a larger and sadder trend in the church, and that is the deliberate creation and maintenance of a gulf between leaders and members.

---

11. I learned recently of a scholar who requested permission at the Historical Department library to see the instructions for handling welfare cases during the 1950s. He was instructed to submit his request in writing, explaining what he would do with the information. He was informed that receiving such permission would require the decision of a committee which would have to meet at least once and perhaps twice to make such a decision, so that he should expect a delay of at least two weeks. Fortunately, the materials for the time period of interest were available at the University of Utah without any preliminary paperwork.

This gap is particularly pronounced when it comes to general authorities and members. According to the handbook, these relationships are characterized exclusively by two negatives: Members are not to "record General Authority addresses given at regional or stake conferences, missionary meetings, or other local meetings" (11–1), and members are discouraged "from calling, visiting, or writing to church headquarters about personal matters" (11–2). Granted, part of the reason for the second policy, though not the first, is to relieve part of the increasingly complex burden for general authorities. This distancing of general authorities from followers has, in my opinion, intensified and accelerated sharply within just the last five years. Let me cite three examples.

First, Elder Dallin H. Oaks's April 1989 conference address, "Alternate Voices," was, in my opinion, an attempt to silence the voices of all but general authorities. He marginalized "alternate voices" within the church, disfranchised members as representatives of the church, and eliminated dialogue and discussion, leaving only the options, for members, of silent listening or "contention."

Elder Oaks's disfranchisement of members as church representatives essentially deals with external or public relations. He uses the term "Church leaders" or "representative of the Church" five times within four crucial paragraphs in juxtaposition to "members" or "volunteers,"[12] which is also used five times.

> Church leaders are sometimes invited to state the Church's position at a debate or symposium. ... But the Church is directed to avoid disputation and contention. Moreover, if a representative of the Church participated in such an event, this could have the unwanted effect of encouraging Church members to look to

---

12. The term "volunteer" is an odd one, since most members of the church have callings that, at least theoretically, come from God through priesthood channels in exactly the same way that the priesthood leader's calling comes. The use of "volunteer" suggests misguided and unwanted zeal.

the sponsors of alternate voices to bring them information on the positions of the Church. ... Church leaders should avoid official involvement, directly or indirectly. Volunteers do not speak for the Church. ... The Church's silence [does not] constitute. ... an admission of facts asserted in that setting.[13]

The structure of Elder Oaks's argument clearly juxtaposes leaders and members. The term, "Church leader," is usually situation specific, ranging from the Primary president at an in-service meeting, to a stake president at stake conference. Elder Oaks, however, uses "leader" to mean exclusively "general authority," a cultural and perhaps theological innovation of his address with which I am very uncomfortable. In this context, the Young Women's general president, a general board member, a missionary, that missionary's president, or a stake president would not be a leader but a member. Thousands of LDS women would perhaps be surprised to learn that Barbara B. Smith's energetic defense of the church's anti-Equal Rights Amendment position during the 1970s and the mobilization of those same women to engage in public protest (while concealing their church membership) was not made as a church "leader."

In short, to Elder Oaks, members are not leaders and, which is more troubling, leaders do not seem to be members. I am disturbed by an image of leadership that defines itself as different in kind from members, that sets itself sharply apart from members, assigns members to be "examples" and "missionaries" for the church, denies that these "volunteers" represent the church, refuses to provide "authorized" representatives except as it chooses (which, I think, implies that it holds itself aloof from dialogue, questioning, or providing explanations which may be discussed), and then also insists that its silence does not become one of the elements of that dialogue. If a friend treated me in such a way, I would not know which to deplore

---

13. Dallin H. Oaks, "Alternate Voices," *Ensign*, May 1989, 28.

first—the naivete of thinking that refusing to converse is not a message, or the arrogance of claiming a relationship but refusing the demands inherent in friendship.

The other two examples involve private, internal church settings. At April 1993 general conference, Elder Russell M. Nelson focused on prescribing "proper priesthood protocol" or "complete deference to … an order of correct procedure."[14] He then devoted the rest of his address to a list of such procedures. The first is to call priesthood leaders by their titles. (I need hardly mention that women have no such titles, so despite valiant efforts at parallel address by scholars such as Neylan McBain, they are always the

---

14. Russell M. Nelson, "Honoring the Priesthood," *Ensign*, May 1993, 38. President Nelson has marked his succession in January 2018 to the presidency of the church by issuing a flood of instructions, many of them characterized as "revelations" to him while all such changes imply his approval. They include banning the use of "Mormon" as a noun or adjective; replacing home and visiting teaching with a more informal program of "ministering"; shortening the three-hour block of Sunday meetings, in place since 1980, to two hours; instituting "Come, Follow Me," a "home-centered, Church-supported" curriculum; equipping missionaries with smartphones; allowing women missionaries to wear dress pants; incorporating high priest quorums into elders quorums (ward seventies quorums had already been integrated into one of the other two quorums); and providing leaders in the U.S. and Canada with "new" guidelines on counseling members and dealing with abuse. "Inspired Direction," *Ensign*, May 2019, 121, lists sixteen such changes made so far during the Nelson presidency. A seventeenth, a training program required of priesthood leaders and those working with children or youth, was announced on August 18, 2019. Although moving in a beneficial direction, it still failed to take the important step of teaching children and youth how to identify exploitive behavior and take steps to stop it. While President Thomas S. Monson's health gradually worsened, President Nelson made other significant pronouncements, among them the policy in 2015 of declaring gay couples who are legally and lawfully married to be "apostates" and excluding their children from church ordinances such as baptism. On April 5, 2019, Dallin H. Oaks, speaking for the First Presidency at a leadership conference, eliminated the second provision and modified the first by declaring a legally married couple no longer to be apostates subject to church discipline although they were still considered to be in "transgression." This "policy" was thus reduced in severity to an "adjustment."

addressor, never the addressee.)[15] When a presiding officer "comes into a meeting where you had been presiding, please consult with him immediately for instruction," Elder Nelson tells bishops and stake presidents. In a meeting, no one speaks after the presiding general authority has spoken. The stake president is to "remain at the side of your file leader until excused." The reason he gives is that the general authority "may be impressed to give additional teaching or direction. And you may also prevent problems. For example, if a member asks a question of your leader that should not have been directed to him, you are there to respond." Apostles honor seniority even to the point of "entering or leaving a room" in seniority.[16] A friend who observed the party of general authorities returning to Salt Lake City after the dedication of the San Diego temple confirmed that they entered the plane in order of seniority.

In May 1993, Elder Boyd K. Packer spoke to the All-Church Coordinating Council, a speech that was reported by the Associated Press within a few weeks as singling out homosexuals, feminists, "and the ever-present challenge from the so-called scholars or intellectuals" as "dangers" to the church, and as having "made major invasions into the membership of the Church."[17] I do not know

---

15. Speaking earlier in the same conference, Elder Dallin H. Oaks began his address, "The Language of Prayer," with a lengthy introduction about the importance in military, judicial, and ecclesiastical settings of using correct titles: "The use of titles signifies respect for office and authority. The words we use in speaking to someone can identify the nature of our relationship to that person. They can also remind speaker and listener of the responsibilities they owe one another in that relationship. The form of address can also serve as a mark of respect or affection." *Ensign*, May 1993, 15. He does not point out that the use of an honorific title by a subordinate reinforces nonegalitarian relationships, emphasizes the power differential between the two, and reduces the psychological and social base of the subordinate.

16. "Honoring the Priesthood," 39–40. Elder Nelson suggests, rather improbably, it seems to me, that John the Beloved reached the tomb before Peter but hung back because "he deferred to the senior Apostle" (40).

17. Boyd K. Packer, "All-Church Coordinating Council," May 18, 1993, 4, photocopy of typescript in my possession.

what the All-Church Coordinating Council is, who its members are, or what its duties are. That in itself is disturbing, since its members apparently have significant responsibilities. But perhaps even more disturbing to me was an anecdote with which he began. He tells of being newly appointed as supervisor of seminaries and Institutes of Religion in 1955 and coming to see Elder Harold B. Lee, who was then just junior to Joseph Fielding Smith. Elder Packer said:

> Elder Lee had agreed to give me counsel and some direction. He didn't say much, nothing really in detail, but what he told me has saved me time and time again.
>
> "You must decide now which way you face," he said. "Either you represent the teachers and students and champion their causes or you represent the Brethren who appointed you. You need to decide now which way you face." Then he added, "Some of your predecessors faced the wrong way."[18]

Elder Packer then related several incidents of "facing the right way" and, not surprisingly, urged his listeners to do the same, by which he meant that they were not to "represent" anyone but the general authorities. They were not to "become advocates" for members who are "hurting" or "think they are not understood." He offered no suggestions for how general authorities may receive information about members or from members. Rather, he warned that when church officers become "their [members'] advocates—sympathize with their complaints against the Church, and perhaps even soften the commandments to comfort them, ... then the channels of revelation are reversed."[19]

My image of the church is of a community, an extended family, in which the different parts value each other, work to understand each other, listen to each other, and try to help each other. I see faces turning in many directions, down to a child, up to an older

18. Ibid., 1.
19. Ibid., 6.

adult, right or left to a friend and back again. Elder Packer's image is a chilling one of only two directions, of rigid role definitions in which leaders speak and members listen, of faces turned resolutely away from those in pain. It is an image of marionettes, of robots.

I think I am not mistaken in identifying this gulf as having been created by the leaders. Yes, members contribute to its maintenance out of an anxiety about orthodoxy, obedience, and celebrity thrills. But in organizational terms, it primarily serves the need of leaders for docile, passive, compliant followers who will not challenge directives, will not insist that their needs merit the same consideration as the leader's desires, or will not expect to be consulted and listened to. It is hard not to see this relationship as self-serving and potentially, if not actually, abusive of the spiritual life of members.

It is fortunate indeed that the religious life of most members of the church is lived in families, neighborhoods, wards, and stakes. Although there are exceptions, these settings function as communities of affection, affiliation, and learning. A man who is a fanatic (and fantastic) scoutmaster today may be a struggling bishop tomorrow and a bored Sunday school superintendent five years later. A woman who may not like the church's financial devotion to the scouting program[20] and who resists the scoutmaster's enthusiasm will teach his daughter in Laurels and be his wife's visiting teaching companion. This man will be aware that there are other opinions about how useful the money spent on scouting is. He will set her apart for a calling in the Relief Society, be grateful for her influence on his daughter, and eat her casserole when his wife has an operation. They will pray with and for each other. The fluidity of callings, the presence and visible contributions of women, and the

---

20. Effective January 2020, the church officially severed its relationship with Boy Scouts of America, replacing it with a churchwide "Children and Youth" program allegedly designed for the participation of girls as well as boys. An unpublicized reason may be the BSA's refusal to continue excluding gay Scouts and leaders.

long-term growth observed in oneself and in others over time all work against rigid roles, an emphasis on protocol at the expense of service, and the systemic devaluing and demeaning of some segments of the congregation at the expense of others. Exposure to real people in real wards, in other words—rather than isolation behind walls of protocol and rules—intensifies my testimony that the gospel is lived out in relationships. Jesus warned his disciples:

> Beware of the scribes, which love to go in long clothing, and love salutations in the marketplaces,
>
> And the chief seats in the synagogues, and the uppermost rooms at feasts. (Mark 12:38–39)

I wonder if this could apply to leaders who insist on strict dress codes, enjoy deference paid to them, and regulate behavior among themselves by strict protocol. I think of the consoling counsel of the Book of Mormon prophet Jacob:

> O then, my dear brothers and sisters, come to the Lord, the Holy One. Remember that his ways are righteous. ... The Holy One of Israel guards the gate. He does not have a servant there. No one can come in except at the gate, and he cannot be tricked. ...
>
> He will open the door to whoever knocks.

The next part of this scripture is often, I think, quoted against intellectuals. But I wonder if it applies to anyone who displaces Christ as the gatekeeper, keeping people out, or pouring energy into rulemaking and rule enforcement rather than the pure gospel of love and good works. The scripture continues:

> He will open the door to whoever knocks, but he hates those who are proud because of their wisdom and education and riches [and perhaps we might add, their special positions or their special access to special information]. If they do not throw away all those things, and think of themselves as fools before God, and become humble, he will not open the door to them.

... the things which are for those who are truly wise—that is, the happiness prepared for the saints—will not be given to them.[21]

Truly, the charge to seek humility and true wisdom is one to which it behooves all of us to pay serious heed. And here, Jesus himself set the example. To settle a dispute among his closest disciples about the protocol of precedence, he stripped off his clothes, girded himself in a towel and washed the feet of his apostles. I believe this model of humble service is one that is still, despite terrific forces in the other direction, alive and well in the Church of Jesus Christ.

---

21. 2 Ne. 9:41–43: Lynn Mathews Anderson, *The Easy-to-Read Book of Mormon*, photocopy of typescript, Feb. 1993. The authorized version of the Book of Mormon renders this passage thus:

> O then, my beloved brethren, come unto the Lord, the Holy One. Remember that his paths are righteous. Behold, the way for man is narrow, but it lieth in a straight course before him, and the keeper of the gate is the Holy One of Israel; and he employeth no servant there; and there is none other way save it be by the gate; for he cannot be deceived, for the Lord God is his name.
>
> And whoso knocketh, to him will he open; and the wise, and the learned, and they that are rich, who are puffed up because of their learning, and their wisdom, and their riches—yea, they are they whom he despiseth; and save they shall cast these things away, and consider themselves fools before God, and come down in the depths of humility, he will not open unto them.
>
> But the things of the wise and the prudent shall be hid from them forever—yea, that happiness which is prepared for the saints. (2 Ne. 9:41–43.)

18

Circles

I wrote this essay about the meaning of the LDS temple in December 1992 and January 1993 at the invitation of a magazine aimed at a popular LDS audience. To the best of my knowledge, its appearance here is its first publication. I last participated in temple rites the first week of September 1993.

I live in a city encircling a temple. I calculate directions and distances in relation to it. Sometimes, as I drive to the temple at five in the morning, long before sunrise, I am alone on the broad streets.

I think without words about what it means to live in a city centered on a temple. I grope toward understanding what it means to possess and be possessed by a holy place. I sense within myself generations who have also turned their faces toward a holy place that is both history and geography.

I sit waiting with the others, men and women clad in white. I read again Solomon's prayer of dedication for his temple. That temple organized the world of his people around it. The climactic verses are a prophecy, foretelling a time of captivity when his people will be taken far away from their temple. Even there, Solomon prays, even then, may "they turn back to you with all their heart and soul in the land of their captivity ... and pray toward the land you gave their fathers, toward the city you have chosen and toward the temple I have built for your name ..." (NIV 2 Chron. 6:38). This is a prayer of circles, of turning toward the center, of focusing attention deeper and deeper toward that center.

On the row in front of me, two older women lean together, whispering softly in German. They are in a land not of their birth, but in this place they are at home. Their faces have the same look. They could be sisters. Or is it just that both of them have the same deep stillness? They know why they are here. They know what they are waiting for.

After Solomon had created his circles, drawing his people around the sacred space created for God, he then invoked that holy presence: "From heaven, your dwelling place, hear their prayer and their pleas," he implored. "Arise, O Lord God, and come to your resting place" (2 Chron. 6:39, 41).

We are creating the resting place within ourselves. Across the aisle sits a young man, dark-haired, dark-skinned. His face is still, stilled. His eyes are closed. He brings his hands together, a repose that is still intense. I feel within myself the same circle close around stillness. I feel a humility that is trust, a waiting that is faith, a quietness that is hope.

I look at the hands of the women in the rows ahead of me. Not their heads. White-coifed, their heads are mostly the same. It is the hands that tell me things: the blue-veined hands of elderly women, joints a little crooked with arthritis, perhaps trembling a little. The smooth hands, sleek with youth, firm and strong. Mostly pink or peach-colored hands. Here and there brown—all shades: golden brown, reddish brown, chocolate brown. Hands with rings or without. Hands with carefully tended and polished nails. Occasionally I see a hand with fingernails bitten raggedly to the quick, and I breathe a prayer for the comfort and easing of the woman who has brought such tension to the temple. They are all the hands of sisters.

Do we not all come to the temple with prayers? Some of us have stopped and written names on the tablets in the hallways, the names of those we remember with love, with grief, with worry. The faith of those we do not know will unite for their healing, body and soul, as we unite in faith for those we do not know. We do not need to know them to care for them. Is there special virtue to the prayers uttered in a temple? Perhaps. My prayers this morning concern most of the same issues I prayed about last night, but surely *I* pray differently in a temple, in this place where the air seems aglow with presence, where even the act of praying is a promise that it will be heard.

It was the assurance of being heard, not the assurance of rescue, for which Solomon prayed, there before his altar in another holy time, another holy place. "Whatever disaster or disease may come," his words fall like rain, "and when a prayer or plea is made by any of your people Israel—each one aware of her afflictions and pains, and spreading out her hands toward this temple—then hear from heaven, your dwelling place. ... May your eyes be open and your ears attentive to the prayers offered in this place" (2 Chron. 6:28, 40, adapted for gender inclusiveness).

What circles and cycles of our life have brought us to the temple? Across the room, an elderly man is nodding, drowsing. The familiar pattern of the ritual words is soothing, comforting, comfortable. A lullaby. On the aisle, a young pregnant woman leans forward, listening hard. She frowns, her brow creasing. A lesson.

I sit in a quiet room, with other quiet people. It is not circular, but it has the feeling of a circle. I feel above me the spires of the temple. How can something so weighty leap into the sky so exultantly? I feel beneath me the gentle waters of the baptismal font, modeled after the oxen-borne brazen sea of Solomon's temple. Deeper still are the ancient echoes of Lake Bonneville, lapping out of prehistoric times. And deeper still are the primordial waters of Genesis that did not yet know the elemental distinction between water and earth.

Stone, sea, and stillness. At the core of the circle, deeper than speech, lies stillness. This stillness is the silence that precedes the syllables of creation. It is the stillness of being that precedes knowing. I come here to remember.

Cromwell, Oliver, 119

Crosby, Jonathan, 156

Crosby, Caroline Barnes, 156

curse (Old Testament), 161–62

Monson, Thomas S., 2, 193, 255n14

Montaigne, Michel, 189

Moore, Thomas, 69

Morgan, Mary Ann, 34

Mormon Alliance, 16n7, 49–51, 65

Mormon architecture, 24–25

Mormon Church, and feminism, 44; as army, 35, 117; as body, 35–36; as community, 257–58; as contract 135–36; as family, 117, 135; as patriarchy, 226; as sect, 136; authoritarianism, 47; boundaries, 107–8; dangers to, according to Packer, 82; fear in, 213–15; human errors, 99–100; infallibility of leaders, 142; intellectuals, 184; judgmentalness in, 70; LGBTI members, 184n1; theology of, 83

Mormon historic sites, 24

Mormon history, 93

Mormon women. *See* women.

Mormon-L, 59

Mother in Heaven, 10, 16, 84, 224

Mother Teresa, 37

motherhood, and priesthood, 225

Mountain Meadows massacre, 44, 89–90, 240–41

mysteries of God, 133–34, 177–79

N

"Name Withheld," 86–87

Nelson, Russell M., 14–17, 243, 255–56, 255n14

Neville, Melanie Hepworth, 12

Neville, Roark B., 12

New Mormon History, 1

Newell, Eric, 58

Newell, Jack, 56

Newell, Linda King, 44, 57–58, 94, 155

Nibley, Hugh, 171

Norton, Don E., Jr., 201

O

Oaks, Dallin H., 253–55, 255n14

obedience, church emphasis on, 146–50

Okazaki, Chieko, 112–17, 223

Okazaki, Ed, 113–14

Olive Branch, 62

Oliver, Mary, 222, 224

P

Packer, Boyd K., and excommunications, 1, 27–28, 33, 93, 148; on change, 151; on confidentiality, 44; on dangers to church, 16, 82, 256–58; on historians, 141; on men's "needs," 232–33; on women's "needs," 228

Partridge, Kody, 210

Pearce, Virginia Hinckley, 237

Peck, Elbert, 21

Petersen, Zina, 99n9

At Calf Creek Falls in 1988 for Christian's baptism:
Paul Lawrence Anderson, Lavina Fielding Anderson,
and Christian N.K. Anderson

Lavina Fielding Anderson, president of Editing, Inc., is a member of the Editorial Advisory Committee of Signature Books, former trustee of the Mormon Alliance and, with Janice M. Allred, co-editor of the *Case Reports of the Mormon Alliance*. She is a former editor and/or copy editor of the *Journal of Mormon History*, the *Association for Mormon Letters Annual*, the *Ensign*, and *Dialogue: A Journal of Mormon Thought*. She is the editor of *Lucy's Book: A Critical Edition of Lucy Mack Smith's Family Memoir* (Signature Books, 2001) and is currently researching *Lucy's Life: A Biography of Lucy Mack Smith*. She is the recipient of the Grace Fort Arrington Award for Distinguished Service (1991), the O. Marvin Lewis Award for Best Essay (1995), the Special Merit Award for Exceptional Service (1995), the Eve Award (1999), co-recipient of the John Whitmer Historical Association award for Outstanding Bibliographical Essays (2005), and the recipient of the Smith-Pettit Foundation Award for Outstanding Contribution to Mormon Letters (2018).

Jana Riess is a senior columnist at Religion News Service and the author or co-author of more than a dozen books, including *The Next Mormons: How Millennials Are Changing the LDS Church*. She holds a PhD in American religious history from Columbia University. She is a Relief Society teacher and the ward historian in her Cincinnati, Ohio, ward.